Manufactured in the United States of America

ary of Congress Card Number 73-86202
national Standard Book Number:
Cloth Binding: 0-911214-57-7
Paperback: 0-911214-45-3

THE
UPWARD
TREND

Harvey Jackins

RATIONAL ISLAN[

S

Conceived in beauty and in strength, but born
In pain and turmoil and in drugged fog
Into a world that makes no sense at all
Without the knowledge of distress' effect
And how the patterns parasite on thinking;
Fenced off from contact with reality
By clumsy pretense socially enforced,
Except for tantalizing glimpses caught
In sky and wild and children's innocence;
We've joined, submissive, in lockstep routine,
Or tried distraught rebellion. Either way
Our precious lives have wasted. We've conformed
To one nonsense or other, bought despair,
Apologized for living, fought for scraps.
We've helped oppress each other, helped exploit
Our fellow humans, gone to war, and killed.

Beneath these tragedies, we've stayed intact,
The best evolved, so far, and to our knowledge,
Of all within our spreading universes,
Still wise up to the limits of distress,
Still loving, thoughtful, caring, self-directed
In intermittent functioning. Our power
Muted and hidden, by ourselves forgotten.

The re-emergence journey's small beginning
Was almost accident. If this could happen
To just one person once, what implications
Might not this have for everyone? We tried.
We guessed, we floundered, made mistakes, persisted,
Moved past the goals of "feeling better", saw,
Unwillingly, the depth of our distress,
Dared to reach past the paired co-counseling step
To classes, groups, communities, the world,
Challenged the chronics. Finally, now, we move
To stopper up the outflow of new hurts
From cruel oppression's nozzels, interrupt
The thoughtless ways we beat each other down.

How strong are we? What power do we possess?
Can any opposition stand against us?
If even one of us makes up her mind
That all unreason end, reclaims her power,
Thinks all the time, and moves, will present knowledge
Suffice to raise the multitudes behind her?

Is the time to come for total re-emergence?
You say. I think you know my answer.

                                        --Harvey Jackins

Table of Contents

FOREWORD

This collection of essays, articles, and reports covers most of the important theoretical developments in Re-evaluation Counseling that emerged between early 1973 and early 1977. These were years of vigorous growth and development in both the theory and practice of Re-evaluation Counseling. Consistent success in emerging from chronic patterns, the challenging of oppression patterns from the society and the confrontation of the nearly universal distress of "powerlessness" are among the landmark developments chronicled and discussed here.

For an introduction, or a fundamental presentation of the basic levels of Re-evaluation Counseling, the reader is referred to *The Human Side of Human Beings, The Fundamentals of Co-Counseling Manual,* and *The Human Situation.* For a description of the Re-evaluation Counseling Communities, the *Guidebook to Re-evaluation Counseling* is suggested.

The number of accredited Re-evaluation Counseling teachers, the number of organized RC Communities, and the number of countries in which co-counselors are active, have all increased at least ten-fold in the period of 1973 to 1977. Probably the numbers of active co-counselors have increased at least this much. Re-evaluation Counseling is no longer a United States phenomenon, but solidly based in the thinking and practice of many countries, with the basic literature appearing in many languages. From early communities of white middle-class intellectuals, Re-evaluation Counseling has been accepted and adopted by working-class communities, blacks, Asians, young people, older people, Latinos, and women's groups.

I think you will probably find this book as exciting to read as I found it exciting to write. We are grappling here with the very frontiers of human re-emergence. Re-evaluation Counseling is not, however, just to be read about or discussed. It is to *use*.

If you are not yet using Re-evaluation Counseling and would like to explore it, you are welcome to write to me at 719 Second Avenue North, Seattle, Washington, 98109, U.S.A. and I will be pleased to help you contact the experienced co-counselors nearest you.

Harvey Jackins
May 15, 1977

This book is dedicated to the co-counselors of the world.

My special appreciation to the thousands of RC Teachers, Reference Persons, and other leaders who have shared with me the fun of guiding the growth of human re-emergence.

My thanks, in particular, to Mary McCabe, to Tim Jackins, and to Katie Kauffman, who have helped most in the thinking and the writing that led to this book.

THE UPWARD TREND

The Growing Edge

The State of the Cosmos *

The World and the Universe In Which RC Operates

There is a general principle that if one wishes to consider an area of activity and think about it, it helps to set it in the largest possible frame of reference. If one can think of a system as embedded in another larger system, one can draw more accurate conclusions about it. Some recent theorems in mathematical logic come down to this: there are questions in any system that cannot be answered in that system. If one embeds the system in a larger system, however, one can perhaps get an answer that will be useful. Let us then back up and, instead of trying to talk first about immediate concerns, try to talk about the whole picture.

We assume, of course, that the universe is real, that it exists independently of our perception of it.

We observe that the universe is dynamic. All of our observations indicate that there is no such thing as stasis (except as a relative term) in the universe. Probably the notion of unchange arises only out of painful emotion. The only apparent stasis in the universe is in our own distress patterns, the illusion offered to ourselves and to others that things are just like they always were--the frenziedly recreated illusion of yesterday persisting today, the illusion we work so hard to reconstruct day by day while the actual situation changes.

TWO GREAT PROCESSES

Observably and as an hypothesis, it is useful to think of two great general processes operating in this universe. One is

---

*Excerpts from a Report to the International Reference Persons' Committee of the Re-evaluation Counseling Communities – January 18 and 19, 1975

the familiar one which has been observed and measured and bemoaned by philosophers in the last two or three genera-tions--the process of entropy, the running down, the second law of thermodynamics, the tendency toward disorder, toward chaos, toward randomness, toward lack of meaning. The other process--which has always been inspirationally defended and which I and a few other people have been speaking about in concrete terms for a few years--is the equally pervasive tendency toward order, toward meaning, toward integration.   This process was viewed a generation ago as an accidental phenomenon that only occurred on our particular planet and in our particular species. It was believed that life and thought were in fundamental violation of the laws of probability and were inevitably about to be snuffed out and disappear.   That view, of course, was based·on a faulty theory of astrophysics, on the notion that planets only arose because of the near approach of another star toward the sun which then tore masses of material out of it by gravitational pull and gave rise to the planets. With better physics and better understanding of how matter coalesces into stars, it is plain that it also usually coalesces into planets around the star.   That realization tears the foundation from under the gloomy notion that life and intelligence are accidental phenomena, existing only because of a fleeting gap in the statistical tables which may close at any minute and wipe them out.

I could and often do argue with ample evidence that the tendency toward growth, toward integration, toward meaning, toward independence, toward intelligence, toward awareness and toward mastery is equally as pervasive throughout the universe as is the tendency toward disintegra-tion.   The two processes are undoubtedly two facets of the same reality. I would guess that the process toward integra-tion and growth is dependent on the other disintegration process, that it is fueled by the other, that in ways that we don't yet understand, the disappearing of stars into black holes leads to the creation of new matter.

When I was young there was a little machine called the hydraulic ram on nearly every farm that had a brook. If you built a little dam in the brook so there was a sizable fall of water over a short distance, this little mechanical marvel would sit there and whomp a thin stream of water up the hill a considerable distance to water your orchards. I'm sure that in the big universe the tendency toward randomness and entropy fuels the equally pervasive tendency toward growth and meaning in a similar way.

Quantitatively the running down is the greater process if it is measured in terms of tons and parsecs. On a qualitative scale, however, growth proceeds faster than disintegration and higher orders of complexity arise much more rapidly than disintegration progresses. We may have some simple law of leverage involved here--some analogue of more force on the shorter end of the lever but more distance on the longer.

THE UPWARD PROCESS AND OUR PART IN IT

It seems to me that our Re-evaluation Counseling activities can be most soundly and confidently viewed as the very leading edge of the tendency toward order and meaning in the universe.

I have this hope that somewhere, even perhaps in our own galaxy, we may have older brothers and sisters who could arrive soon and take us by the' hand, explain some present mysteries to us and give us a few boosts over the hard spots. It's probably a good guess as well as a hope, but we don't have any knowledge of their existence yet.

Certainly we ourselves, we humans, are far out on the trend toward order and integration. As far as we know, we are on the point of it. However it happened, here we are. Our sub-species is, as far as we know, the most highly evolved expression of the upward trend in the universe.

We have been and are in this position whether we have been aware of it or not. I think it will tremendously accelerate and ease our handling of this role to be aware of it, to begin to apply intelligence to the question of intelligence, to apply awareness to the question of awareness. There are certain intuitive attempts in this direction being made here and there, but I suspect that we are the only group who are likely to undertake it in a serious, consistent way at this point in time.

This is not because we are chosen people or any kind of elite. There are much smarter, more gifted and more functional people outside of our ranks than we yet have in them. Our special position is one of the side effects, one of the spinoffs, of the accidental re-discovery of the discharge and re-evaluation process. Just as discharge and re-evaluation have coincidentally resolved many ancient philosophical dilemmas, so they also, as fringe benefits, have given us the realizations that it is possible to think all the time, that logic is a dependable guide for us to use whenever possible and that feelings are not, the possibilities that we can be aware of awareness and that we can think about thinking, that we can commit ourselves to thinking all the time.

Just to reach this kind of a periscopic turn-back perspective upon our functioning will in itself greatly expedite what we are about. We may have begun as the helpless unaware pawns of an upward rising process, but we don't have to stay that way. We were lucky that we happened to get caught up in being alive, in having the ability to think, in finding the means to re-emerge from distress. Now we need to capitalize on our luck awarely, to plan our further advances. Chris once said at bedtime when he was four, "Animals and plants are lucky; they get to be alive. We are even more lucky because we get to think, too." I have never heard it said better. We also lucked into discharge and re-evaluation and have come out smelling like a rose so far, but we don't need to stay on this unplanned level. This is one of the problems before us in Re-evaluation Counseling. Having realized that regular co-counseling is some kind of a conveyer belt under our feet moving us in a good direction, we must not relapse into mindless co-counseling or taking-it-for-routine co-counseling or wait for the light of full intelligence to strike us someday while we go on saying "again" in shut-down voices.

There is an intuitive reach for this knowledge that we can organize our own progress. This morning, perhaps, we can take a new kind of look at the possibilities. All kinds of things had to happen before we reached this point.

THE MEANING OF GOOD AND EVIL

The notion of evil has been so misused that people are in flight from it, in revolt against it, and correctly so. Yet I think we can now define evil and good in meaningful terms. Good could be defined as any manifestation of the upward, integrative trend in the universe. Evil would not be the existence of the disintegrative trend in the universe, because that is undoubtedly necessary. The compost heap must exist to fuel the next season's flowers. We can say, however, that evil is allowing the process to take over unnecessarily, allowing it to slop into or defeat the upward process. To sacrifice a child's life in order that the crops may prosper was evil when it happened. To burn Stradivarious violins for fuel is evil under most conditions. To allow the contents of a cesspool to splash on clean silk, that is evil. To relapse into non-thinking when thinking is possible is evil.

WE HAVE A CHOICE

We are assuming some version of the axiom of choice. We are assuming that at least sometimes it is possible to choose. All our experience would indicate practical support for this. Even though we correctly insist on the attitude toward another person as client that she or he has done and is doing the very best that she or he can do, that attitude cannot hold for ourselves as clients. We must hold firmly to the attitude that there is at least a zone of choice for the first person, singular or plural. Our observations and experience tend to confirm this. Patterns compel only to a certain point.

5

That point may be 99 and 99/100% in the case of a deeply distressed person, but there is always at least a little sliver of choice left as long as the person is alive. People who are in better shape have a larger zone of choice, more chance of choosing to act on restimulation or not, more chance of choosing to keep thinking or to abandon thinking. The past is compelled, fixed, because it is the past. The future does always offer us some kind of choice.

The integrative trend in the universe is familiar though not usually identified as such. We reach for various concepts to try to identify it and grasp it and deal with it. Certainly being smart, using one's head, is part of the trend. So is cooperative action, acting as if we were our brother's and sister's keeper. Taking no action without concern for how it affects all the factors in a situation is sometimes preached and, in the past, hardly ever practiced. Nevertheless, this part of the upward trend is surfacing.

THE MEANING OF LOVE

One name we have for this upward trend in the universe is love. I think love, which is often distorted and emerges in so many forms, is exactly that. What we reach for with this great yearning that sends the songster beating his guitar around the word, is just exactly an intuitive recognition that the integrative tendency in the universe is what it is all about. Our place in this trend is the essential meaning of our exist-ence. The wild songs that love is all that matters are reaching for a truth even though they have relied more on sentiment than on logic until now.

We can make the transition from sentiment and say clearly and logically that this *is* what it is all about. Love, the functioning of intelligence to enhance the process of which it is a part, is one of the highest expressions of this good trend in the universe.

Linking together these frontier functions of the good trend, these intelligences, these awarenesses* in mutual effort,

*Awareness, I suspect, has something to do with intelligence being applied to intelligence. It is certainly beyond what we have found intelligence to be--a higher function.

in mutual support is what we are trying to talk about when we say "love". We may glimpse love in an intuitive sense when we lay our warm skins against each other and hold on tight for awhile; but it can also be looked at very logically as trying to break through to new levels of function. Obviously, everything and everybody functions, flourishes, flowers and operates much better when these intelligences and the entities that bear them, take no action without thought for everyone else's survival. We have said, as a principle in RC, that any really good solution is a good solution for everyone, that there are no real conflicts between the survivals of different human beings. That has been one of our expressions of this principle.

I think that's sound. This can help us cut through a lot of fog and confusion. We can quit keeping our inspiration in one compartment and our good thinking in another.

THE ROLE OF RC LEADERSHIP

By a series of accidents and hard work and interactions, we're sitting on the point of the point of the needle of this rising arrow, this "good" tendency in the universe.

I have said we have 50,000 co-counselors. I haven't any accurate notion of how many co-counselors there are. The figure is exaggerated in the sense of how many we could put on the mailing list at one point. In another sense I think it is low. There are far more people who are trying to use Reevaluation Counseling in some form and with some success than that. We can talk about this in much more detail in our discussion of leadership, but we know we have a large number of people trying awarely to play a conscious role in enhancing this project.

We have a much smaller group of people who are taking big responsibilities, the Area Reference Persons, etc. This group here, the International Reference Committee, is set up as an advisory group, a consultative group. It may eventually have to become something else. It may have to take on a structural responsibility to cope with our growth; but, if so, I think we will have to do it very carefully.

As of now, this group is the leading body of the RC Communities. At this point human affairs have come to the point of needing knowledge, understanding, awareness applied to them. Progress has come to the point that active, aware, guidance of the process needs to take place. A group of intelligent human beings should and can play a decisive role in steering the whole upward process. This is where I think we are. The opportunity has fallen into our laps.

We can goof, and it is certainly possible with the best of intentions to goof. We could, theoretically, even wind up in a personal or group defeat. The entire movement that we are representing here could, conceivably, lose its way or be defeated. We cannot expect a guarantee of success ahead of time on anything so important. I propose that it would be ridiculous for us not to try, however, to accept the challenge, to succeed.

A KEY PROCESS

The process that we call Re-evaluation Counseling plays a crucial role in future progress. It isn't the only important upward process in the universe, obviously. There are thousands of equally basic, equally important upward processes that have to go on. RC will play a crucial role, however, simply because it is the untangling process, the until-now suppressed and hidden healing process for the problem of human irrationality.

Irrationality has, until now, plagued all humans, the only known group of entities that have had the opportunity to become intelligent and loving. From the time of the emergence of intelligence, it has been burdened and has been buried beneath the weight of distress patterns inevitably resulting from the conditions of life in an unmastered world. Once begun, such distress patterns were transmitted inevitably from generation to generation, by restimulated rehearsal and then, once social structures were involved, by systematic procedures. The process of Re-evaluation Counseling plays this key role of releasing all other human potentials.

We rejoice in the whole range of human progress as it moves forward on many levels. Anyone that keeps up to date on scientific developments can't help but be thrilled at the tremendous amount of insight and understanding physical and biological scientists are achieving in field after field.

There is just one sector where human progress has been stalled and where the other fronts have been held back because nothing has moved here. Our opponent, the disintegrative tendency in the universe, has a salient deep into human affairs, the salient of human irrationality. Counseling is the weapon for liberating this salient. RC is the process, increasingly effective, that is beginning to untie the leash from the stake in this area. Real movement forward in the direction of uncluttering human intelligence and allowing it to operate is taking place in and around Re-evaluation Counseling. Attempts are being made elsewhere and in other ways, but compared to what takes place in Re-evaluation Counseling, very little happens. The best attempts of the various therapies and self-improvement systems, the dozens of schools of phychologists and psychiatrists, the human growth movements and the inspirational teachers, all accomplish very little. They are interesting as social phenomena and there are things to be learned from their occurrence and their multiplicity, but they are by no means effective. None of them have even a small part of the overall grasp of the situation or of the effectiveness of RC. What we have learned to do is small yet, compared to our future knowledge, but enormous compared to anything else. The mastering of the processes of discharge and re-evaluation, the acquisition of practice and theory, the building of the community, the mutual support, the interaction with the society around us-- all these things that have become and are becoming parts of Re-evaluation Counseling together constitute a crucial process for the future of humanity and the upward trend of the universe. The liberation of human intelligence from individual distress patterns is well-begun and will continue until every human is free.

The fight for progress, the fight for human re-emergence goes on in lots of sectors besides this one of individual re-emergence from irrationality. The whole world-wide movement to eliminate exploitation and end oppression is certainly in this direction. Exploitation and oppression of humans is outstandingly evil. Whenever someone profits by another person's distress, disintegration is intruding into and ravaging progress and goodness. All the liberation movements of humankind are very much a part of the upward trend of the universe.

Most of them are not yet rational or aware. By and large, they are fueled by reactive processes as yet, still fueled by distress, by the intolerability of one distress being countered by another distress. Fear is being overcome by hate and rage, passivity is being challenged by despair. Nevertheless, they are in the upward direction and they are fueled. The long-range inability of an oppressive society to work is a factor that moves to overthrow the factor of oppression itself. The world forces for liberation are still moving blindly, but they are moving in the direction of progress; eventually, they will move decisively and nothing can stop them. They are beyond interruption or suppression and the logic of their development will push them in the direction of becoming rational and aware. They will necessarily interact with the struggle that we have begun to free people's minds from distress patterns.

At this last La Scherpa workshop, the discussion of this interaction surfaced and was continued at Suhuaro I. At first there were some objections to discussing sexism, racism, and oppression at an RC workshop. Then there was a very good discussion. The conclusion was that we have to necessarily tackle sexism, racism, adultism toward children and other forms of oppression both inside our community and outside as an inherent part of what we are doing. The workshops concluded that to do this is implicit in RC itself. If we do not, the workshops reasoned, then the daily load of distress visited on our co-counselors by oppression is likely to make them lose their war for re-emergence even if they win battles in their sessions. They may be gaining in their co-counseling sessions, but they are losing in between times by the dead weight of restimulation from the oppression, invalidations and putdowns, of many of which they may be still unaware, having been heavily conditioned to accept them without protest.

WE NEED TO INTERACT WITH OTHER UPWARD TRENDS

We meet as leaders of the particular movement of Re-evaluation Counseling. We have been concerned most with a particular kind of negative force in the universe--the distress recording on individual humans. We are surrounded by many other forms of entropy: death, decay, discouragement, disease, disillusionment, recession, inflation, unemployment, poverty, oppression, war and all the rest.   Against these, however, move many counter tendencies, counter-forces. They operate generally on a far less aware level than we do, but they are important tendencies. Everywhere, including the very worst conditions, there are humans waiting to be released and guided to move in the direction of freedom, intelligence, awareness, love.

Given our awareness, our theory, and our practical abilities, however, we do have certain responsibilities. We can do a poor job or a good job about those responsibilities, but it seems to me we can't refuse them. It's like once becoming a parent. You can do a poor job or a good job of being a parent from then on, but you can't quit being a parent. Whether we face it or not, the implicit opportunity and responsibility are there. If we face it, then we will have to keep thinking; thinking about our correct relationship to all humans.

RCERS NEED TO BE AWARE AND INFORMED

Beyond question, the world situation will lead soon to enormous struggles, since many people are going to have to fight or starve.

It is important that we leaders in Re-evaluation Counseling know these matters, understand these things. The people in the world around us are going to be more and more involved and it is important that we be intelligent and informed in our contacts with them.

We in Re-evaluation Counseling happen by accident to be engaged in probably the most fundamental change that humanity has ever been engaged in--the re-emergence from the oppression of the distress patterns that have covered humans from the very beginnning of time. We are engaged in a long-time, ongoing project. Others have glimpsed the necessity for remolding individuals even after political and economic liberation, but have guessed that three or four generations would be necessary and didn't know how it would come about.

OUR IMPLICIT RESPONSIBILITIES

We need to constantly improve our mastery of RC theory and practice but not stop there. We can't afford to be wise about RC and ignorant about economics and politics. We have to know what is going on. I think if we don't fill these responsibilities it will weaken our basic struggle against the distress patterns.

LEADERSHIP

To be a leader of other humans is an inherent part of being a full-functioning human. In the re-emergent future all humans will take their turns at being leaders of others. The general population has been systematically invalidated and discouraged in this as in other respects. The people who have come into RC carry these patterns. To continually help more people to become free to be rational leaders is a big part of building healthy communities.

Leadership will tend to emerge spontaneously but it's going to be a very slow process unless we awarely and thoughtfully promote it. It's like the difference between gathering food from the wild forest or raising crops. We have a responsibility to open new doors as fast as we can to any-body who seems ready to start moving in this direction. Permeation and the use of our techniques outside will bring excellent people in the Community to enhance their func-tioning where they are but also to train our teachers to keep opening new doors for them. Of course we praise and encourage each person's progress where she/he is, even if it's at a very slow rate. We need also, however, to continually have long range progress in mind and expect more from each one so that she/he is not allowed to circle the moon when her/his current goals run out.

LOOK FOR THE BEST

In the very nature of things, it is correct to seek out with special care the sparklers who can quickly begin to play a significant role. This is actually in the interest of all people. We are not turning our backs on the neediest. This is the workable, long-range way to reach the most distressed persons, the persons who most deserve our sympathy (if anybody deserves "sympathy"). First we gather together the sparklers, accelerate their development, get a unity of pur-pose, theory, and policy and then take off. This is the way to acquire the resources to eventually reach all people.

The criterion in choosing people to cultivate into leader-ship is not just where the person is now. That's not as crucial as where they have the possibility of growing to in a reason-able period of time. In discussions in the Communities I

am often asked, "Why don't we recruit a big shot or a cor-
poration president, or a minister (we might get his whole
congregation)?" I don't think I need to belabor the point--
you don't recruit her followers when you recruit a leader.

*   *   *

Where people are has some bearing. If a person is surviving well and being responsible, that tells you something
about what kind of shape he/she is in.

The sparkler that we are looking for is a person who is
re-emerging, who is eager to grow, who wants to regain complete humanness. We are looking for the worker who has
happy children. She may be on ADC but her children are
happy. He or she is the one we need rather than the well-to-do
person who has the trappings of success because he/she
has "adjusted" to society. We need to look for the sparklers
who are already intelligent and aware, who still think most
of the time, who still care about others, who will burst forth
to elegant functioning with a year or two of good co-
counseling.

LOOK FOR NEW LEADERSHIP AWARELY

We have practiced this kind of search intuitively. The
more we are aware of doing it, the more we think about what
we are doing, the better. We are looking for treasure. We included some poorly functioning people in the early years and
it wasn't a mistake. We learned a lot that we had to learn.
On the one hand, we proved in practice that the most distressed person whose fore-brain had not been physically
damaged could recover just like anyone else if given enough
resources and support. It was necessary to prove it in practice. On the other hand, we learned that it is too exhausting
to build with people like that at the beginning. At this point
we know our energies should not be invested on long shots or
nearly lost causes. We know we should be prepared to let
RC not develop in a place for quite a while rather than put
it in the hands of someone who is going to muddle things up.

This is a break with some of our past practice. It is all right to learn, to change. We are not obligated to our past mistakes. We can be assured that if we recruit sharp people who can face and accept the full content of our program they will be with us for good. We don't need to entice them with any other bait than just exactly their participation in what we are doing. We offer a chance to think clearly, to have a life full of purpose, to associate with people who are going somewhere, a chance to recover full humanness step by step as we figure out how. This is sufficient inducement to people to bring in just about anybody we want.

If after we have promoted someone to leadership, we discover we have a clinker on our hands, no matter how good that one looked before, we don't stand there and bemoan the fact that it gives out clinking sounds. We let that one go. There are people with patterns we won't be able to straighten out while they are holding positions of teachers or leaders or perhaps, even while they remain within and disrupt the Community. We haven't made many mistakes, but we have made a few and we will make more; but we are not obligated to our past mistakes. When the readout says blown fuse, we face the fact that a fuse has blown and don't just stand there and say that the fuse shouldn't have blown or plead with it to unblow.

Really caring about such a person includes not colluding with the chronic pattern or letting it operate in the name of RC to confuse other co-counselors.

The key problem for all of us who are leaders in RC is exactly developing new leaders. When a leader talks about over-commitment and fatigue, I think he/she is really talking about the underside of the real problem--the recruitment and promotion of new leaders. Even with the greatest enthusiasm, the greatest effort, the greatest loving of people, if we don't face the development of new leaders as a continual necessity, we won't be functioning well.

I don't think we can develop leaders without loving them enormously. To ask the prospective leaders to enter on this kind of growth, without the feeling of being personally loved and cared about and forever supported would be just too frightening for most of them. The few people who can start out without that kind of support will have to be very aggressive and this will turn out to be a pattern as often as not. When it is we have real difficulties. We must love, support, encourage. At the same time, we must be ruthlessly and completely realistic about what patterns we run into. We can't know ahead of time that our most promising prospects are going to be unpatterned and superb in every respect, or even that the patterned difficulties that show up will only make things difficult for himself or herself and not for other co-counselors or the Community. We may run into very disruptive patterns that we couldn't have anticipated. When we do we need to act in complete realism and not in terms of sentiment in how we handle these people. We won't punish them because they have patterns or denounce them because we are disappointed in them, but we will move to shunt them out of the role they can't handle into one that they can handle.

The growth of leaders is, I think, our key problem. Our own growth ourselves is a problem for us. There are other people in RC who should be coming to this level of leadership that aren't here yet. We present members of the International Reference Committee have no long range monopoly on this spot. Some of us may not keep growing fast enough in this next period. Although we have done good work, we cannot coast on past achievements. Mel was saying it well; if we are realistic, we will be delighted to have someone we trust take our place as a leader. There are always other important responsibilities for us to handle and enjoy.

On the other hand the very opportunity to function at this level is a great stimulant. So that if we are realistic and ruthless about each other's patterns we all can continue to grow. The experience we gain from functioning like this is going to be very difficult to provide to new people coming up. The most brilliant of the younger and newer people are going to have to scramble to catch up and we are going to have to take pains to inform them of the things we have had a chance to learn these last few years.

What is the policy on who will be leading International Workshops?

I would say that anyone who leads an International Workshop, except in very special cases, should be able to adequately represent our complete policy, including being aggressive about Community building and aggressive about going after people's chronic patterns; that they must be able to teach the whole theory instead of just leading a nice workshop. In particular, it seems to me, that no one should plan to lead any workshops outside of her/his Area unless his/her own Area is in excellent shape. We will ask people to have excellent home bases where they function well before they go to lead anything elsewhere. Otherwise they are going to teach a weak variety of RC, just by example, if nothing else. We haven't had this criterion until this last year. We have come to this criterion now. The results of incomplete leadership at International Workshops have not been good enough.

It was decided at the Reference Persons' Workshop that no one should organize or lead workshops in his/her own Area without the approval of the Area Reference Person and no one should organize or lead workshops outside his/her own Area without the approval of the International Reference Person. I think we will have to be more strict about this to stop some of the circuit-riding, eager-beavering workshop leading that has sometimes left people in new regions with a very inadequate impression of RC.

COMMUNITY

In a sense the RC Communities date from 1950 when a few people began hanging around my office in the University

Building. In a sense they date from the ongoing classes we tried to organize to keep people actively co-counseling in Seattle in the 50's and 60's. In the present form they date from 1970. Margot had started a class in Morrisville before that and planned to keep Inge teaching. A little group formed around her class when she moved to L.A. in late 1969. Spring of 1970 saw the real beginnings. A lot has happened since then.

The second stage of the Re-evaluation Counseling Communities themselves started with the RC picnics and Saturday night socials in Santa Barbara. These intuitive attempts to set up some kind of organization finally coalesced in the meeting at McGuire House. The teachers from Southern California, from Santa Barbara and Los Angeles and San Diego met and argued over a draft of guidelines that I proposed. I took it away and re-drafted it and re-submitted it. Finally the stormy first Reference Persons' and RC Teachers' workshop that fall became a constitutional convention where the idea of a responsible relationship was actually hammered out and the official Guidelines adopted. The Guidelines we have now were worked out there in most particulars. They have been refined and extended since, but the basics were agreed upon at that time.

The Communities have proved themselves viable and workable to an amazing degree. The Guidelines type of relationship has worked. Theoretically, we have no illusion that our present Community organization or the present Guidelines are the best Guidelines or the best relationship possible. Probably on many counts better ones can and will be worked out. We do have a workable one, however, one on which wide agreement has been reached, and one with a self-renewing character to it. It works. It has been violated and ignored a lot in practice, but it is there to come back to and to correct to. The more experienced and successful Communities are sticklers for Guidelines. You can practically tell how well a Community works by how much attention its leaders pay to the Guidelines and how closely they follow them. It makes a decisive difference in the way they function.

The idea of Communities has worked. It arose spontaneously. We didn't anticipate it. It was forced on us. We had to face the need and play an aware role in developing it.

Our Communities have been successful. We proposed for them to guide the spread of co-counseling across the surface of the globe. In the second year we established clearly the idea that co-counseling should be international, that we would tolerate no national boundaries. We now have geographical groupings and one world community. I think this is important.

We have been very successful considering our initial resources. Other movements have organized and have spread. Very few of them have been completely self-generated in terms of finances and resources and ideas 'the way RC has. Relying on our self-sustaining financing has been hard, sometimes. Some RCers have dreamed of foundation grants, but being on our own has given us valuable and necessary independence. Longfellow said of the Village Blacksmith, "He looks the whole world in the face and he owes not any man." We don't owe anybody anything and we have been able to keep our policy pretty much our own. Fears and "what ifs" have inhibited some Communities, but we have not sold our independence in exchange for some support. We have not been bribed or bought off in any sense. We would be in a much different position if we had started off with a Rockefeller Foundation grant.

GROWTH

We now have many organized Areas and Sub-Areas. We have over a hundred teachers outside of organized Areas, many of whom are leading groups of co-counselors larger than our first Areas were. We have become a lot more particular about when we set up an organized Area. The tiny ones we used to set up were a mistake. There's a lot more growth than the number of our Areas indicates. We have good strong teachers outside organized Areas as well. We have over 600 accredited teachers worldwide.

THE FOUNDATION

The Re-evaluation Foundation was organized because of the insistence of some people that it could replace our Outreach funds, that we could collect the money we needed from people who had lots of money. This was nonsense, as we might have expected, but the Foundation has turned out to be convenient. Outreach funds are now going through the Foundation.

There is still a very real possibility of raising some tax-deductible contributions outside the Communities. It should be possible to raise money outside our class and workshop contributions. I don't know how but it can be done.

The Foundation has become a valuable adjunct to the Communities in terms of its acceptance and disbursement of the Outreach Funds. It's expensive and it's bureaucratic and it's awkward, but it's also accurate, legal beyond any question, and very accountable.

INTERNATIONAL WORKSHOPS

One of the outstanding features of our Communities has been the intercommunication and growth achieved through International Workshops. The workshops themselves have been remarkable events. The first major workshop, Buck Creek I, was held four and a half years ago. Of the 38 people who were there, probably 30 or more are now teaching RC somewhere.

There have now been 16 Buck Creeks, 35 Kirkridges, 37 La Scherpas and innumerable others scattered at other locations. These workshops have financed a good deal of our outreach. They have accelerated people's growth and development and spread RC knowledge widely.

They have been strikingly successful, almost without exception. There have been a very few where naive leadership gave a poor impression to a few people. There have been a few others where eager leadership did a partial job. Everybody was happy -- both the leaders and the people attending -- but some of the things a workshop should accomplish were missed -- community building, new leadership evolvement, etc. An International Workshop should achieve a number of things. It isn't all having good sessions and giving people good directions in front of the body. Little harm has been done, however. Even the poorest workshops have been good.

OTHER WORKSHOPS

From the International Workshops have spun off the most amazing variety of Area Workshops, local workshops, regional workshops, class workshops, one-day workshops, special topic workshops, cooperative teachers' workshops, etc., etc. On almost any weekend a dozen or more RC workshops are in progress somewhere. It is as if humans had finally discovered how they had always wanted to spend their weekends. Theory, policy, and practice sometimes get a little bent or diluted at these functions, but the discussion and openness also seems to furnish a kind of self-correcting function, as long as the participants have had access to the correct theory and policy beforehand. Overall, the effect of these workshops is excellent and the wide range in costs makes it possible for any RCer to share in a workshop experience.

LITERATURE

We are still weak on literature distribution but improving rapidly. The Communities have distributed considerable basic literature. Our basic books are no longer being published at a loss as they were for a long time. Sales of the Manual are able to make up the loss on some of the new items that are being published. Much of the cost of *The R.C. Teacher* and *Present Time* are still being paid by Personal Counselors with some help from International Outreach.

PRESENT TIME

I think the Communities have developed a marvelous organ in *Present Time.* It is a completely distinctive emergence of people's literature, of thinking people's literature. There is more thought in those 32 or 40 pages than in many encyclopedias. It is a great source of encouragement to people to think. People see their own thoughtful thinking in *Present Time* and their future thinking is enhanced. They are encouraged to write further. I'm especially proud of the Excerpts from the Mail. Katie's questionnaires have been another special tool for drawing people into thinking and contributing.

THE AREA NEWSWETTERS

Present Time has many descendents in the Area Newsletters. They have really proliferated. Their growth has been very much of a spontaneous development. They often start as a simple listing of starting times for classes (which is what the 1950's *Present Time* in Seattle did). Then an issue or two later there is a theoretical article a paragraph long and "please come to the public lecture." Already some of them are more elaborate than *Present Time* was a few issues ago. How many of you have seen the New York City newsletter? It is set in elegant type and very impressive. The content of the (Palo Alto) *Peninsula* Newsletter is excellent. The Boston Newsletter (*Boston Time*) has become a major publication with big articles. There are many others. The names range all the way from the *Newsletter from Podunk Flats Community* to *The Crumpled Tissue.* I think the production and distribution of these is of great importance. Many groups of people are learning to think about and communicate theory and its organizational application. The existence of these widely distributed groups of editors will give sturdiness to

22

our Communities and afford a training experience in thinking, writing, editing, and publishing that it would be very difficult to furnish any other way. I hope in the future that copies of each Area newsletter can be sent to each Reference Person so each set of editors can learn from each other.

THE SPECIAL JOURNALS

The R.C. Teacher has been a great help to our teachers and continues to improve. Now we have *Classroom* and *Seeds and Crystals* and *Sisters*. We have *Pensamientos* and the *Asian-American Newsletter*. We have *Handicapped But Not Incapable* and we have *Well-Being*. We are going to have newsletters for black RCers, for RC lawyers, for RC social activists, for RC priests and nuns, for RC young people.

These publications are a new inning in the ball game. Through them we are going to unleash a great deal of creative thinking and communication--and actual permeation of the societies. I will want to look over the first few issues of each before they go to press. We want them to be consistent with our theory and policy and we will push to raise standards of typography. We want them to be quality publications soon. With experience the concerned groups and their editorial boards will become semi-autonomous with less and less supervision from the International Community. To have these varied groups of people who will have learned to put out a theoretical organ, learned to think, write, edit, publish and distribute to their own constituencies will be a resource beyond price in the interesting days ahead. We are not starting these special journals just for the fun of it. We are starting them for effective permeation and application of RC in the whole of society.

OUR ORGANIZATIONAL PRINCIPLES ARE WORKING

Our Community organization format has proven itself viable in a variety of different situations. The occasional demand that it be changed or modified or distorted "for national reasons" in new places have turned out to be reactive. The few places where the organization hasn't worked well are where it hasn't been really tried because some pattern "knew better."

REASONS FOR SATISFACTION

Our Communities are going so well that we could be tempted to just sit and gloat over them. They are doing just *so* well. The blank spaces on the map are being filled. The Mid-West United States is now spotted all over with stable Communities. An experienced teacher has moved to Mississippi. There is a contact in Arkansas and teachers in Tennessee and Kentucky. Hector in Mexico City is persisting. Ryszard is continuing to teach in Warsaw. His class is doing exceedingly well. England is doing very well. You heard the good news from France. The beginnings of unity at last -- agreement that France Venier shall be Reference Person. Brussels is flourishing. Daniel has asked for a few more teachers to be certified. Amsterdam and Geneva are excellent. Germany and Sweden are fine. Those who didn't get to meet Ian Newman should know we have a fine new Reference Person in Tasmania. He has been able to attend some workshops with Mary and me. The situation on the mainland of Australia has shaken down to about four effective teachers. Yukio Aki is applying RC in the Christian Social Change Groups in Japan and finds that it is very effective. Good teachers and classes in Ireland and Scotland.

LEADERSHIP

The crucial question before the Communities is still exactly the question of Leadership. We have good or adequate leadership in almost every Organized Area and many newer places as well *for a beginning level of RC.* For the kind of RC that will be necessary for our inevitable, individual and community growth we are still very short. There are still too great variations in effectiveness and leadership in organization between different Areas. Our best leaders are outstanding and are models for the rest of us to grow by. Our best Communities are excellent examples, also. It is a question of bringing the general level up to these.

There is no important problem facing any Community in its growth anywhere that isn't being or hasn't been solved in some other Area already. If we can have enough communication between the Areas on these things then no one need be alone and at a loss with a problem. Some Community or other has met a similar problem and come up with at least a possible solution to it. We just need enough communication. There are several Communities who have excelled organizationally. Certainly Boston, Albuquerque, Brussels and Palo Alto are outstanding. In numbers Santa Barbara and Los Angeles are outstanding. What these Communities have done, if concretely communicated, would be of great benefit to others. New York City has changed greatly this year. Good things are happening both in numbers and activities. It would be good for the rest of us to know what has made the difference.

THE QUALITY OF LEADERSHIP

We have some upcoming leaders who will accept leadership, who want to be leaders and will accept the responsibility and requirements that go along with it. This has taken a little time to get this far, to get the acceptance of the Mary McCabe principle, to develop a willingness to fight for soundness of policy, an unwillingness to tolerate vagueness and discrepancies and distortions. But our leaders must aggressively go beyond this to be creative. At least one leader in an Area has to have fire in her eye for getting the show on the road and doing it right, has to have great joy in solving the problem and seeing that things move, has to be able to care that things happen. The best caretaker leader isn't enough. It takes going beyond that. It is an analogue of where we are trying to get our co-counselors to -- that they care about each other enough to notice where each is still being stupid because of a chronic pattern and will reach out a hand and intervene. We must care enough about our Areas to intervene with a teacher, to check up and to see whether someone is teaching well or not. If she is not, find out why not. If she can be helped to teach well, help her. If she is not ready, help her stop teaching and find someone who is ready. We must learn not to wait for crises. We need to become accustomed to the notion of staying ahead of the game, dust off our capacity to be thrilled to see that things are done right and to move on them aggressively.

This zinginess comes in all kinds of flavors. I don't think that anybody can model on anybody else. But there is some kind of a general need here.

We have excellent leaders. We have a large number of them now. We have over 600 teachers. We have over 150 Reference People and Alternates. We have such outstanding leaders as Emma and Roberto who aren't directly involved in Reference jobs. We have leaders who are keenly, consistently, joyfully seeing that new leaders develop, who are trying to put themselves out of jobs so they can take on tougher ones.

CARING ENOUGH TO INTERVENE

This analogue of caring about each other enough to intervene in a misfunction is a requirement for effective leadership. We cherish it where it surfaces -- where it doesn't we have patterns. We need to learn how to reach through certain leaders' patterns and shake them loose, how to be ruthless about not letting a leader misfunction in a slot for a long time, while we hope "that the pattern will go away" and we need to learn how to do this without at the same time invalidating the leader. How can we be honest and direct and deal with these things instead of pussy-footing around? How can we grab ourselves by the seat of our pants and shake the lead out and get back to thinking all the time? How can we get beyond just thinking of things as they come to thinking ahead, taking initiative, grabbing the reins? These are key questions before our Communities.

How will we solve the as yet unsolved problems of dividing large population Areas into small Areas? How can we interrupt several years of teaching simplistic counseling, teaching counseling insufficiently in some large Areas?

With all the questions facing us we need to remember that our Communities overall are in just excellent shape. Every one of them has some problems, of course. Bureaucracy is intruding into this one. This one hasn't raised enough finances to operate on. This one is an appendage to a campus instead of really getting into the Community where the strength is. This one's leadership is involved in susceptibility to hurt feelings. They all have problems but they have all been growing beautifully! So many good things are going on. Thousands of people are finding real living in a way that no one else but RCers are. Even the primitive co-counseling is working so well. We are growing faster than seems possible. We are developing leadership faster than anyone ever did. There are so many good things. We can rejoice in them and go on to the next challenge.

THEORY

WHAT GOOD IS THEORY

Good theory is the clear summation and generalization of successful practice plus logical deductions and conjectures from such practice (which are clearly identified as deductions and conjectures).

Bad theory arises out of distress patterns, either directly or indirectly. Human progress has sometimes been laid waste by theories arising out of distress patterns and then reinforced by reactionary social forces. The effects of distress in preventing thinking sometimes leads people to make up theories out of dreams and out of their sensations of the moment.

Any good theory begins with a summary and an intelligent explanation of the common elements in successful practice. Certainly ours does. We are almost alone in the field of human behavior in that strikingly successful *practice came first* and we carefully evolved our theory to explain and guide what was *already working* (in contrast to the usual psychologist's beginning speculation and the following attempts to warp, suggest, and misinterpret human behavior to fit the speculation.)

NEED FOR A THEORY ABOUT THEORY

The power and consistency of our theory are still not generally appreciated even within the RC Communities. We still have people active in RC who assume that RC theory is similar to psychological theories or human growth theories and think that perhaps some of those would work just as well.

In part, this is because we haven't been explicit enough about the role of theory, the importance of theory. Almost all people in a society such as ours have been conditioned against theory, in particular against daring to think for themselves. They have been told they must take someone else's word for authority, accept someone else's dictates. This lies heavy on people's minds. Also, their acquaintance with theory has been almost entirely with oppressive theories, false biased theories used to cheat them.

Beyond that lies another difficulty. Incoherence is one of the results of invalidating people. It handicaps much of the population. People find it difficult to put their own ideas into words well enough to communicate with each other. On the other hand they hear opportunists who are trying to take advantage of them for oppressive purposes being very glib and coherent about deceptive and reactionary "theories." This often leads to a kind of general blind rejection of theory, to pragmatism, to eclecticism, or to defending weird speculations by asking, "how do you know it isn't so?"

This rejection of all theory because of bad experiences with bad theory is understandable but it cannot be given in to. It is similar to the also familiar rejection of the whole notion of leadership by people whose whole experience with leadership has been with oppressive leadership, but we have also learned not to give in to that. We must fight for the actual existence of leadership, of a correct leadership, or we are disarmed. This is so with theory as well. There is a broad, general resistance, understandably, to the acceptance of theory. This must be combatted by clear explanations, by communicating, in effect, a theory about theory.

CLASS ATTITUDES

Middle-class intellectuals who become co-counselors tend to more quickly hear and consider our theory. Their educational background makes it easier for them to take the first steps toward understanding it and trying it. They will tend to have more difficulty, however, in understanding its profundity, its dependability, the importance of not mixing it with contradictory elements from other theories. This is because part of their educational conditioning has been to collect theories like bags of nuts, not to find one that works, nor to apply it, improve it, and make it consistent, but to simply make a collection, to be pragmatic in their choice of theory from time to time, seeking through the libraries of the world or the journals which they read for one more alternative, not understanding that theories are meant to be *applied*.

As people from the working class and the Third World come into our Communities, they will tend in general to have more initial resistance to acceptance of our theory, will be more suspicious of theory in general. We will need to explain clearly and patiently, not only what our theory is, but its importance to individual and Community progress. When the Third World and working class people have accepted the theory, however, they will generally be more devoted to its consistency and its consistent application than our middle class co-counselors. Once the theory has shown its use to them, once they have seen its benefits, they are likely to be very devoted to it and defend its purity and rigor carefully.

HOW RC THEORY EVOLVED

One of the important steps in the construction of RC theory was the very early decision to not take anything on faith, to not borrow anything from previous theories, to not look to existing theories of psychology or human growth or anything else for ideas, to not assume anything or believe anything to be true just because someone had said that it was so or had written a book saying that it was so. We decided to make a fresh start, to include in our theoretical generalizations only the data from experiences that we ourselves had with people, only the actual, successful experiences of re-emergence through counseling that happened in our own experience.

One reason for this was that at the time it seemed plain that no existing theories of human behavior worked well enough or led to good enough or consistent enough results that their assumptions and principles should be given any credence. This was true and has remained true. Slowly, however, we have come to realize these other theories not only do not work well and show no or poor practical results, but also that they are reactionary in their content. The theory of psychoanalysis, for example, portrays humans in an unhuman way. In practice, it becomes a tool for degrading people, for limiting their goals. This is true also of even the most optimistic of the modern humanistic psychologies or human growth theories. Their most positive conjectures are too limited to fit the reality of human beings. The best of the Perls and the Rogers and the Maslow theories (and these men are very positive human beings) would leave people disarmed in the full job of re-emergence by the gaps in their positiveness and the limitations they unawarely leave on the goals of humanity.

This decision of ours to make a completely fresh start in our theory was one of the really important decisions in the evolution of RC. From then on, our theory evolved on the basis of very careful summaries of our very successful practice.

DECISION FOR RIGOR

Another decision was to be rigorous, as completely rigorous as we could be. I think that we have been exemplary in refusing to kid ourselves, in refusing to accept anything in our theory simply because we would like to believe it was so or because it would be a convenient generalization.

Possibly this consistent rigor from the beginning owes something to the existence of a chronic anxiety pattern. I don't think I can claim that my intelligence was functioning that clearly at the beginning. It would be wrong to say that I was lucky in having a chronic pattern of anxious scepticism, but perhaps it would be correct to say that I was lucky that I didn't have a chronic pattern of thoughtless enthusiasm. I was very suspicious on questions of theory, not only of anyone else's enthusiasm but also of my own. I have remained consistently reluctant to accept any new portion of theory until it has survived the fire of sceptical questioning and attack.

When my first co-counselor and I sat down to discuss what had happened to my first client, this was one of the things which we did, at my insistence -- question all of our enthusiasms. We faced clearly at that time the possibility that the marvelous things that had happened to my first client were self-generated, were the result of a spontaneous cyclical process, that perhaps the counseling that I had done had nothing to do with his dramatic re-emergence. We faced that possibility first and then treated as an alternative conjecture the possibility that we had stumbled onto something very profound and very important.

THE DETAILS OF BEING RIGOROUS

The theory has grown in this way, with good rigor, with consistent scepticism turned on anything new. No part of our theory has been added without overwhelming evidence. Each new portion has been first treated as a conjecture and has then faced a number of challenges before it is accepted as even a tentative conclusion. Each new guide or rule or principle has been clearly labelled as an hypothesis until the evidence was overwhelming that it was a useful generalization.

I remember, a few months after my professional one-way counseling and classes began, getting some of my students to listen to me while I made a list. What do I actually know? I asked myself. What am I sure that I know? I concluded that I was fairly sure that when people cried a lot they felt better and seemed to function better; that there were some indications that a lot of shaking had a similar effect. I didn't mention laughter at that point. There was great enthusiasm among my students for many other conjectures, but I wasn't willing then to go beyond those two points as a summary of what I really knew.

The theory has evolved with a critical attitude turned on each portion of it all the way. I think this has been excellent for its consistency, and its slow growth has been a good growth.

Ours has been a scientific theory in the very best sense of the word. We have been at least as rigorous as the theoretical physicist whom most scientists look to as a model for generalizing only from sufficient evidence. When our experiences with clients weren't sufficient in number or variety to uphold a generalization yet, we kept our tentative explanation labeled as an unproven conjecture, however hopeful we felt about it. We have been careful to avoid that most familiar misuse of logic, the generalizing from too few examples.

There is a kind of "new theory", so-called, which arises spontaneously in the co-counseling communities over and over again. I get one or two "theoretical" papers a month, proposing patterned speculation as theory that I am asked to take seriously and publish. Often a clearly patterned tag is attached, such as the statement that "you must accept and publish this as RC theory or you will be invalidating me". Sometimes the patterned character is subtler and harder to detect. There are other "contributions" that are simply a rewriting of existing RC literature. These are theory "created" in the same sense that the lazy high school student "creates" a book report by copying one out of the encyclopedia. To resist this kind of patterned "need" to participate in "creating" theory without any hard thinking and rigor will be an ongoing necessity as our Communities develop.

THE SCIENTIFIC METHOD

RC theory has arisen as a careful, inductively logical structure, each accumulation of carefully scrutinized experimental data finally generalized into a tentative conclusion. This conclusion has then been used to predict other possible phenomena that can be explored in co-counseling. If the results of these explorations when critically examined over a long period of time are in good enough agreement, then we can draw another tentative conclusion. Each conclusion is stated as a conjecture to begin with and accepted as a useful generalization only after a great deal of evidence.

Our theory grew in its early stages in this way -- by the use of inductive logic. It is important to realize that inductive logic is a sufficiently powerful tool to reach useful generalizations, but that ultimately it has some limitations. It is always, in a sense, shaky. In using inductive logic (which is the logic on which the physical sciences are based) one needs to realize that any "law", any generalization from examples, is always based on a limited number of examples. The nature of the generalization can always be modified or overthrown by a counter-example which may show up any day. The next experience may cast a serious doubt on your generalization even though the previous twenty-three all supported it.

This needs to be faced and accepted. I think only painful emotion would ever stand in the way of our accepting this. In this generation, most theoretical physicists have learned to be happy facing this, have learned to eagerly anticipate contradictions showing up because they know they are going to lead to a good period of intellectual activity while an improved theory is hammered out. (Even physicists a generation ago were often still emotionally attached to the conclusions they personally had reached and were sometimes willing to fight hard for an outworn idea.) The little joke which we reprint from the Seattle Science Center in the pamphlet on Distinctive Characteristics indicates the limitations of inductive logic.

It is important that we realize that our theory and our "laws" are just like the theory and "laws" of physics and chemistry. They are actually conjectures with enough experimental support that they are useful as generalizations. That's what a "law" inevitably consists of in an inductively logical structure. It can be overthrown by new evidence. When it is, this is a good thing, because the new evidence usually leads to a more correct and wider generalization. If your previous generalization was carefully made, it usually turns out to be a special case of the new, more general "law". For example, Newton's "laws" of gravitation turned out to be a special application of the general "laws" of relativity describing how the more general "laws" operate over no more than interplanetary distances, no greater than medium-sized stellar masses, etc.

FRONTIER QUESTIONS

Do you see any new developments happening in RC theory?

I can think of a couple of interesting developments that we are not yet ready to generalize about. One is that there is apparently considerable evidence that a significant amount of re-evaluation, including some kind of disposing of tension, takes place while people are dreaming. We're not sure whether there is enough overt evidence of discharge as we think of the usual processes of discharge to use that term. It's true that people chuckle and mumble in their sleep and are known to sweat and shake and cry, but it seems as if a good deal of re-evaluation takes place with the main overt indication being eye movements.

It is good for us to be aware of this information. I don't think we need to be in any hurry to incorporate it yet into the structure of our theory. We don't have enough rigorous evidence ourselves yet. The data that we have is from other people's experiments, and I think we would have serious questions about the rigor of their procedures and the assumptions on which they based their experiments. There does seem to be something at least akin to re-evaluation involved in dreaming that we will one day understand and include in our theory.

There is also a process of which we have much more direct knowledge ourselves that we have not been able to describe rigorously yet. This is the process that takes place when a client who has been isolated from other humans (almost any client) finally makes close and real contact with another person, usually with the co-counselor. I have sometimes called this a "coming home" process. There may be lots of the usual kinds of discharge too, but some of what takes place is not, at least obviously, in the usual modes of discharge. Something very profound happens. The client will "melt" into the counselor, long sighs of relief take place, and often great waves of heat come off the client. Something very profound is happening here, and it is certainly very akin to the other processes and directions that we have called discharge and re-evaluation. We need more experience with it, we need to examine and think about it with more rigor. I have talked about it at workshops and have sometimes demonstrated it, but I haven't yet tried to write it up in our regular literature because I don't think we know enough about it as yet to do this.

There are many other frontier questions. We are reaching out into the unexplored areas in many ways. New conjectures arise continually out of my experience and out of the experience of many other co-counselors.

Most new conjectures do not stand up, of course. A majority, as we might expect, turn out to be rooted in patterns. They are nearly all, of course, very well-intentioned. Most proposals come from good people who honestly "feel" that they have a great insight and want to generalize it into the theory. However, excitement and a feeling of conviction can and often do arise out of patterns and by themselves are not enough reason to include an idea in our theory.

GROWTH WITH CARE

Our theory continues to grow. It is of great importance that it not grow carelessly. The sceptical rigor which we have turned on new developments since the beginning (even though at first in a patterned way) needs to continue to be turned on any new theory in a rational way. Our attitude toward any proposed additions to our theory should be one of rigorous scepticism. Additions should meet highly specific criteria and be added only after a long period of testing and much experience.

INSPIRATION AND PROOF

I think it is important that we realize that inspiration is an excellent guide to experimentation but *must not* be a guide to the *acceptance* of theory. Every other meaningful discipline has had to learn this -- the difference between the process of conjecture and the process of acceptance.

Conjecture, hunches, inspiration are essential. One doesn't increase one's understanding of phenomena rapidly by simply routinely grinding away at it. For co-counseling to reach the next ten million people it cannot rely on old routines. We must always try, in any session, to come up with a new, inspired way of counseling. We must always expect to make fresh discoveries or our application of co-

counseling will not work well enough. We must play hunches, we must try new things.

What is important is that we not confuse a hunch or one apparent success with a theoretical conclusion. Even an apparent success is just one indication. If the test tube turns blue once, let's see what the first ten thousand test tubes do before we generalize.

The theory was developed to begin with in the way that the theory of physical science, of physics, for example, was developed. Experiments, repeated, rigorously checked on, led to generalizations, subject to revision always in the light of further data, but becoming more and more dependable as they were tried out in practice more and more times. Explanations made in the form of conjectures were accepted into the theory only after attempts to disprove them or find some simpler explanation had failed.

NOT A SOCIAL "PSEUDO-SCIENCE"

I think our co-counselors generally need to realize this is not the way the so-called social "sciences" have usually operated. Few if any of the social "sciences" on few if any occasions have qualified as a science in the rigorous way that the physical sciences do and that Re-evaluation Counseling has done. It is still the general practice among the academic community in these fields to rake together a number of observations, put together the best overall description of them they can think of, call this a theory, and work at supporting it with additional data-gathering or experiments designed to support that particular description rather than to establish the reality of the situation. This is a problem throughout the social "sciences". It is, of course, especially one in psychology, which has seen little or no scientific rigor applied ever.

A new development in RC came in the early 1960's. As with many of the key developments in RC, much of the thinking and support and persistance for this was furnished by Mary McCabe. Everyone who knows her intuitively recognizes the central importance which Mary has for Re-evaluation Counseling. Not many, however, would know unless they were very close to the situation what a tremendous role her thinking, nurturing, encouraging, and insisting and persisting has played in the development of the theory itself. I have been the spokesman for nearly all of the theoretical developments but my speaking out is always the result of long-term encouragement and insistence and thoughtful counseling on the part of Mary.

AN ADDITIONAL LOGICAL STRUCTURE

What happened in the 1960's was that we began to create a parallel structure in our theory based on *deductive* logic, parallel to the existing system based on inductive logic. I was moved to write the *Postulates* at that time. Partly this came out of my wanting to be very sure and very aware of what I was assuming to be true about people in my work with them and in the development of the theory. By then I had heard many examples from my clients and students of the mistakes that their unaware assumptions had led them into. They would say to me, "well, everybody knows this," and then would tell me some obvious nonsense, widely accepted but nonsense. I think I was concerned that I not kid myself in some similar way.

Whatever the motivations involved (and some of them were rational), with Mary's thoughtful encouragement and persistence I wrote the *Postulates* and began informally checking out all the existing inductive conclusions on a deductive basis.

In the first place, were the *Postulates* consistent with each other? In the second place, could the theory of counseling as we had attained it in the early 60's be derived deductively from the *Postulates* without the experimental evidence which had led to the theory in the first place? Third, if there were portions of the existing theory that I could not derive deductively as yet, the question was, was that part of the theory inconsistent with the things that I *could* derive deductively from the *Postulates*?

This checking out process has been carried out ever since, mostly informally and intuitively. It isn't down on paper yet, and I'm not sure that there is any rush in getting it on paper, but it has been carried out. Innumerable numbers of my sessions as client have been spent in checking this sort of thing through, and many conversations with Mary and other experienced counselors have taken place on this topic. We have found no inconsistencies.

The existence of this deductively logical structure has been very reassuring. We have overwhelming reason from a whole new direction to be confident of the essential correctness and workability of our theory. We can be much more certain of the logical consistency of our theory, much more sure that a conclusion or generalization in one area is not in conflict with another conclusion or generalization in another area. The *Postulates* and the deductive structure which has arisen out of them has contributed greatly to the unity and cohesiveness of our co-counseling movement.

REASSURING TO CO-COUNSELORS

In ways which I didn't expect, the *Postulates* have played an important role in supporting and reassuring people's own thinking. It is very reassuring to people to see the beginnings of RC thinking out in plain view and realize that these are assumptions that they too can make with good heart, that these give a picture of the world and the universe and the nature of human beings that they would always have liked to assume to be true.

A SOURCE OF CONFIDENCE

The double-checking on what we are doing made possible by the two logical structures gives all of us, and, in particular me, a great sense of confidence in dealing with challenges or problems. I can usually tell quickly whether a challenge issued to the theory is a sound one or not, and I am not alone in this confidence. Many co-counselors have by now integrated this double-checking of our theory into their common practice.

When we've had a problem with any of our leaders, it's usually the case that, because of their background and distresses, they have never understood the notion of logical consistency and still practice, awarely or not, eclecticism, pragmatism, picking and choosing without regard for logical consistency. The only test people in this condition have learned to apply is whether something works the first time they try it. That is not sufficient. Rigor requires that the test not only work one time, because it could work that one time or few times for the wrong reason (and often does temporarily). The test is that it has to be consistent with everything else that you do and fits into the general theory as well as "works".

TWO PROCESSES IN THEORY GROWTH

It is probably worth discussing two important, distinct processes in the building of a theory, or the building of any logical structure. Both are necessary, but when they become confused with each other they do not work well.

The first of these processes might be called inspiration, conjecture, playing hunches. This is very important in the functioning of human intelligence.

A mathematician, for example, could operate on very careful deductive logic and set up the axioms or assumptions for a mathematical system, check carefully that they are consistent with each other, add the necessary undefined terms and definitions. Without inspiration, he could then grind out a very large number of theorems all of which would be carefully proven to be true in the assumed system beyond a shadow of doubt but almost all of which would be of no importance whatever. Instead the creative mathematician must play hunches, must seek to speculate on what important results or theorems he can possibly think of that might derive logically from his assumptions. He labels these significant results *conjectures* and then seeks to prove them rigorously.

The process of arriving at these significant conjectures is a process that calls for the greatest freedom in thinking. Flash answers, fantasies, brainstorming, any process at all that allows complete freedom and encouragement for speculation is in order here. No thought is too wild to be considered and put down on the list of conjectures in this portion of our thinking. All the effort of the individual thinker or the group of thinkers at this point needs to be directed to resisting any attempt to be careful, to challenging any and all strictures in the formulation of interesting possibilities to be thought about.

The second process, however, is the rigorous checking and proving (or disproving) of these conjectures and here, one's attitude becomes completely different if one wishes to have dependable results. The acceptance of a conjecture as a valid conclusion or generalization must come only after the conjecture has been proved beyond a shadow of a doubt (if one is using deductive logic) or reinforced by repeated experiments or experiences all of which are challenged and criticized in all possible ways before they are accepted and of whom it is demanded that they actually lead to the conclusion in question and could not possibly be interpreted in any other way. To admit a generalization into any theory including the theory of Re-evaluation Counseling requires that it first pass the test of being attacked, questioned, sprayed with acid, scraped and blowtorched. The ones that survive belong in the theory, and they will be in better shape and better formulated when one has finished attacking them than they were when first proposed. Any proposed addition to the theory must first survive the attempt to be torn down, to be disproved in any possible way. The Vatican used to appoint what they called a Devil's Advocate to seek to destroy any claims of a proposed saint to canonization. We must play the role of Devil's Advocate before accepting any new theoretical principle or generalization.

Again, there are two processes here: First, speculating, looking forward, looking for new directions, new growth of theory. Here anything is welcome, the wildest idea is fine. There must be no strictures against putting the conjecture on the list. But when it comes to acceptance then we who have been such fond, welcoming friends to the new idea become its deadliest enemies and only if it survives our attacks does it become accepted as part of our theory.

POLICY IS PART OF THEORY

Our theory is growing. Sometimes people listening to me review fundamental principles at a workshop wonder if the theory has been completed. This is not so at all. Our theory is continually growing in a very live and healthy way. People sometimes don't recognize large parts of it because we often call it policy, but this newly emerging policy is very much a part of Re-evaluation Counseling theory. The emergence of Communities, the rules of relations within the Communities, the process of permeation, the proposals for interaction with the other integrative forces and trends in the universe that we talked about yesterday, all of these are very much part of theory. Of course it continues to grow at the basic levels as well. We have a much clearer theory about paying attention to a client now than we had a few years ago. More powerful and effective counseling results from it.

A HISTORY OF PUBLICATIONS

A continuing problem is effective communication of the theory that has been evolved and as it evolves. The first book that we planned was called "The Future of Man" and it has never been published. It is sitting in manuscript. In trying to get it ready, Mary and I came to the conclusion that we

needed a succinct introduction to Re-evaluation Counseling
first, so we put my introductory lecture down on paper and
rewrote it and rewrote it until it became *The Human Side of
Human Beings*.   In the process, we worked with a good
algebra text as our model. We didn't want to publish it until
we felt that we could not improve on any word, any comma,
any period in it. I think our care with that first book was a
very fortunate thing.

Publication actually started with several forerunners of
the *Fundamentals of Co-Counseling Manual*. We used to
make them by hand in vestpocket size, little lists of suggestions for counseling effectively. Close after those came the
holiday poems which are now collected in one section of
Zest is Best. These contain a good deal of theory in a very
basic sense. Mary recognized their importance before I did
and insisted that I write them and distribute them. It turned
out that people who got them also liked and appreciated
them. Some of our first validation from people distant from
Seattle came from the responses to these Christmas cards.
A great deal of theory is said better in the poems in *Zest is
Best* than it has been anywhere else. Many people, if not
most people, can hear and remember the things said in verse
better than they can prose.

MANY CONTRIBUTIONS TO THEORY

Recently articles in *Present Time, The R.C. Teacher*
and the other RC publications have become important ways
of communicating theory to the Communities. Mary is now
writing more, a development that is welcomed by all of us.
People respond with enthusiasm to her articles. Many of
our more experienced co-counselors are starting to contribute
to theory. Using quotes from letters in *Present Time* and
The R.C. Teacher has played an important role in this.

When I have asked people to write theoretical articles,
the responses have often been not too successful. People
apparently become self-conscious at the thought that they
were "writing an article" and wrote very stilted ones. As I

began to quote a phrase or two from letters in *Present Time*, however, I noticed the writers' letters contained longer quotable excerpts for the next issue of *Present Time*. As the process continued, it became possible to lift excellent short articles out of many of the letters. Apparently, writing a letter in a white hot urge to communicate something important thrusts aside many of the barriers to writing and allows the writer to communicate without self-consciousness and to the point. Real contributions to theory are often made now in the longer excerpts from letters in our publications. (Emma Ramos-Diaz' letters have been outstanding, but many, many readers of RC have had theoretical articles appear in the last year.)

We have adopted a restrictive posture toward publishing articles purporting to represent an RC position or RC theory outside of our own publications. We insist that such publication have prior official approval from the Community. We haven't always been able to enforce this rule on non-RCers or ex-RCers, but it is obvious that it has had a salutary effect. A great deal of nonsense that would have otherwise been published has been discouraged. The articles that have appeared without our approval have not been disasterous because, in part, the knowledge of our firm policy in this respect has led the writers to attempt to be more responsible than they might otherwise have been.

We have a small problem here which I think is being handled. This is an occasional attempt to use RC theory and the popularity of RC for a kind of free ride in doing academic dissertations. We have asked that academic RCers not do their dissertations on RC unless their project is first checked with the International Reference Person for correctness in representing RC and also that the project be one of *real scholarship*. We ask that RC not be used for a "free ride", for filling a frozen need to publish or get a dissertation done or something like this. This will always be a gray area, but I think we are handling it pretty well.

MORE PUBLICATION

The most important challenge, of course, is to publish more theory ourselves. This becomes a crucial question.

There has been some apparent conflict for me between concentrating on writing and publishing more theory versus getting around to see the Communities and meet with people at workshops. Workshops do a marvelous job of communicating theory and practice, and bring immediate results in the growth of new leadership and the growth of Communities. I have made an aware choice these last three years to put in most of the time available at workshops and relegate new books of theory to second place.

New books will appear, however. The recent theoretical articles in our magazines will need to be rewritten somewhat for book publication. There are enough published articles for another "collection" book beyond *The Human Situation*, and it should be published before long.

THE ROUGH NOTES

Amazingly good communication has been achieved through the Rough Notes volumes -- The Rough Notes from Buck Creek I, The Rough Notes from La Scherpa I, and The Rough Notes from Calvinwood I (the first classroom teachers' workshop). These have had profound effects on the development of teachers even though they are in oral rather than written language. The practice of some Areas of buying these expensive volumes and having them on loan for circulation has worked so well that we can recommend it to all Areas. We are also trying to sponsor travelling sets of these books outside the organized Areas.

THE CASSETTES

The issued cassettes have also been an excellent shortcut for communicating theory. The language of a cassette includes a lot of arm waving, of course. Oral language, at least my oral language, is much different from written language, yet people seem to be able to hear theory accurately to an amazing extent. One of our goals is to have a wide variety of cassettes available from the excellent lectures and workshop discussions of the last few years.

THE APPLICATION OF THEORY

Our theory does not operate in a vacuum but in a concrete situation. The leading edge of our theory and practice has for some time been the growth of our Communities and, increasingly, our interaction with the society at large. It is possible to let these new developments create a problem for us, to let ourselves divide into those primary co-counselors and those primary community builders or leaders. The pull to do this will be there, but we must resist it. All of us must keep progressing through our own co-counseling and all of us must also learn to think all the time and take responsibility and lead in our Communities and in the world at large.

The fulfilment of our humanness requires playing, at some time and in some areas, the role of organizing and leading other human intelligences. This tendency to separate this from co-counseling sessions themselves is one aspect of a general reactive, patterned tendency to compartmentalize the different aspects of co-counseling and to neglect some phases while we concentrate on the parts that are easy for us. We are countering this pull directly with the idea of the inevitable development of co-counseling -- discussed in the talks that I have been giving at workshops and in the articles in *Present Time*. We're trying to show that it is all together -- to make plain that permeation of the society is really necessary in order for one to go on having good sessions; that one can't just concentrate on good sessions and have everything work out. Not only is our Communities permeating society a requirement for us to go on having good sessions, but having good sessions ourselves is necessary for the permeation of society. We need to understand that it is all tied together, that new persons have to have a good session before we can expect them to become interested in counseling, that co-counseling is harder than counseling and being counseled, that recruitment is an inevitable development, that Community building will follow, and then permeation, that Re-evaluation Counseling is all of one piece and needs to be understood and cooperated with on all fronts even if we concentrate more or less of our efforts in one area at a particular time.

AREAS OF DIFFICULTY

There are perhaps three areas of difficulty in the use of RC theory at the present time that we can identify. One such area is the perhaps inevitable reactive tendency to sloppiness, to lack of rigor. This arises everywhere and it arises with all of us. The patterns of any person pull at one to be sloppy.

The wave of "set exercise" teaching that arose in some Areas and was caught and clarified and checked at the La Scherpa teachers' workshop last summer is an example. Here was a pull to be sloppy, to quit thinking, but make up a list of little "fun" set exercises to do and call that RC teaching. It wasn't bad that it came out in the open at the workshop, that was very good, of course, but how widespread it appeared to have become among the teachers was an indication of how far sloppiness can go in actual practice. After the article calling for an end to this "set-exercise" teaching was published in *Present Time*, approving letters from students came in from nearly every Community, letters saying, "I knew there was something wrong and I'm so relieved that it's not happening anymore."

Another widespread difficulty is the tendency to isolate Re-evaluation Counseling activities from reality, to treat co-counseling as an escape from the real world, an escape from living. This will keep co-counseling from working as well as it should.

I don't mean that co-counseling and the Co-counseling Communities should not serve as a sanctuary intermittently. This is part of RC's function, of course. We need to be able to come to a co-counseling session or co-counseling class or to come back into the Community to catch up on one's discharge and re-evaluation and emergence, to allow one's wounds to heal, to correct one's compass and charge one's batteries; but only in order to prepare to crank up our motors, throw our vehicles into high gear, and roar out the gate for another assault on the world in general.

Fear patterns are taking over when this retreating and huddling takes place. In the grip of them, co-counselors huddle with each other instead of making friends in the real world where the bulk of their potential friends exist. They violate the "no socializing" principle and then make all kinds of rationalized defenses of the error. Some people retreat from community activities to their classes because they feel safer and more comfortable there. Some people stop participating in classes because they "only want to co-counsel". Of course their co-counseling doesn't work well if they don't continue to participate in class, of course the class doesn't function well enough unless people are looking out, reaching out, permeating the society around them, reaching new people and making new friends and cooperators of them.

The retreat behavior is a dead thing. It's a reactive entropy-pointing tendency to degrade RC, to adjust it to patterns, to reach compromises with patterns. We are lured to "not make so much effort" and compromise with the entropy forces. To give into this is death, not only for the theory but for us. We will not achieve permanent immortality this way. We will not even have a few years of being fully human if we lose our way on this question. This reactive tendency must be battled intransigently. We keep our flag flying when we make no adjustment, no compromise in terms of our overall direction. (We will make *tactical* compromises with the devil, let alone with a pattern; but *only* for its overthrow.) Never can we settle for being "comfortable" in a reactive way. Tactical compromises must always be on the way toward strategic victory or they will spell defeat.

OVERSIMPLIFICATION

In a way, the third difficulty is an expression of the second. This is the tendency to keep RC too simple, to not grow in our use of RC, to not apply it in anything but the most simplistic ways. This patterned tendency has often defended itself under the slogan, "the client is in charge of her own material." It's true that I once said this at a workshop. I didn't believe I had said it until someone played the cassette back to me. I had said it in such a context, however, that the meaning was not at all the one it appears to have when it is quoted in defense of never going beyond permissive counseling. Connie Lindemann put this tendency in sharp words. She said, "Well, that's what I learned, that you validate your clients and you get them to discharge, and they will eventually get their heads out". I'm afraid this is pretty much how RC is interpreted in some of our Areas and among some co-counselors, but it is not a correct statement. It is so incomplete as to be very misleading.

Of course we are very glad when our new students in a Fundamentals class learn this much in their first eight weeks. They learn to listen to their clients without interrupting or interfering. They learn to let them cry, they learn to let them bring up the material they wish to and say what they want to about it. That's a great deal to learn in the first eight weeks. A great deal of conditioning from the culture has to be shrugged off to get this far, but this is *only starting* to learn co-counseling.

The great bulk of the reactive thrust into our lives from patterns is in the *chronic* patterns. The overwhelming weight that crushes us down is in *chronic* patterns. Unless we go beyond the permissive approach, we are helpless with chronic patterns, and only accidentally will we win victories over them. (It is accidental if permissive counseling happens to contradict a particular chronic pattern so that it works against it. The fact that this sometimes happens delayed us five years in getting a clear picture of what a chronic pattern was.)

In general, to successfully attack a chronic pattern *requires the word from outside*, requires the thoughtful observation of the counselor and careful creation and offering of the direction that will send the client against his/her feelings, against his/her adjustments, against the heavy weight of the chronic pattern.

Larry Morgan said at a recent workshop, "Every teacher has got to care deeply and in detail that every student get rid of every bit of reactive material. The teacher has to think about the student and guide him or her and encourage him or her, and insist on her or him moving against chronic patterns, and has to open doors and place challenges before her or him until she or he does." Co-counseling that remains simplistic and doesn't go this far will be a trap.

Every counselor has to care enough about his or her client to observe what the chronic patterns are and has to plot and plan against them, has to create and give the word from outside that will bring the client head-on into a successful assault against them. Every teacher has to care this much about the students in class. Every Reference Person has to care this much about every teacher. We on this committee have to care this much about every teacher. We on this committee have to care this much about every single Reference Person and teacher.

COMPLETE RE-EMERGENCE IS OUR GOAL

We can't conceive of resting and being permissive and acting indifferent while someone muddles in confusion and turns the bright co-counseling sword into a rusty pile of junk, turns co-counseling into a trivial thing. This is where our battles are, to take our re-emergence all the way through permeation, all the way to where we're guiding the other integrative processes in the universe. The automatic evolutionary processes are not the only ones that are important. Our deliberate, aware intervention to free each other from the bondage of chronic patterns, to free each other to be complete humans, must operate.

WE WON'T PERMIT DISRUPTION

We will apparently have a few occasions where people in the grip of certain chronic disruptive and destructive patterns will have gotten into our Community. We have had four occasions in the last couple of years when such people had to be made to choose between cooperating and following the theory and the practice or leaving the Community. We can be patient only up to a point and then such patterns must be separated from us. For the sake of our present co-counselors and for the sake of our appearance before the world of human beings, it must be clear that what they are doing is not Re-evaluation Counseling.

Such actions will be rare, to be used only as a last resort when we do not find any way to interrupt the pattern. Our basic tool in clarifying theory and policy is our endless willingness to explain, our willingness to demonstrate, our ability to be zingy and sharp in holding nonsense up to the light.

All our leadership needs to become fiercely aggressive on these questions of the purity and the continually growing character of our theory and policy. Where someone has been leading and teaching and co-counseling wrong, we have to have it out with them until they understand what's wrong and how they can do it right, and if they can't understand it in a reasonable time, we have to insist that they quit teaching or quit leading.

When a pattern is the enemy, sometimes you have to be fierce and intransigent even though you, of course, also have to be skillful in the way you make your attack. Sometimes you will have to swing a fierce hatchet of criticism and requirement.

Usually the people that I am fierce with later agree and are appreciative for the intervention once the difficulty is surmounted. I'll give you that for your long-range comfort, but short-range there will not necessarily be any comfort for you. It is tough to lovingly but fiercely interject correct theory and policy where the chronic patterns are threatening to take over the individual's progress in co-counseling or their teaching or their leadership in the Community.

We co-counselors owe it to each other to intervene sharply and fiercely with each other in the areas where we are not thinking or acting intelligently because a chronic pattern has us shut down and deceived. This is what really caring is about, and we have to grow up to this point.

What Do We Know?
What Have We Learned?*

Re-evaluation Counseling and the Re-evaluation Counseling Communities are flourishing in almost every respect. Large numbers of excellent new people are coming into our Communities. Experienced co-counselors are persisting with their co-counseling. Important permanent gains in re-emergence are reported by thousands of individuals from all sections of our Communities. Our leadership corps is expanding and maturing. We seem from every point of view, to be much more aware and confident of what we are about, to be reaping more and more satisfying results on our way to our long range goals.

At this time, on the eve of our fifth International Reference Persons' Workshop in the fifth year of the existence of our Communities, it's worthwhile to review our position. What do we know? What have we learned? What important conclusions can we draw from the present situation of Re-evaluation Counseling practice, theory and organization?

The following seem to me to be at least some of the important ponts:

I. We have learned that RE-EVALUATION COUNSELING WORKS AND WORKS INCREASINGLY WELL.

Dependable, fundamental, significant gains are made toward the re-emergence of our complete human natures and abilities whenever co-counseling is pursued correctly and assiduously. Real, permanent, satisfying changes and achievements are regularly reported by large numbers of co-counselors in our Communities.

*Preliminary Report to the International Reference Persons' Workshop – Buck Creek XVIII, July 14, 1975

II. We have learned that COOPERATIVE EFFORT AND COMMUNITY ORGANIZATION ARE NECESSARY FOR THE MOST EFFECTIVE USE OF RE-EVALUA-TION CO-COUNSELING.

We have experience with co-counseling in many different situations: the isolated person in the process of training a co-counselor, small groups trying to learn co-counseling together, classes outside of organized Areas, and many stages of Community maturity all the way to large, well-organized, well-led Communities of co-counselors. The evidence is very clear that the existence of the strongest and best Community organization that we can attain is a decisive factor in improving and enhancing individual co-counseling. Any co-counselor can expect to progress much faster in a strong co-counseling Community with clear, able leadership.

III. We have learned that RE-EVALUATION CO-COUNSEL-ING COMMUNITIES DEPENDABLY GROW, FLOUR-ISH AND MATURE IN AN EXCELLENT MANNER IF THE ALREADY-ATTAINED POLICIES ARE APPLIED RIGOROUSLY BY ABLE LEADERSHIP.

There is hardly any kind of problem confronting any Community which by now has not already been solved or is in the process of being solved by another Community. Difficulties seem to stem not from external circumstances nor from absence of sufficient policy guides but from failure to really carry out already existing policies.

IV. We have learned that ANY NEW POPULATION CAN BE REACHED WITH OUR BASIC THEORY AND POLICY IN SPITE OF NATIONAL AND CULTURAL DIFFERENCES.

Cultural differences do not require modification of our basic theory and policy but they do require care that cultural patterns (which are *not* part of our theory and policy) not be unawarely extended to or foisted upon the new populations as if they were part of Re-evaluation Counseling.

Our early attempts to "adjust" RC to requirements put to us by some people in new cultures, requests that we modify RC to fit the peculiarities of new cultures, have turned out to be patterned requests in every case. Large numbers of people in the populations involved have welcomed an accurate version of RC and found it workable. There is, however, an unaware residue of taken-for-granted nonsense in the United States and Western cultures which is correctly objected to by the new populations. We need to be aware of this and free our working versions of RC from it before we offer RC to the new people.

V. We have learned that THE MASTERY OF RE-EVALU-ATION COUNSELING THEORY MUST NOT STOP AT THE FUNDAMENTALS LEVEL.

Fundamentals co-counseling works extremely well, and will work better and better as the participants become more skillful and more aware. It will remain the foundation of all co-counseling, even at later stages. Successfully grappling with chronic patterns and assisting the individual to emerge from them does, however, require a qualitative change in addressing a client. It requires making a more aware distinction between the client as a person and the client's distresses. It requires increasingly warm and aware support and validation and assistance to the person and increasingly sharp, intransigent, flexible contradiction of distress. In general, except for fortunate circumstances, to begin to emerge from a chronic pattern requires "the word from outside", from someone playing the role of counselor, someone who has earned the trust of the client as a person and can communicate skillfully and well a direction which will seem reasonable to the person but which will contradict and begin the discharge of the chronic pattern. This direction needs to be increasingly accurate and specific for the particular chronic pattern, but it also needs to be a possible direction, it needs to seem reasonable to the client to attempt it. A workable direction against a chronic pattern must not seem to be the blank face of an unscalable cliff or the client will resort to pretense or unawareness in order to appear to follow the direction.

VI. We have learned that OUR COMMUNITIES SHOULD BE PREPARED TO DIVIDE BEFORE THEY EXCEED 200 CO-COUNSELORS IN NUMBER.

Effective leadership from Reference Person to teachers and from teachers to co-counselors is necessary for the best functioning of the Communities and consistent re-emergence by co-counselors. The development of additional leaders should have been achieved long before 200 co-counselors are active. Certainly it is difficult for one set of leaders to provide leadership to more than 200 people.

VII. We have learned that AN AREA OR SUB-AREA ORGANIZATION SHOULD BE FORMED WHEN THERE ARE ABOUT THIRTY ACTIVE CO-COUN-SELORS, TWO OR MORE TEACHERS, AND WHEN ABLE, PROMISING LEADERSHIP IS AVAILABLE.

Setting up Area organizations has not in general worked well until there are at least two teachers and at least 30 active co-counselors. Until this point of growth, leadership can be effectively given by a teacher in contact with the International Communities leadership. To set up an Area organization before someone is familiar with and ready for the responsibilities of being Reference Person is often to create more problems than it solves. Functioning leadership rather than the existence of a structure is what makes an Area effective.

VIII. We have learned that LEADERSHIP TO WORKSHOPS AND CLASSES OUTSIDE THEIR OWN AREA SHOULD BE EXTENDED ONLY BY LEADERS WHO ARE FUNCTIONING WELL AT HOME AND WHOSE OWN AREAS ARE IN GOOD SHAPE.

We have no need for leaders who make a "career" of leading workshops even though it is an inviting occupation and it is easy to rouse enthusiasm from co-counselors when one can visit briefly and then leave. One of the responsibilities of a workshop leader is to develop new leadership during the course of the workshop and also to assist the permanent growth of the Community where the workshop is held. A person who has not done a good job of organizing his or her own Area is not likely to be effective in assisting another Area in this respect, hampered both by lack of accurate knowledge and lack of being a good example. Those who are effective leaders in their own Areas, however, will know what they are talking about and will have the conviction of confident achievement behind them. They are less prone to seek to run the workshop on a popularity-winning basis, but more to look after the long-range needs of the Community.

IX. We have learned that RE-EVALUATION COUNSELING AND LIBERATION MOVEMENTS ARE COMPATIBLE.

We have learned that the basic liberating role of Re-evaluation counseling, the freeing of the individual from the pattern, is supportive to and is supported by efforts of people to free themselves from social, economic and political oppression. The initial suspicion and fear of Re-evaluation Counseling often held by people active in social liberation can be overcome by good communication.

X. We have learned that THIRD WORLD AND WORKING CLASS PEOPLE ARE READY TO ACCEPT AND USE RE-EVALUATION COUNSELING IF IT IS PRESENTED CORRECTLY AND COMMUNICATED WELL.

Fears that the basic theory and practice of Re-evaluation Counseling would not be understood by people whose concerns are surviving under and emerging from oppression have turned out to be groundless. Any difficulty until now in involving such people in Re-evaluation Counseling turns out to have been the timidities and other patterned attitudes of our present membership, rather than anything about the theory or practice itself.

XI. We have learned that PUBLICATIONS DEVOTED TO THE APPLICATION OF RC THEORY AND THE PERMEATION OF RE-EVALUATION COUNSELING INTO SPECIFIC AREAS OF HUMAN ACTIVITIES ARE WORKABLE.

Our special journals for communication between co-counselors who wish to apply the theory in permeating their own particular areas of interest and activity have met with enough of a response and participation to indicate clearly that we are on the way to developing a very important channel of communication in this respect.

XII. We have learned that SPECIAL WORKSHOPS ARE VALUABLE IF THEY ARE ORGANIZED AROUND COMMON INTERESTS OR COMMON GOALS RATHER THAN AROUND COMMON PROBLEMS.

If co-counselors who share goals and interests in the real world communicate together and use the tools of co-counseling, they in practice turn out to be very supportive of each other. Co-counselors who attempt to get together to discuss a common problem on the other hand are under pressure to pool their distresses, resonate with each other, and arrive at incorrect policies and programs.

XIII. As a result of our large amount of teaching experience, WE HAVE A CLEARER IDEA OF WHAT THE MAIN FUNCTIONS OF AN RC TEACHER ARE.

The key functions and modes of teaching for an RC teacher seem at present to be:

A. To communicate the theory verbally in classes;

B. To communicate the theory in print and recordings by introducing, making available and selling all RC literature and tapes, including the special interest journals, to the co-counselors and the class members;

Part of the natural functioning of a human intelligence is the organizing of other intelligences together for common effort, toward common goals, achieving common successes.

D. We have learned that good leadership operates much more by example than by exhortation. Teachers and leaders in RC need to be aware that one of the facts of life is that everything they do or don't do in their lives is noticed and widely discussed by students and co-counselors and, unhappily, by their patterns. An old saying sums it up, "What you *do* speaks so loudly to me that I cannot hear what you *say*."

E. We have learned that a person should be accepted into leadership only when that person is actually ready and will be able to function responsibly. (The fact that such persons may have to discharge certain distresses and feelings as they assume leadership does not by itself, of course, mean they are not ready.)

F. We have learned that the kind of eagerness for leadership which seeks to fill a frozen need to be recognized as a leader is not a qualification for leadership nor is the ability to pretend to be a leader. Actual readiness to lead in a rational way, for rational motives, must be present before a person is asked to take leadership.

G. We have learned that a key function of a leader is, immediately on assuming leadership, to begin training one's own replacement and additional leaders.

H. We have come to realize that a good leader does not do the thinking *for* the group, but instead elicits, gleans, collects, assembles and integrates the best thinking of every member of the group. She or he selects by careful listening and then remembers the brilliant, sparkling thinking of group members, separating it from all the distressed nonsense, and collects and integrates this into a complete, consistent program with the gaps filled in by the leader's own thinking. The entire integrated program is then communicated back to the members of the group and the acceptance of it as their program is secured. This is *possible* to do. To do the thinking *for* the group is not.

I. We have learned that good collective thinking and fruitful discussion on the part of any group requires that a leader of the group prepare and present proposals on the questions at issue at the beginning of the discussion. To say "this is a problem, has anyone any ideas?" does not in general lead to a good discussion but rather to all kinds of patterned responses. On the other hand, if the leadership places as complete as possible a set of proposals before the group, even if the proposals are mistaken or less than optimum, the group will tend to respond thoughtfully, either accepting, amending, substituting or otherwise improving the proposals, with thinking involved, rather than the patterned response which the failure to present an initial program will elicit.

XV. We have learned that THE USE OF SECTION ORGANIZATION AND LEADERSHIP IN ANY LARGE WORKSHOP ENHANCES THE FUNCTIONING OF THE WORKSHOP AND PROVIDES AN EXCELLENT MEDIUM FOR TRAINING NEW LEADERSHIP FOR THE COMMUNITY.

As our workshops, particularly the International Workshops, have grown larger, we feared for a loss of the intimacy and warmth that we'd experienced in the smaller workshops. With the evolving of the section organization scheme, however, this warmth, closeness and intimacy has been fully recaptured and the richness and variety of a larger workshop has also been made available. The organization of a workshop by sections has in effect given us small workshops within a large workshop and has been of great advantage to the workshop attenders. The use of section leaders and assistant leaders and the organization of special meetings and discussions with them has provided a useful training medium for new leadership. Where it has been possible, the use of the more experienced people as *assistant* leaders with promising but less experienced people taking the role of the *leaders* of the sections has been profitable. It has allowed the new people the experience of actual leadership and has allowed the more experienced people a chance to learn what has often been difficult in the Communities, the art of supporting new leaderhisp and helping it to mature and "grow up".

XVI. We have learned that THE INSISTENT PATTERNED PULL ON TEACHERS AND LEADERS OF RC TO RESORT TO "SET EXERCISES" AND MECHANICAL ROUTINES OF LEADING OR TEACHING CAN BE RESISTED WITH AN AWARE POLICY.

We have learned that this pull can be resisted and overcome by awareness of the problem and by raising the issue with the co-counseling community in general so that co-counselors and class members also awarely watch that this sort of non-thinking activity does not creep into the work of our teachers and leaders.

XVII. We have learned that CO-COUNSELORS CAN, WITH CARE, ENGAGE TOGETHER IN ADDITIONAL ACTIVITIES WITH A CO-COUNSELING CONTENT BUT CANNOT, IN GENERAL, SUCCESSFULLY ADD ADDITIONAL RELATIONSHIPS TO THE CO-COUNSELING ONE.

It is clear from experience that co-counselors can and will be able to carry on many activities with each other as long as *the content of these activities is essentially co-coun-*

seling, that it is directed to assisting each other toward re-emergence into full humanness. It is also clear that adding additional relationships to the co-counseling relationship is not yet workable if it ever will be. Efforts to add these additional relationships have not been supportive of, but rather a hindrance to, the re-emergence of the parties concerned. This seems to be uniformly so whether the individuals "guiltily" violate the blue pages in secret or whether they construct elaborate rationalizations and justifications for the additional relationships. It seems to be clearly true that a co-counselor should construct any additional relationships beyond co-counseling only with people outside the Re-evaluation Counseling Communities, that otherwise the addictive pull to try to fill a "frozen need" is so deceiving that irrational, non-survival behavior always results.

XVIII. We have learned that THERE ARE WORKABLE GUIDELINES (OF WHICH WE NOW KNOW AT LEAST THE BEGINNING RULES) FOR CO-COUN-SELING BETWEEN MEMBERS OF GROUPS WHICH PLAY OPPRESSING AND OPPRESSED ROLES TOWARD EACH OTHER IN OUR SOCIETY.

We have a great deal more to learn in this area. As a beginning it seems clear that members of an oppressed group should not in general be expected to listen to members of the unoppressed groups work on their distresses in this area (racism, sexism, etc.). (The members of oppressed groups will find themselves having to do enough of this through the compulsive behavior of other co-counselors or through accidental circumstances to test their mettle. What is important is that we awarely seek to avoid imposing this on them wherever possible.)

It seems clear that clarifying discussions need to take place first in the separate groups (at workshops, etc.) so that the safety and lack of cross-group restimulation can allow the issues to be clearly formulated and then the various groups should communicate to each other in an organized manner in a joint meeting. It also seems clear that such distresses as racism should be worked on with co-counselors of one's own group and that permissive counseling alone will not in general suffice even to bring them to light against the occluding shame and guilt.

XIX. We have learned that DISRUPTIVE BEHAVIOR BY INDIVIDUALS IN A CO-COUNSELING CLASS OR CO-COUNSELING COMMUNITY ("MAKING TROUBLE FOR THE LEADER OR TEACHER") CAN BEST BE UNDERSTOOD AS AN ATTEMPT TO COMMUNI-CATE SOMETHING TO THE LEADER OR THE TEACHER.

At the present we can suggest a list of five possible, general messages which such behavior may be trying to get across to the teacher or leader. These five messages and the general tentative responses to remedy the indicated difficul-ties follow. The disruptive behavior may mean:

A. The person is trying to communicate that he or she lacks enough information or has incorrect informa-tion in the area. This is implicitly a request to the leader or teacher for correct information or for correction of the incorrect information. The remedy is to patiently explain and explain and explain.

B. A signal that the person is being expected to work or be counseled at a level that he or she is not yet ready to handle. The remedy in this case is to back up, to ask the person what she or he would like to do and then listen patiently (through perhaps considerable preliminary dramatization) until able to hear the communication of what he or she feels he or she can handle and what she or he is ready to tackle. You can then remove any premature expectation from the person. In rare instances the message may be that he or she is not yet ready to be in RC or in co-counseling.

C. The person is exhibiting a pattern to you by dramatizing it and thus implicitly requesting help with the pattern which she or he is dramatizing. "Every dramatization is a call for help." The remedy in this case is to assume the counselor role and with skill and persistence find a way to help the person with this problem or to demonstrate to the person's regular co-counselors how to help with it.

D. The person being "difficult" may be testing the leader, the counselor, or the teacher. The person may be seeking reassurance that the co-counselor, leader or teacher will not give in to the distresses, will stand up to them, will hold the line against them. The remedy, the correct response in this case, is of course to stand firm, to hold the line, to strike an attitude of loving, sometimes amused, warm, flexible intransigence against the dramatization. The payoff will come when, having tested the resistance and finding that it will furnish sufficient contradiction to his or her distress, the person begins to discharge, often voluminously.

E. The person is trying to signal that the leaders, teachers or counselors are unawarely acting in a mistaken way, are acting out of their own (often chronic) distress or out of a mistaken conception of the situation. This should not be the *first* possibility to be considered by the counselor, teacher, or leader. To leap to this first is often to fall into one's own guilt patterns and abandon the person who is asking for help in one of the four other situations listed above. However, if checking out on the other four persistently does not bring a solution, then it is important that each of us keep the possibility in mind that first person singular is acting in a distressed way. "Keep your faith when all men doubt you, but make allowance for their doubting, too." The remedy, of course, is to have a session or a series of sessions as a client, to examine the possibility that *you may be pushing your distress* at the person, remembering that the theoretical possibility of this exists with everyone else and that thus, implicitly, it could even be true for the first person singular, no matter how righteous or defensive you may be feeling at the moment.

XX. We have learned that THERE ARE CHRONIC PATTERNS OF SUCH DEPTH AND SEVERITY THAT OUR PRESENT RESOURCES, BOTH INDIVIDUAL AND COMMUNITY, WILL NOT SUFFICE FOR ASSISTING THE VICTIMS TO EMERGE WITHOUT DAMAGE TO THE PERSON OR COMMUNITY OR WITHOUT THE DRAINING OFF OF RESOURCES FROM EQUALLY WORTHWHILE AND MUCH MORE PRODUCTIVE CHANNELS OF WORK WITH OTHER PEOPLE.

We have learned that screening of the people entering our Community is absolutely necessary for our optimum development and for the attainment of our long-range goal of reaching and assisting everyone in the world to re-emerge.

It remains a good rule that one should not bring or take into class or Community anyone that the person doing the recruiting will not be delighted to have as a co-counselor.

We do not yet have the facilities, resources, or organization to cope with deeply distressed victims of very destructive chronic patterns and such destructive patterns do exist in large numbers in our present distressed society. Individuals whose distresses are destructive to our Communities need to be screened out or separated from our Communities just as rigorously as those whose patterns threaten or impose on individuals. The individual whose patterns seek to misuse our Communities, misrepresent Re-evaluation Counseling, destroy our unity or confuse the consistency of our theory are fully as irrational and destructive to the success of our project as those who are destructive of individuals. The pretexts of "democracy" and "intellectual freedom" should not confuse anyone. These individuals are "free" to do any-thing they want outside of RC but not to exploit it or misrepresent it from within our Communities.

XXI. We have learned that THE HANDLING OF OUR OUTREACH FUNDS THROUGH THE RE-EVALUA-TION FOUNDATION IS A WORKABLE PROCEDURE.

The awkwardness in added paperwork has not kept our outreach funds from operating well under the new set-up. I think we can have every expectation that outreach be in better supply and that the Foundation will engage in many projects supportive of Re-evaluation Counseling from funds collected outside our Communities.

These are some of the outstanding features of our current functioning, our insights and our knowledge.

Another Look
at Re-evaluation Counseling *

In the general point of view which we adopt:

The Universe is real and exists independently of our thinking about it.

The Universe is dynamic, is in a state of constant change.

Change takes place in two general directions:

Downward change towards randomness, uniformity, and disintegration, and

Upward change toward complexity, integration, order and meaning.

As part of the upward change trend, entities arise which attain increasing, though limited, freedom over random events and act with some independence to accelerate the development of integration and meaning. In our experience living creatures are examples of such entities.

INTELLIGENCE ARISES

Living creatures in their evolution tend toward development of an ability to cope with the environment and to impose their survival and attainment of their goals on the environment by creating new responses to each changing moment of reality. In our experience, human intelligence is an example of such an ability.

*First printed in Present Time No. 22 – January, 1976

The development and experience of human intelligence leads to *awareness* of the environment, of oneself, and, eventually, of one's relationship to the environment and to other intelligences, and of the potentials inherent in these relationships. Awareness is hard or impossible to define but its existence as a superior function arising out of intelligence is felt subjectively and is also supported by objective evidence.

REALITY OBSCURED

The functioning of human intelligence and the flourishing of awareness has been obscured and inhibited by the phenomenon of human irrationality, arising out of the vulnerability of intelligence to disruption by the intrusion of the disintegration trend of the universe upon it before that intelligence is experienced and informed enough to protect itself successfully. This intrusion of randomness and lack of meaning into the sphere of human intelligence is known to us as "hurt" or "distress". It perpetuates itself through the mechanism of the *"distress recording"*, through the contagious spread of such distress recordings to other intelligences, and through the institutionalization of these distress recordings in oppressive societies.

CORRECTIVE PROCESSES

Corrective processes to counter the installation and perpetuation of distress patterns spontaneously arise. These undo the effects of hurt on human intelligence, dissolve distress recordings, and allow the intelligences to proceed, individually and cooperatively, to resume the initiative in inter-relation with the Universe, and care and mastery of it. These counter-processes have collectively been described as *discharge* and *re-evaluation*.

AWARE APPLICATION

Aware appreciation of the discharge and re-evaluation processes, and aware application, enhancement, and acceleration of these processes has finally appeared in the current period, in part, at least, because humans finally acquired enough information and enough mastery of the environment. This phenomenon has been named Re-evaluation Counseling and Co-counseling.

Re-evaluation Counseling is a new phenomenon or entity in the real Universe. It is of decisive interest and importance to human intelligences at this stage of the development of the Universe. To examine the phenomenon in the context of the Universe and of human affairs enhances both the system and the examiner.

THE EXISTENCE OF CHOICE

Although we assume the objective existence of the Universe, modifiable by our thought only through concrete, real processes, yet the position, attitude, or viewpoint from which we examine the Universe or any part of it will always be to some extent the result of a *choice*. Understanding any phenomenon well requires that it be examined from several perspectives. Some possible perspectives are of little value or negative value (if based on distress pattern illusions). Other perspectives yield valuable information. (An example of the first is viewing a container of beverage as "half-empty" rather than "half full". An example of the second is examining light as a "wave" phenomenon and also as a "particle" phenomenon.)

Past efforts to view the phenomenon of Re-evaluation Counseling as a "therapy", as a "mutual self-help" self-improvement program, as a community of determinedly loving people, as a needed catalyst for the liberation struggles of all groups of oppressed peoples, as a "leading edge" of the upward trend in the Universe, have been helpful.

ANOTHER VIEW

It is also possible to view Re-evaluation Counseling as *a process for attaining a more accurate picture of reality*, particularly the reality of human nature, of human intelligence, of human relationships, and of human capabilities, by removing the occlusions upon it. These occlusions are caused by lack of information, by mis-information, and, especially, by the illusions created by distress patterns.

We have much previous experience that continually corrected and improved directions *against* distress patterns become more and more accurate approximations of reality. Approaching these areas of reality in this way, we are led to persistently and repetitively ask each other questions like the following:

How intelligent must you logically be?

How good are you?

How much do you love another person?

How much do you care about your co-counselor?

How intense bad feelings and how heavy discharge are you willing to experience in order to recover yourself fully?

How long do you want to postpone doing this?

How thoroughly will you commit yourself to be with your client and actively, aggressively insist on the persistence and support which will dismantle her or his chronic pattern?

Discharge and insights will tend to occur in answering these questions.

Any difficulties in giving wholehearted responses to any of the above questions betray the precise locations of the interfering distress. A question of the form:

What gets in the way of ----------? (e.g. you realizing you are totally good?) and eliciting the immediate "thought" from the client can effectively guide discharge and re-evaluation against the confusion of chronic distresses.

PUT TO USE

Determined, *persistent* action on the part of both client and counselor are clearly and logically indicated to implement the foregoing.

To attempt a fresh perspective such as the above can lead, not only to a clearer understanding, but to rewarding accuracy and persistence in the achievement of complete re-emergence in a finite amount of time.

The Nature of Theory*

I want to talk this morning about the basic notion of theory, to discuss the theory of theory.

There are some common difficulties with the whole question of theory. These difficulties appear at many places in the co-counseling community. On the one hand, there are such tendencies as trying to settle questions that need to be thought about by instead saying, "Harvey says. . ." On the other hand, you have some resentment expressed, not only at Harvey, but at an explicit, written, firm theory. There are some feelings that the leaders of Re-evaluation Counseling, and particularly Harvey, are intolerant and narrow-minded because they insist on not thoughtlessly borrowing contradictory ideas or practices from various psychologies or human growth movements.

I think that confusion underlies both these kinds of difficulties, and that these confusions are not peculiar to us but come into Re-evaluation Counseling from a confusion in the general society.

COMMON FALLACIES

We have been told, from many sources, for example, that there are such things as "absolute truth". We hear in some religions that there are propositions which must not be thought about, which must be accepted without question. On the other hand, there are philosophies extant which condemn consistency as narrow-mindedness and extol eclecticism, pragmatism and changing your mind about everything every day. I think that this situation can be

*Talk at Madison V, R.C. Teachers' Workshop – May 9 - 14, 1976

examined in a way that will do away with most of these difficulties, but it will require for many of us a fresh look at things we have taken for granted.

ALL INFORMATION IS NEEDED

In the first place, I think we must face and accept that all our knowledge, all our pictures of reality, consists entirely of mental models which our own intelligences have constructed. Not only is there no possibility of attaining absolute truth or absolute knowledge about anything, but we can never even make direct contact with the reality that surrounds us. All our concepts of the reality around us are mental images constructed by us from little flashes of electricity that travel along our nerves from our sense organs to our forebrain. If I say I am in direct contact with this chair, it is not strictly true. I am receiving little flashes of electricity from the nerves in my thumb, and from the frequency and intensity of those flashes construct a notion of the hardness and solidity of the chair. The way the electricity flashes along my optic nerves allows me to construct a notion of "orange" color about the rug. That is all the information we ever have of the universe, the flashes of electricity coming through to our switchboard in our frontal lobes.

A SATISFACTORY SITUATION

To face this does not increase our insecurity because it turns out that in practice we can construct mental models of the reality around us that are as accurate a description of that reality as we wish.

If we wish to be more accurate, we simply need to make more effort. We may need to construct additional sensors such as telescopes and microscopes, but we can do so.

Not only is this true, but any two individual's different mental concepts of the reality around them can be made to coincide, can be brought into just as close agreement as desired, if each secures sufficient information, discharges the distress patterns which introduce confusion, and allows for the difference in viewpoint of any two observers. By this last we mean that an observer on one side of a house can say "the house is red" while the observer on the other side of the house can say "the house is white", and they can then agree "the house is white on one side and red on the other side".

This way in which we approximate the nature of reality turns out to be as useful and desirable as we need. Once having realized this, we can also realize that the whole desire for "absolute truth" or "absolute reality" arises only from the insecurity of human distress patterns. If the patterned desire to know everything "exactly", in an absolute sense, could be fulfilled, we would then be in the terrible dilemma of eternal boredom.

A CHOICE IS NECESSARY

With this digested, we need to be rigorous about another basic question. One cannot state in any absolute sense even that there *is* a reality or that the universe is *real*. One must choose between *assuming* that it is real, or that, since we have a conception of it, *assuming* that it is a projection of our minds. Whole schools of philosophers have adopted each of the two positions and both schools have erected systems that are logical and consistent within themselves, on each of the possible two assumptions.

Re-evaluation Counseling, along with the physical sciences in general, chooses to start with the assumption that *a real universe does exist, independent of our perception of it.* We choose to start with this assumption for the reasons that this assumption leads to more interesting results and to more satisfactory lives. These are good reasons and are quite sufficient. In practice, this assumption of the reality of the universe underlies almost all human activities. Even the idealist philosophers who avowedly start with the assumption of no real universe, eat their breakfasts each morning as vigorously as if they were real. The usual practice, however, is not a careful enough basis for rigorous thought on important questions. We prefer to say clearly that we do start with this assumption of a *real* universe and reject any ideas or any mental models that are not consistent with this. We *assume* that the universe is real.

A DYNAMIC REALITY

We observe that the universe is dynamic, that in every manifestation it is in constant change, at greater or lesser rates of change.

REALITY IS CONSISTENT

We also assume that the universe is consistent, that the reality of any portion of the universe does not make untenable the reality of any other portion of it. If such apparent inconsistencies appear, we assume these are caused by lack of information or lack of understanding of the phenomena. As a result of assuming the universe to be consistent everywhere, we place the requirement on any theories which we erect about the universe that these theories be consistent as well.

THE USE OF INDUCTIVE LOGIC

In seeking to comprehend and develop theories about the portions of the universe in which we are interested, there are two principal acceptable methods. I will call one method the method of inductive logic. This is the method mostly used by the physcial sciences. This consists of observing the working of various portions of the reality we're interested in and generalizing from what is common to these particular examples for a description (a "rule", a "law") which we hope will cover all such examples even though we can only examine a limited number of cases. Generalizing from particular examples is the main principle of physical science, of inductive logic. For example, if we freeze some distilled water many, many times and it always freezes at zero degrees Celsius, we generalize from these experiments to the statement that distilled water freezes at 0 degrees. The physicist used to call these generalizations "laws". Modern physicists are more aware that they are always, in a sense, conjectures, always subject to revision in the light of future data which may not fit the generalization. When these generalizations are made carefully and thoughtfully, however, they are usually only superseded by being included in a more general law or generalization of which they become a part. If an experimenter eventually notices that at high pressure water consistently freezes at a slightly different point than zero degrees, she or he will create a new generalization which takes into account the changes in the freezing point with regard to pressure while the old generalization becomes the limited case for atmospheric pressure only. When Newton's generalizations about gravitation were superseded because they no longer described some known events accurately enough, they became a special case of the more general laws of relativity.

PRACTICE CAME FIRST

Re-evaluation Counseling theory developed, in the first place, on the basis of inductive logic. Successful practice came first. The theory arose later as an attempt to explain successful practice which had already taken place. This has not been the rule for most so-called "social sciences". Today, especially, in the era of a collapsing society, many theories about people are seized upon and promulgated that are purely the result of introspection. Particularly in the field of human behavior, rigor and care in setting up and interpreting experiments has been almost entirely absent. This is, in part, the result of general carelessness but in part results from pressures to serve the interests of oppression in that society. A rigorous theory of economics, for example, could not be taught in the universities without threatening the foundations of the present society and its ruling class. A premium is thus placed upon intellectual nonsense in these fields. Intellectuals often take refuge from these pressures in eclectism and pragmatism, these being a cloak for non-consistency in thinking and for irresponsibility toward the implications of one's "theorizing" for the oppressed people in the society.

RC began accidentally. Something very interesting and positive happened to one person who was allowed to cry at length. The results were so interesting that attempts were made to duplicate them. Enough success attended these efforts that within a few months there was an obvious need for some generalized explanation for what was already happening in practice. This corresponds exactly with the physicist inducing general laws from particular experiences.

NO ABSOLUTES

Many different theories can be constructed to fit any set of observations. A particular theory survives and is valued, not only on how well it fits the facts (this is basic), but also on how useful it is in predicting what new attempts at useful activity should be tried, how consistent it is, how understandable it is, and how much use one can make of it in guiding one's practical activities.

The theory that we call Re-evaluation Counseling is not necessarily the only explanation that could be made about successful counseling practice. It is simply the best guesses that we have been able to make as to why these successes happen. To say this is not to yield authority to "theorists" who are sure that what they are saying is "absolute truth". We are much closer to the nature of reality than they are. We are secure enough to say these are guesses, and having said this, we can be quite positive about them in that they have proven to be very useful guesses that have been carefully checked for consistency, that have continually led to new, useful areas of practice. Such key concepts as the sharp distinction between the human intelligence and the distress pattern, or the notion of the distress pattern being composed of frozen intelligence and unusable information which is converted by discharge into liberated intelligence and useful information, for examples, have proven to be very powerful and effective in guiding peoples' re-emergence.

RESPECT FOR PEOPLE, NOT WRONG THEORIES

Insecure people coming into Re-evaluation Counseling sometimes have a conditioned "respect" for current "official" or widely-publicized theories. They may feel that my confidence in RC theory is arrogance. They charge me with being "intolerant" of other theories. This is true. I am. I have little respect for much current nonsense.

This should not be taken to mean, however, that I am intolerant and arrogant toward the people who follow these other theories. This is *not* true. Psychologists and human growth leaders and sociologists are good people trying to do good things, and sometimes succeeding. Many professional "therapists", for example, are giving some support and help to distressed people that we in the RC Communities are not yet ready to take responsibility for. In my opinion, however, they are hindered rather than helped by their "theories". It is their essential human nature and their caring rather than their theories which operates to what good results they achieve. I think it is ridiculous for any theory to claim to be useful in this field if it does not distinguish between distress patterns and the flexible human intelligence, for example. How can one possibly lump them together, as almost all these theories do, and achieve any useful results?

Although as with any scientific theory, any part of RC theory is subject to revision at any time that real, verified evidence contradicts it, its validity, consistency, and usefulness are well-established. It must and will be defended vigorously against any careless intrusion of contradictory concepts.

ALIVE AND GROWING

RC theory is by no means completed. Profound additions to the theory are currently taking place on many fronts. They are often not recognized as theory because they are of such immediate practical importance. Many co-counselors regard these advances as practical questions or current policies rather than as theory. Yet our current examination and analysis, for example, of the oppressive patterns installed systematically by an oppressive society and the means for eliminating them will, as understanding evolves, have as great importance to our re-emergence as the familiar Spectrum of Techniques concept.

We are farther along in our understanding of the chronic pattern, but we are still engaged in working out much of this theory.

We are starting many special journals whose function is not only communication, but also to assemble a group of thoughtful editors and writers on these particular topics, to create and apply a theory in these special fields.

A SECOND LOGICAL STRUCTURE

The theory of Re-evaluation Counseling developed only as an inductive structure until the early 1960's. At that time, though our results were known only to a narrow circle of people, they were so exciting, so rewarding, and so important that we made an attempt to strengthen theory from another direction. The consistency we had been able to achieve had been of the greatest importance in the further development of the theory and in the practical work. We sought for a means to improve the consistency still more, to make it still more rigorous and dependable. The means we chose was to try to erect a second logical structure alongside the original inductive one.

The now familiar list of 24 "Postulates" or axioms of Re-evaluation Counseling was drawn up. These, of course, were in some sense drawn inductively from experience, as all sets of axioms are, but the usual intuitive leap was made in setting these assumptions up without avowed recourse to the reality which underlies them.

(The source of any set of axioms or postulates does lie in observation of reality, but, since any conclusions drawn from observations of reality are subject to contradiction by some future observation not yet made, in order to have a completely consistent logical structure, one states the axioms without recourse to the reality from which they arise.)

We simply say of the 24 "Postulates" that "we assume these things to be true". We state these as a *starting point* for this new logical system. So, in this new logical system, these are not to be questioned and the truth of any further developments in this system depends only on the truth of what we started with, and, of course, the logical rigor of our development. We say, then, that "Our conclusions are true if our starting point is true". We *do not say* flatly that our conclusions in this system are true with reference to reality.

From these "Postulates", then, we sought to deduce rigorous, air-tight conclusions which would be in accord with the generalizations we had reached from practice.

MORE DEPENDABLE CONSISTENCY

We have had considerable success with this. This gives us the advantage of more dependable consistency for our theory. If one accepts the 24 "Postulates" as assumptions, then the logical conclusions deduced from them are dependable and consistent. If these conclusions are reinforced by our generalizations from experience, then we can be much more confident about what we are doing about our practical work.

One system gives us touch with reality. The other system gives us consistency. So Re-evaluation Counseling has attained a more reassuring consistency and dependability than most scientific systems, and this in an area of work where consistency has previously been almost entirely lacking.

LONG-RANGE IMPORTANCE

Many co-counselors as yet know or care little about this. Conditioned to be suspicious of theory, which in the past has often been used to oppress them, they are satisfied with the pragmatic results. They say, "I don't care about the theory. RC works for me. That is what matters". This is understandable, but these basic questions are of great importance in the development of the future, not just of Re-evaluation Counseling, but of humankind.

QUESTIONS

If you say any theory consists of making guesses, won't this make people feel insecure about the theory?

No, it is rather the person who is insecure in his or her understanding of the theory who feels that he or she has to fiercely insist that this is the truth, the truth, the whole truth, or engage in "arguments" with other equally rigid views which are more shouting matches than arguments. If we can remember to say, not *"This is the theory"* or "Harvey said so" but rather that this is the best explanation we have been able to work out of why our practice works so well, people will be able to hear us better.

Would you clarify what you said about the existence of the universe and our perception of it?

The idealist schools of philosophy assume that our perception creates the world, that there is no sound unless someone hears it, that apparent reality is a projection of my mind or God's mind. We assume that the universe would be there even if we didn't notice it. There is no "proof" of one or the other viewpoint, but you must assume one or the other and stay with it in order to be consistent.

Why do you think people resist theory? I would think they would enjoy it.

In general, they do. The human mind loves theory inherently. Theory is an expression of its intelligent functioning. Most people in this society, however, have seen false theories used as weapons to oppress them. From this can come a rigid distrust of all theory. We have to be patient with this at first. I certainly agree that the mastery of theory is necessary for our full emergence. In most approaches to human behavior we have an "expert" who knows the "theory" and a "patient" who is acted upon. One of the distinctive features of RC is that we try to put the full theory in the possession of the client.

Can you give an example of how the requirement of consistency helps in theory and practice?

A number of clients cried very hard, when we paid attention to them. A number of other clients didn't discharge when we paid attention to them. Our theoretical notion of consistency led us to think that all clients would cry if the conditions permitted, since all clients desired the results which the ones who cried attained. Therefore, consistency led us to continually try to find different things that the counselor could do so that the others could cry as well, instead of assuming that people have different natures, that some can cry and some can't.

Powerlessness Is A Fraud *

REALITY HAS BEEN OBSCURED

Until the present period the nature of reality has been largely obscured for all human intelligences. Partly this is because we are able to observe directly with our senses only a comparatively narrow range of information about the reality which surrounds us. For example, relationships between very small objects, such as atoms or molecules, or the relationships between galaxies or other objects of that size, are not obvious to evolving human beings until they have acquired a great deal of information in the more easily available size ranges and have invented instruments to extend their senses into the microscopic and macroscopic worlds.

Obscuring of reality by the volume of the information coming from it or by the limited range of our inherent sensing systems is not the only, nor the most serious, source of ignorance and misinformation. More confusing and more of a problem until now are the effects of distress patterns distorting our interpretations of the information received. Almost certainly distress patterns were affecting us even before our flexible intelligences evolved. Distress was probably already being perpetuated by the familiar (to us) mechanism of acting out hurt, previously done to us, against someone else, long before we were humans. Possibly not once in all human history to date has an intelligent human infant had an opportunity to view reality for more than a few instants at a time without the intrusion of a restimulated distress pattern or patterned distortion of information offered by other humans.

*First printed in Present Time No. 24 – July, 1976

Once distress patterns become installed in social structures (and this probably happened even before the emergence of formal societies) the nature of reality became systematically distorted. Community fears were perpetuated through "teaching" of the taboos, propitiations and other rituals associated with primitive religions. When exploitative societies came into being it became to an exploiting human's apparent advantage to perpetuate the oppression of another human. The economic advantage to be attained by keeping, not only oppressed people, but the whole society locked into false pictures of reality which appear to support the oppression led to many social structures (schools, churches, propaganda ministries, etc.) whose function was largely in this direction.

WHY DO WE DOUBT OUR STRENGTH?

It is plain that there must be a real reason why human beings (including those of us who have made a great deal of progress through the use of RC) have continued to be timid, ineffective and long-suffering in the face of mistreatment, social injustice, plundering and pollution of their environment, and repeated wars and economic crises.

It seems now that there is a real reason for this passivity, that the reason is one that we can do something about, is something that we have the tools to deal with. What has been holding up progress is a heavy layer of distress, installed very early on all of us, whose content is that situations which oppress and threaten us are beyond our powers to change and that we must "adjust" to them.

What nonsense! We already know well that the essential nature of the human being is to be in full charge of everything, to take and keep the initiative, to benevolently master the environment. A fraudulent concept and feeling of powerlessness has been perpetrated upon us and locked in by distress.

Perhaps many co-counselors will feel that they were already aware of this. I was, too, but not really -- not in the aware sense I am now.

HOW AWARENESS HAPPENED

The breakthrough came in a class I was leading. I had asked the class members to listen to me and respond afterwards to an impatience I felt about the slowness of co-counselors to take decisive action. I asked, since almost all decisive advances in RC theory had come when we rejected limits (*complete* responsibility, *complete* appreciation, etc.) why were co-counselors insisting on respecting some invisible barrier when it came to acting in the wide world?

I mentioned the economic crisis, the deterioration of the environment, and the continuing reactive drive toward nuclear over-armament and the danger of holocaust as reasons, not to panic, but, it seemed to me, to take decisive leadership in human affairs. "What is holding us up?" I asked.

I received responses of reassurance (that we were really doing just fine already) and also some resentment was expressed at what felt like invalidating criticism by me.

THE CRITICAL ANALOGY

Then Liz Kunz spoke.

"I don't hear what you're trying to say, " She said. (I am paraphrasing her words from memory) "But I keep thinking that maybe you are trying to say something analagous to what I discovered by learning about sexism.

"I have always been a hard-working client, " said Liz. "I have discharged heavily ever since I got into RC. But when I learned about sexism it made a great deal of difference in my counseling. I had been discharging with my goal being to reach a place where I wouldn't be hurt by the things that happened to me anymore. When I saw sexism for what it was and realized I could reject it and fight against it instead of going on enduring it and discharging on it, it gave me a big short cut. That realization will save me hundreds of hours of counseling work in my re-emergence. I wonder if you are trying to get at something like that?"

I became very excited. I shouted "Of course! Powerlessness! That has to be it! That has to be *the* distress that we have gone on respecting and treating as if it were reality."

Once said out loud it was obvious. I even found that I had been using the word repeatedly myself during the last few months, in workshops and in writing. But to *almost* face it and be aware of it is not quite the same as *really* being aware of the situation. My thanks to Liz Kunz.

I propose, of course, that all of us in RC declare an end to any respect or tolerance for feelings or attitudes of powerlessness, that we treat them as the patterned distresses they must be and pursue them with discharge. Power to the Person!

STEP BY STEP

This is one more of the crucial realizations that one-by-one emerged from the patterned confusion in which we began our re-emergence. Insight by insight we have gained a better and better concept of the reality of ourselves and the universe.

A good deal of the development of Re-evaluation Counseling theory and practice has consisted of shedding the obscuring notions and concepts which give a false picture of reality and attainment of a more and more accurate picture of what the universe and its contents are really like. (A crucial area of this revelation has been what we humans and our inherent relationships are really like.)

If we view the development of RC in this light, we can see why we had to begin with timid and tentative conjectures. It was a bold step to think that since a few people felt better after they cried it might be good for all people to cry. We had to go against universal conditioning that people shouldn't discharge and that one should interrupt and condemn their discharge if one wished to be helpful.

It was another step forward to think about (and eventually try) seeking discharge *deliberately*, pursuing it persistently instead of settling for what occured accidentally or for as much as permissive counseling alone would bring.

Heavy, rigid traditions of hierarchy and dependency had to be challenged to realize that people could take turns at counseling each other and being counseled, that reversible co-counseling was long-range workable. In spite of many initial difficulties and appearances to the contrary the underlying reality turned out to be that exchanging co-counseling is inherent in human capabilities and works exceedingly well.

THAT THOROUGHNESS IS POSSIBLE

Considerable intense work, mostly with one-way clients, had to take place before we could be sure that discharge could be exhaustive, that it could be persisted in to completion, that the distress pattern could be "cleaned up completely." Such thorough, exhaustive counseling produced profound and permanent improvements and dramatically better levels of human functioning for the client.

These insights and practices emerged slowly. We often acted intuitively on each of these principles before we realized them as principles; i.e., our practice moved in that direction before we awarely generalized the importance of what we were doing. This has been true with each succeeding set of developments of our thoery.

It was an important new realization that taking a turn before group attention could use the multiplied awareness of the group to discharge certain distresses faster and more thoroughly than with a single co-counselor. This had happened incidentally in Re-evaluation Counseling classes many, many times before it was recognized as a general phenomenon which could be planned for and taken advantage of deliberately.

THE OVERTHROW OF THE CHRONIC

Several such insights occurred in the development of our skills against chronic patterns. It was a turning point to realize that a chronic pattern was not just "heavy" but that it acually played all the time, constantly restimulated by the conditions of ordinary living. It was a further important step to realize that a chronic pattern could recharge itself and regain its dire effectiveness through dominating the individual between sessions as much or almost as much as it could be weakened or done away with by discharge during sessions. This made it clear that to eliminate a chronic pattern requires that a direction against the pattern be held between sessions to "starve" it of the restimulation which would otherwise keep it operating.

It was a fresh insight to realize clearly that a counselor's "word from outside" contradicting the pattern could save the client much fumbling and misdirection in beginning discharge of the chronic pattern. Later still came the realization that one must be ruthless (though skilled and flexible) in attacking the chronic pattern of one's client, but that, at the same time, one must be warm and loving and supportive to the client himself, or herself, and refuse to let any identification of the pattern with the person take place.

COMMUNITY SUPPORT

From the very beginning of RC, there were supportive, cooperative relationships within the group of co-counselors. Personal Counselors, which was for about 20 years the main vehicle for the development of Re-evaluation Counseling, functioned with a semi-volunteer staff, able to keep going because of the mutual interest and sense of companionship and purpose which was felt by the staff people and the co-counseling students.

As co-counseling began to spread across the United States and the world, the newer co-counselors began to reach for an organized relationship with each other and this culminated in the Guidelines of 1972, revised and kept up to date many times since then. It was a key insight that a "community" relationship between co-counselors could stabilize and expedite their re-emergence greatly by adding safety, variety of co-counseling resources, increased possibilities of consultation and responsible modeling.

The functioning of the RC Community has uncovered a good deal of the reality of inherent relationships between human beings. The RC Communities have functioned as pilot plants or experimental projects for realizing how good and supportive rational relationships between all human beings could be in the wide world.

CHALLENGING OPPRESSION

The next important realization was slow in coming to clarity, though it was grappled with for several years. Challenging oppressive attitudes which we found coming into the RC Communities from the society around us finally brought the realization that attitudes of sexism, racism, adultism, anti-Semitism, ageism, etc. were directly interfering with the successful functioning of co-counseling and were denying the full benefits of co-counseling to many people in the oppressed end of relationships while preserving inhuman attitudes destructive to people in the "oppressor" roles.

This took a long time. At first reluctantly and now enthusiastically it has become the policy of the Communities to challenge oppressive patterns directly. A systematic effort on this has begun, and as workable techniques for discharging and re-evaluating on oppressive patterns have developed it is plain that we have revealed the true nature of another large portion of previously obscured reality and have exposed the usual attitudes in present societies as false, destructive, re-inforcing of patterns and rooted in distress. Thousands of co-counselors are presently excited and jubilant at realizing that their progress to re-emergence can be greatly accelerated by rejecting and disassociating from the patterns of oppression which they have been victimized by in the past. The until-now unchallenged reinstallation of distress by these patterns can be decisively interrupted, saving thousands of hours of discharge and years of time in re-emergence.

As we come to see what human beings "should have been like all along" and are really like inherently, as we begin to repudiate the notions of "human nature" and human society that we have previously accepted as inherent or necessary, (but which we now can clearly see are simply accumulated distress and the socially reinforced regeneration of the distress) new frontiers of progress open up before us.

ALL IS WELL

All is going exceedingly well in the development of Re-evaluation Counseling.

All is going well in the growth and the maturing of the Re-evaluation Counseling Communities. The program adopted for the past year has been carried out and is being carried out quite successfully. The level of co-counseling is maturing. The Communities themselves are maturing well. Chronic patterns are being challenged with considerable success.

Oppressive patterns are being challenged in our counseling by the development of workable new techniques, by special workshops, special newsletters, and by joyous commitment against oppression of Communities and community members who were often fearful of this development a year ago, but are enthusiastically pursuing it today.

The future looks extremely bright. We have much room for satisfaction. Yet, I think, and I think co-counselors will in general agree with me, that there is some reason for impatience with the present effectiveness of Re-evaluation Counseling in the world at large.

A significant number of co-counselors have absorbed the theory very well and have integrated it into their lives. They are successful in everything which they tackle. Yet the world as a whole, on the level of governments and national policies and on the content of most people's lives, continues to pursue reactive policies of increasing hardship and want, of wasting the earth's resources, of pollution of the environment, and of a slow reactive grinding in the direction of nuclear war.

WHY DO WE HESITATE?

Why have not individual RCers as yet played a decisive role in turning the tide of human activity in the other direction? What is holding us up from decisive action, from speaking out clearly enough of the things that we know well so that large numbers of people will hear us and will act in a rational, human direction?

(What was Vachel Lindsay trying to tell us about in his poem, "It is the world's one crime its babes grow dull. . . limp and leaden-eyed"?)

I think we can at last put a name to the obstacle. As in all previous theoretical breakthroughs the difficulty seems obvious once we notice it. Things I've said and written in the last few months reveal that I've *almost* said this many times. It may not even seem new to the reader and yet *to realize it awarely* is a new and decisive change.

AN ENEMY EXPOSED

The name of this unchallenged distress is *"powerlessness"*.

It shows up in every case of oppression. It dramatizes itself in every lack of initiative, in every insight not acted upon.

We have known for some time that the real nature of human beings is to take the initiative, to move aggressively on problems. We've known that the almost universal behavior of not moving decisively has to be something wrong. What can be wrong? If it is different from the inherent nature of human beings it has to be a pattern. If it is a pattern, then it has to be an extremely widespread, nearly universal chronic pattern. And it has to be an extremely heavy chronic pattern to explain the enormous amount of apathy and passivity present in the population.

Of course! All human beings that we have knowledge of (including the most advantaged) have gone through a long series of devastating experiences, while small children, of having their self-determination and their own decisions on the conduct of their lives thwarted, defeated, smashed, derided, and stomped on in every possible way.

All of us are born with a sense of being in charge of our universe, a full expectation of an immediately co-operative rational universe waiting for us, ready to carry out our wishes. An infant is not powerless. A human infant is possessed of a very powerful voice. In a rational environment that voice alone would be enough to see that prompt action is taken to carry out the child's wishes. The intuitive feeling a child has of being in charge should correspond to reality.

THE SOURCES ARE PLAIN

But the environment into which the child is born is a very messed-up and patterned pseudo-reality. Expecting to deal with humans, the child instead has to deal with patterns. Expecting cooperation and love, the child receives invalidation and opposition. It is little wonder that by the time the child is grown, he or she feels deeply and chronically that "there is nothing I can do about it", "you can't fight city hall", "I just do what they tell me", and similar expressions of discouragement, despair, apathy and surrender. This accumulation of defeating early hurts has to be the evil substructure of almost all patterns, both the patterns of oppression and patterns of individual invalidation.

If we can name it, we can find a way to challenge it and remove it. It will undoubtedly be called by many names in the future. I name it "powerlessness" for now. Remember the name. Use it. It is the next major adversary of our re-emergence, coming into clear view. Don't let it sink back into unrecognized obscurity and domination of our behavior.

Certainly everyone of us has had many incidents of having the power to run our own lives denied to us by the adults around us or the forces of society. The distress in these experiences which has kept us apathetic or timid is waiting for discharge. The distress may be very heavy and it may take all our counseling skills to contradict it enough to discharge it completely, but we have many skills by now.

There are many possible techniques to be tried on this. To hold up to view our excuses for not taking charge of the world could bring discharge. To review the list of all memories of being powerless will bring the incidents to light, at least. We can ask, "What would our most admired heroine or hero do?" One way is certainly to ask our client to tell the story of the "powerless" incidents in the way they *should* have happened, as fantasies in which he or she *kept* the power. The general rules of safety and support, of balance of attention, of persistence with discharge to completion, will apply.

NO DISRUPTION BUT ACCELERATION

To challenge powerlessness will not distract us from the successful counseling we are already doing on our individual chronics or on the ending of internalized oppression. It will be found to be residing in them all. To see it clearly and to reject its claims to be reality will simply accelerate our re-emergence in every way.

We will need to furnish each other safety and reassurance in dealing with such universal heavy distress. We will need to keep our theory clear and in view. We will need to cheer each other on and never pool our timidities, discouragements or apathies.

If this can happen in the next few months (and I doubt if there is anything more crucial to our well being and re-emergence) then I think we will see large numbers of RCers in close communication and good contact with people in the wide world, moving decisively to end the perpetuation of distress, to end the threat of nuclear holocaust, to end the ongoing oppressions of unjust societies.

The Development Of New
Leadership*

People begin Re-evaluation Counseling or come into the Re-evaluation Counseling Communities at many different levels of competence and experience. In spite of our increasing care in screening for our Fundamentals classes, we still find some students who take a long time to understand the effective use of co-counseling. They are drawn to the Community at first more because of the fellowship and warmth and the group activity which is open to them, rather than from any understanding of the theory. Sometimes these students sit in class and discharge only when everyone else is discharging. On occasion some have not co-counseled for more than a year. When these students create no problems and are not a drain on the resources of the rest of the class, they are welcome. We have enough experience to know that eventually they too will begin co-counseling and take the road to emergence that the rest of the co-counselors have taken.

SOME BEGIN SLOWLY

Some other beginning co-counselors will seem to be concerned entirely with their own distresses and feel that they have to concentrate on these rather than take any interest in the broader applications of Re-evaluation Counseling as a philosophy or for social change. These people are welcome in our communities as well. It should be possible for any person who comes into Re-evaluation Counseling meeting the teacher's screening criterion, that is, "someone that the teacher would be delighted to co-counsel with", to progress at their own speed. Many co-counselors need to

*First printed in RC Teacher No. 4 – June, 1974

"sit on the back burner", to go through the elementary theory many times, to discharge steadily for a long time. When they have solved the problems that preoccupy them at first they can (and will) spontaneously take an interest in the wider implications and activities of Re-evaluation Counseling.

INACTIVE ARE NOT LOST

Other beginning co-counselors quickly solve the problems they brought into co-counseling and appear to "drop out", satisfied and happy with the results but appearing to be uninterested in co-counseling further. This is certainly a correct use of co-counseling--to take your gains and use them in the world. (Actually, all these "inactive" co-counselors intend on some level to resume co-counseling at a later date or "when necessary" and consider themselves and should be considered by all of us as continuing members of our Communities.) We have no minimum level of activity that a co-counselor must meet to be considered a Community member. "Once a co-counselor, always a co-counselor."

MANY ARE EAGER

Being clear on this, however, we also need to note that *large* numbers of co-counselors who have experienced any significant discharge and re-evaluation become permanently excited about the broad implications of Re-evaluation Counseling, wish to have a part in spreading the knowledge of Re-evaluation Counseling to other people, and look to the impact of Re-evaluation Counseling on the world for a good deal of the inspiration and meaning in their lives. There are thousands of co-counselors who would like to take a more active and a more leading role than they are doing at present in communicating Re-evaluation Counseling widely and assisting its permeation of society.

LEADERSHIP NEEDED

To realize this at this point of time coincides with some present realizations about the state of our Communities. Our Communities have grown explosively, have become remarkably stable, have developed fine teachers and Area Reference Persons in almost every case. Now, partly because of the growth, they are faced with some new problems for which new solutions must be found.

Some of our Communities have grown so large that there is no longer effective contact between the Area leadership and the individual co-counselors. Great variations also exist in the amount of effective contact between the individual teachers and the students who have taken or are taking classes from them.

The rate of development of new leaders has been very rapid in the early stages of most Communities, but once a stable leadership emerges and the Community is functioning well, some kind of an inhibiting effect tends to prevent the emergence of additional leaders (at least with the speed with which the first ones emerged). This does not imply any wrong actions on the part of the existing leadership or teachers. Some kind of cultural phenomenon exists here that inhibits the growth and development of additional leaders. It must be confronted, identified, and overcome.

Our Communities start with the general premise that we should have only as much structure as is actually needed to support and extend co-counseling and the activities that flow out of it. Some Communities have nevertheless developed strong structures with fixed jobs and roles and relationships. These have often been worked out very intelligently *by old standards* and have worked well *compared to other organizations.* Yet it is plain that some kind of identification with older organizations and older relationships has taken place and that these structures do not necessarily fit Re-evaluation Counseling needs well.

ADVANCE NEW LEADERSHIP

We have, on the one hand, large numbers of people eager to be more active and effective in leading and communicating Re-evaluation Counseling activities and on the other hand a shortage of leaders of high caliber. We have at the present time perhaps a dozen Re-evaluation Counseling leaders who are so able and well-grounded that any one of them could be counted upon to re-found the Re-evaluation Counseling Communities and direct their spread throughout the world population if Re-evaluation Counseling ever had to start over. In terms of the world population and the world situation, at least a thousand such leaders are needed.

We need to think concretely of what steps we can take to multiply the numbers and effectiveness of our leadership.

LEADERSHIP FUNCTIONS

Leaders are necessary in any human group activity. If more than two people attempt to work together, someone must lead or the activities will falter. The leadership may be intuitive, subtle, unrecognized, untitled, but *at least one person* in a group activity must assume the responsibiltiy of thinking about the group and its goals and progress as a whole for such a group to function well. *At least one* leader is required, which means that there can be more than one. Theoretically, every member of a group could play this role of thinking carefully about the group as a whole, and such a group would be very successful. In practice, *at least one* must assume this stance. Even where a meeting leadership rotates from meeting to meeting, at least one person must *think about the series* of meetings and where the group is going as a whole, must think past the individual meeting leader's concern as to how he or she can organize one good meeting or, again, patterns will eventually intrude, and the keen, purposeful direction of the activity will be lost.

An effective leader need not brandish a title. In some circumstances it is better that he or she does not. The most effective leader keeps his or her leadership unobtrusive and has many people carrying out leadership functions. Yet *at least one* individual human intelligence is needed to think about the group and its activities as a whole. This is a crucial function of leadership.

The job of the leader is not to do all the thinking for the people in the group which she or he leads, but rather to call forth, note and assemble the brilliant thinking *from all members* of the group. Even the most patterned of persons has some areas of knowledge, insights and keen thinking. The effective leader will draw on these resources from all the people that he or she leads, will put together the brilliant thoughts or fragments of thoughts which are furnished by others, and will add her or his own thinking to fill in the gaps. The leader's job is to produce a complete and consistent program from the brilliant though sometimes fragmented thoughts of the people he or she listens to, and then communicate this integrated theory back to all the members of the group and secure their acceptance and their support for it. This is another key function of leadership.

KEEP STANDARDS HIGH

We will be promoting hundreds and possibly thousands of co-counselors to be new teachers in the year or so ahead. These will not automatically be chosen from among those who insist they are ready to teach or lead and demand a chance to prove it. Sometimes the insistence is a pattern which will create trouble in leadership or teaching. We will also be looking for the good, responsible persons whose fears and self-doubts interfere with their eagerness to teach but who, if encouraged to teach, will discharge as they do so and emerge quickly to be fine teachers.

In boldly promoting large numbers of new people to teaching and other leadership positions, we cannot afford to give up the standards of rigor and correctness of theory and policy which we have striven to establish over the last two years. Our teachers and our leaders must understand Re-evaluation Counseling theory and must communicate it correctly, free from admixture of contradictory notions. Their lives must be good enough examples of rational living to communicate theory and the possibility of such practice to their students.

Without giving up rigor and care, it should still be possible to promote large numbers of sharp people much faster than we have in the past year.

MOTIVATIONS

The acceptable motivations for becoming leaders in Re-evaluation Counseling need to be looked at. The older group of leaders never had a chance to become confused about opportunism. There was simply no prestige or monetary rewards connected with Re-evaluation Counseling in the days of its development. It was all hard work and subsidizing the work out of one's own pocket.

In recent years, however, Re-evaluation Counseling has come to new areas as a movement of great prestige, with a devoted following, whose workshops are always packed, whose teachers and leaders are obviously trusted and supported by large numbers of people.

This has misled a few individuals into concluding that leadership in Re-evaluation Counseling could be a way to achieve "instant professionalism" for themselves without hard work, or a way to achieve a large income for themselves by taking advantage of the popularity of Co-counseling, or an opportunity to build a little "empire" of co-counselors where their "authority" would be unquestioned. Since these motivations were often concealed, a very, very few of these individuals temporarily assumed leadership in Re-evaluation Counseling Communities. Some of them, with a little prompting, accepted a direction against the patterned motivations, discharged sufficiently, and found rational motivations to become and remain effective leaders. Others are no longer in leadership.

There *are* rewards in being a teacher or leader of Re-evaluation Counseling. It is of great assistance in one's own re-emergence. To awarely attempt to be a model of rationality for others is to subject one's patterns to severe contradiction and speed up their demise.

It is also rewarding to associate with other leaders in the common effort. To communicate and work with peers who are assuming responsibility and leadership equal to your own is to share a precious fellowship.

The basic reward must be, however, the consciousness of being effective in a meaningful effort. What we are doing *matters* in the most profound sense. Our lives have *meaning*. What matters, as the modern Chinese would say, is to "serve the people."

A young co-counselor said to me recently, in a moment of insight, "Once you understand the difference, who would want to spend their lives any other way than in making things right for everybody?"

NO UNNECESSARY STRUCTURES

We must reinstate critical thinking against unnecessary structures in our Communities. We have put forth a correct principle since the beginning that we would set up only those structures which directly fulfilled our needs. Old patterns die hard, however, and fairly elaborate structures which are in themselves time-consuming and give little support to co-counseling have arisen in some Areas. To dismantle these unnecessary features without disrupting the Community involved will take thought and skill.

It seems probable that no Area Community should grow much beyond 200 co-counselors in number (perhaps 100 is a better figure) before it divides into sub-Area Communities. It seems equally probable that no sub-Area should long exist without being assisted to grow in both leadership and numbers to where they can become independent Area Communities.

GROWTH, NOT SLOT-FILLING

We have searched for competent people to perform the various leadership functions which our Communities need.

We have tended to feel delighted at having found "an editor" of an Area newsletter, for example. Our competent Area Reference Persons seem to "settle into" their jobs, and various other functionaries also.

I think that a "slot-filling" attitude has tended to creep over and obscure the "people-developing" attitude with which we began to think about leadership for our Communities three years ago. This is understandable but unacceptable.

STRENGTH IN COMPETENCE

It is time that we awarely realize that the strength of our Community lies not in structure but in competent people. Perhaps we should ask people in the future to take leadership jobs only until they have mastered the skills involved in that particular job and then encourage them to move on to other functions so they can learn to become all-around leaders of Re-evaluation Counseling. Can we say to each leader on every level, "As soon as you have mastered this job and have trained someone to do it as well as you did when you started, we have a more challenging and interesting job waiting for you"?

Should any experienced assistant teacher who understands and supports the theory and the Guidelines and whose observable chronic patterns threaten no scandal to the Communities, and who wishes to teach, be encouraged to do so as soon as he or she finds students outside the present members of the Community?

Shall we propose to our teachers that each must use one or two teaching assistants, *that they train these to be teachers*, and, if the assistants they have are not ready to be so trained because they need more time for co-counseling, that they yield the place as assistant to another promising person?

Shall we ask any Area which lacks an Alternate Area Reference Person to think and move on the question until one is decided upon and accepts the job? Shall we require that the Alternate Area Reference Person share in leadership responsibilities from the beginning and plan that the Reference Person and the Alternate exchange jobs for a "second term", after which, unless the Area is divided by that time into two or more new areas, the former, more experienced, Area Reference Person assumes other important jobs for the Community, or outside the Community, in outreach, or in permeating the larger society with the ideas and philosophy of Re-evaluation Counseling?

Some Common Pitfalls in the
Way of Thinking All the Time*

Considerable excitement has been generated in many of our Re-evaluation Counseling Communities, over the concept of "thinking all the time", sometimes called the "Mary McCabe Principle". The idea of completely resisting the addictive pull to indulge in non-thinking, "reactive resting", or lapses in the responsible use of our intelligence represents a transcendental point similar to the earlier decision for appreciating oneself "without any reservation".

It is plain that "thinking all the time" has already become an important direction for many of our co-counselors, that as a kind of master direction it helps oppose all patterns by keeping one's intelligence in gear and making the effort to be rational at all times.

In doing this, certain common difficulties arise, certain mistakes are easily made. The most common difficulty, of course, is the intrusion of the individual's unique distress patterns, unawarely substituting for rational thinking. Some mistakes, however, apparently arise out of the culture -- out of the conditioning the culture has put upon us -- and serve to hide our individual distressed mistakes from us.

SOME COMMON DIFFICULTIES

I've tried to list the common "illogics" which people fall into, the traps and the pitfalls which interrupt our thinking and are likely to pass unnoticed because of their familiarity. Following each, I've tried to quote a typical expression of each such mistake.

*First printed in Present Time No. 19 -- April, 1975

One, taking strong feelings or sincerity or passionate conviction as evidence of being rational; taking them as an acceptable substitute for critical, logical examination of the actual situation. (Remember, there's nothing as "sincere" as a pattern.)

"He seemed so convinced of what he said that I thought surely he must be right."

Two, generalizing from too little information. One example is not sufficient to prove a general point nor even to indicate a useful generalization. A wise old folk saying goes, "one swallow doesn't make a summer".

"All Indians always walk in single file. At least the only one I ever saw did!"

Three, not being clear and aware about the ideas one is taking for granted in starting one's thinking (not clearly facing and stating one's axioms or postulates or assumptions). It is fairly common in our culture to think logically on the wrong assumptions and wind up with a disastrous conclusion. High government officials are particularly predisposed to this error.

"I always assumed that women liked to be bossed."

Four, unawarely honoring old strictures that have been imposed upon one in the past against depending upon one's own judgment. A lot of this happens to us as we grow up and it is hard to remember that each person is really in charge of his or her own universe and it is his or her responsibility, necessity (and eventually delight) to think clearly about everything, questioning all propositions until one has convinced oneself logically that they are true.

"There are some things you can't think about. You just have to take them on faith."

Five, assuming that one's own feelings and experiences are representative of everyone's feelings and experiences. The universe is full of variety. Many humans have different stores of knowledge, different viewpoints and different goals than we do.

"I know just how you feel."
"This is the way this works for people. I know from my own experience."

Six, assuming that thinking can always be "easy". It's true that being intelligent is the natural way for a human being to function and that thinking really is less work than allowing the pattern to dictate one's actions. The addictive pull to not think can be strong, however, and, as long as patterns exist, one must be on guard and make the effort to check that one is really thinking.

"You're asking me to think all the time and that's H-A-A-A-R-D."

Seven, assuming a too narrow viewpoint on goals, especially in situations implicitly involving oppression, exploitation, or conflict. We have all been the victim of misrepresentation by unjust societies and the oppressive forces within them about what is "good for us".

"What's good for General Motors is good for the country."

Eight, failing to question the values enforced on one as part of one's education and upbringing. These enforced values may, or at least some of them may, be good values, but they should be questioned and should be reaffirmed only if they stand up under questioning.

"The United States would never fight an unjust war."
"More industry is good for everybody."

Nine, deciding that a conclusion one reaches after a number of experiences or experiments which all agree with each other is now a "law" or "flat rule", instead of remembering that it is at most a "useful generalization" which has at least some validity but which we cannot know is totally and universally valid, and may, in fact, be contradicted by the next experience.

"Any piece of paper has to have two sides. I've never seen one that didn't. What do you mean, a Moebius strip?"

Ten, failing to take into account the longer range implications of a decision or an action. What seems advantageous short range can turn out to be a very bad error long range. One needs to think of the interests of everyone concerned and be sure that the action is in everybody's interest before one can be sure of the correctness. A short-sighted view is likely to be an incorrect view.

"It's very handy to have the lake right here beside the factory. We can dump all the waste easily, and get rid of it that way."

Eleven, confusing a compulsive patterned "idea" with a true, rational hunch or intuitive insight. Real intuitive insights or hunches represent some of our most brilliant and unfettered thinking but it is also true that they need to be checked on rigorously that they are actually logical as much as the time and circumstances permit, simply because patterned compulsions often disguise themselves as brilliant insights.

"It finally came to me that what I really needed was another drink."

Twelve, rejecting an intuitive insight or hunch without trying to check it out logically to see if possibly it is correct, failing to take into account that the intuitive leap is a valuable and often necessary part of thinking correctly and completely complements the rigorous checking out and proving which should follow it.

"It was just a guess. Forget it. We'll do it the hard way."

Thirteen, failing to allow for the difference in viewpoint of two different people. Oppression appears very differently to the oppressor, to the oppressed, and to the bystander. If the viewpoint of the observer is taken into account, then agreement between any two observers can be reached to any desired degree by communication and the elimination of patterns.

"How can you on the other side of the house claim the house is red, when I can see very plainly that it's white on my side?"

What examples can you add to the list of these familiar pitfalls and gaps in thinking intelligently all the time?

The Rational Needs of
Human Beings *

There is a great deal we don't know about rational relationships between humans as yet because the phenomenon of human irrationality has interfered with and obscured this area. We hear about some famous friendships-- Damon and Pythias or David and Jonathan or the Three Musketeers--All for one and one for all--and we hear about examples coming out of wartime experiences. The distress patterns are sometimes pushed aside by the overriding urgency of a desperate situation and the people involved sometimes get into close contact with each other and come to depend on each other. Often the best examples of profound, mutually supportive relationships are from extreme stress situations. So as far as saying precisely that this or that is what relationships should be like, we just don't have clear data yet.

This does not mean that we are completely ignorant or have to be pragmatic or eclectic. There *are* clearly discernable trends. We can make good guesses at what rational relationships will be like by looking at the directions in which people are moving as they recover more and more of themselves. We are not, any of us, yet in a position to urgently need precise knowledge of a completely rational relationship anyway until we have done much more work and are able to function that way, but it is valuable to know what the direction is that we are going. I would like to comment on what I have observed and then speculate a little beyond that.

It is useful to recall exactly what a distress pattern is-- it is a literal recording of *everything* that went on during the time of the distress. Sometimes we hear co-counselors talk-

*Talk at New Windsor II – October 12 - 14, 1974

ing about the "motives" of recordings. This is misleading; they have picked up some confusion from other systems of thought. Distress patterns don't have motives, they are scratchy grooves in some kind of recording. They are a literal reproduction of what went on during a past time of hurt, complicated by later additions because, of course, additional layers are added on through restimulation. The entire content of a distress pattern is simply the accumulation of superimposed recordings of what went on in a series of miserable once-upon-a-times.

"FROZEN NEEDS"

If one of the factors that were present during the distress was a need, an unfilled need, that unfilled need becomes part of the recording. In co-counseling slang we refer to it as a "frozen need".

Let's start out with the sources of irrational relationships. We have relationships between patterns, of course, (look at any marriage)--but behind the interlocking of patterns there is often the phenomenon of a human trying to fill a frozen need. This leads·many relationships astray.

We have become clearer recently about the impossibility of meeting or filling frozen needs, have gotten a better look at this phenomenon. Once we look awarely it's apparent that most human beings as they currently function spend a good deal of their efforts toward other people in trying to fill a need *that was recorded.*

Once we look hard at them it's fairly obvious that most presently-observable attempts at adult relationships are attempts to fill frozen needs. Most seeking for spouses is an attempt to get parented. In fact, a great deal of our activities with other people are attempts to find parenting that we needed or didn't get, so that the need froze.

With a clearer perspective from lots of experiences we come to the fact that a frozen need cannot be filled, it can only be discharged. If you didn't get that parenting when you should have gotten it, you are never going to get it. Worse, if you "fortunately" find another pattern that appears to give the appearance of filling your frozen need then you are in deep trouble. The two patterns walk off into the sunset.

I think most of us have observed at some time or other a "devoted" couple of whom people might say, "Isn't that nice, so devoted, after 10 years of marriage they have eyes only for each other." Sure enough, they have eyes only for each other. They stand and say soupy things back and forth. Yes, it's nice, it's nice, it's lovely, it's lovely, it's lovely; you gradually get sick to your stomach. No one can stand to be around them long because one knows intuitively that it's inhuman. They are acting out these recorded little roles and are helplessly stuck in them. If you can get these people to discharge, they may temporarily hate each other, but eventually feel only relief that they have gotten out of the compulsive "sweetness".

CAN'T BE FILLED

Frozen needs cannot be filled. They can only be bade farewell to. It's similar to the fact that you can't bring the lost beloved who died back to life. You can only face the fact that s/he died, say goodbye repeatedly while you sob from the bottom of your being and finally find some peace in realizing that you haven't lost anything that you ever had, and that there is more to life than what you have lost. I imagine that most of you have had experience in cleaning up or at least partially cleaning up something like this. It is very worthwhile to clean it up completely if you can bring yourself to do it.

The frozen need can only be farewelled and discharged. (This doesn't mean that as a counseling tactic you won't try to catch the frozen need off balance by appearing to over-fulfill it in order to get discharge started.)

FUTILE TO TRY

You undoubtedly have known someone who set out to
have you fulfill some frozen need he or she had. You remember how tiresome that became. They called in the middle
of the night. They had you doing their shopping for them.
You kept trying to find some way to make them feel good.
They were delighted and full of grateful appreciation and
cried a lot on Tuesday, but on Wednesday the ante had
gone up. What you did on Tuesday no longer overfulfilled
and brought discharge. It wasn't enough. They now needed
your attention for a few more hours per day. You can't fill
these needs, you can only help discharge them.

There are frozen needs for lots of things besides
parenting. Whatever need was around at the time of distress is what is present now as a sort of demanding fossil.
There can be a frozen hunger, a compulsive hunger, if the
person was hungry during distress. Sometimes the hunger
was the distress, so now they chronically have a huge appetite. Sometimes a client coming out of heavy fear and getting
the first chunk of heavy fear off, goes wild with appetite.
I have had a professional client say, "I can't go on. Have you
got anything in the icebox?" and go back and eat all the
way through the stale bread. (It might have been better if
I could have kept them discharging but my chronic hunger
pattern sympathized with their hunger and I let them go.)

Any need can become frozen. So we look with skepti-
cism at simple sentimental descriptions of people's "ideals"
for relationships because they are quite likely to be recorded.

RATIONAL NEEDS

Are there some rational needs? With this warning in
mind, can we get a picture of what a rational relationship
might be?

Yes, apparently there are rational needs. These rational needs can get frozen by distress and have to be discharged to be free, but apparently they are an ongoing need for human beings even when the humans are free from distress. These needs exist even for mature, in charge, human beings. Not all of the needs involve other people directly.

NUTRITION

There certainly is a need for good nutrition, for adequate amounts of good food. We have a lot to learn here. The choices that immediately confront us are not inviting. We can go on eating the processed frauds that are pushed by heavy advertising, empty calories baited with sugar, salt and fat and laced with dangerous chemical flavors and preservatives. Or we can trust academic nutrition experts to prescribe adequate diets and ignore the obvious irrationalities of their viewpoint--the unaware warping of judgment by tradition and by the pressures of the commercial food industries. Or we could go over to the farther-out school and eat by unchecked hypothesis and mystic slogan.

The plain fact seems to be that if there is going to be an adequate policy on nutrition we are going to have to think it out because it doesn't exist. The commercial advertising school is probably poisoning much of the population. The far-out school is a great thrower of light on the stupidities of the academic nutrition viewpoint. (You have heard that "everybody needs fresh milk." Recent research has indicated that only a tiny minority of the population can digest fresh milk after they are two years old.)

Yet the health-food school is riddled with inconsistency and irrationality, illogical conclusions. We need new thinking there. We need food. We need good nutrition.

EXERCISE

We need exercise. This is something almost entirely obscured in the American culture. Most people work very hard when they have to and the rest of the time they watch TV. Yet there is no question that fun exercise is an essential need for everyone. Someday we will break out of the TV conditioning and make vigorous physical games a common activity again.

Both nutrition and exercise also generally tend to involve relationships with others. We don't like to eat alone and exercising alone is about as boring as anything I can think of.

CLOSENESS

There are other real needs. There are other needs that seem to be real, to be rational, seem to be inherent in the actual make-up of the human being. Some of them we have discovered or re-discovered in Re-evaluation Counseling. All some people know about RC is that we try to encourage meeting one of these needs--the need for closeness. My understanding of this was very slow to evolve. I don't know all about it yet. We have got so far as saying people should have a minimum of four hugs a day. There are people who don't know anymore than that about RC and think it's great on that basis. There are even a few institutions where hugging has become common practice and the people have no notion that it was started by an RCer.

The fact that people actually cannot remain emotionally healthy without physical closeness with other humans regularly was obscured in our culture. It's still obscured for most of the population.

It was completely obscured for me. There was no closeness for anyone where I grew up. It took my clients in the throes of heavy discharge to convince me that I should hold their hands or, later, put my arms around them. I suffered terribly from my own fear and embarrassment, but I did notice what a big difference it made in their ability to discharge.

Check on the quality of hugging. Is it good? Some places in RC it deteriorates into unawareness. The patterns take over.

(Demonstration) Can we demonstrate hugging?

First, some of the familiar ways you shouldn't hug.

I didn't see that.

I hugged myself behind her back. I didn't really touch her. A person acting like this is afraid he might notice that she has a body. That wasn't really a hug. It was a glassy, unaware avoidance. The essence of good hugging is awareness. Here she is. A delightful person. May I hold you? She feels so good, so warm, so soft. Just exactly the right shape. Our phoney culture has identified this, through imposing distress, as sex; but sex is one thing and closeness is another. As little as we have been able to do to get the distress off of sex compared to how much there is on there, we *have* moved far enough that most people in the RC Community can pretty well see that closeness has essentially nothing to do with sex. They are completely separate things. You can enjoy closeness with someone four times your age or one-fourth your age; and this is just great. There are other clues besides our own experience. Our closest cousins, the great apes, spend their days grooming each other. Apparently closeness is a real need. This seems to be a rational need, the need to be close to one another.

TOUCH

A little separate from closeness is touching, (The separation may be just for the purposes of communication.) We have a real need to touch awarely, to touch another person. There is healing in the touch. "Mama kisses it and makes it well" is a very real phenomenon. Focusing outside attention on the hurt allows one's own attention to get outside the hurt and re-evaluate it. The pain is felt and finished, and healing does progress very rapidly.

It's good to touch, just to touch. Although our culture proscribes this, and also tries to tie it up through distress with sexual feelings, it's a very separate thing. Awareness, again, of course, is everything. To be really aware of touching and being touched. The aches and pains that you didn't even know were there surface and dissipate if somebody strokes your tired head or tired feet after a long, hard day. We need to touch each other and we have rational intuitions in this direction.

BEING LOVED

There seems to be a continuing rational inherent need to be loved. This, of course, has been widely celebrated and agreed to, although the meaning of love has been greatly distorted by our culture.

RC has several definitions of love, because we certainly haven't intellectually encompassed the whole concept yet. The workhorse definition, the one that seems to be most useful in coping with problems is that *love is the way people naturally feel about each other if they don't have any distresses in the way.* They love each other to the degree that they know each other. The more they know each other the more they love each other. It's simply there, you don't have to impose love and you don't have to manufacture it. Rather, love is there if you get the distress out of the way. I think all of us have had at least glimpses of this feeling, this experience. When we give our clients a good session, when the clients are discharging well, then the lid or facade is jiggled enough so that you can see underneath it to the real persons and you fall in love with them forever. I have fallen in love with every client I ever had and I remain in love with them. The love can get obscured or occluded, of course. If they dramatize at me and kick my crutch out from under me I may forget that I love them because of my distress. But the basic relationship is there, you don't have to manufacture it or impose it.

We need to feel loved, we need to receive love, we need to feel that there is some human somewhere who has, at least potentially, this loving attitude toward us.

LOVING OTHERS

Now this need is widely celebrated and we are not breaking any new paths in saying this. What I think we do need to say, and clearly, is that far more important than the need to be loved is the need *to love*. This is enormously more important than receiving love, than being the recipient of love. You can get along without being loved over long periods of time if necessary, but if you have allowed your outlet of loving others to be sealed then you are in trouble, you are in real trouble. There are devastating effects on people who have allowed their ability to love to get plugged up.

We don't have to allow it to get plugged up. The last cover of *Present Time* is quoting Mary McCabe on just this question. "To love someone is available to all of us. Let us therefore think on what are the rational means of accomplishing this--and then act." This we can realize. It may be very difficult to obtain love or an expression of love from someone. If you are in a strange place and you don't know the language--to find and receive love may be hard.

Giving love is always possible, however. This is very much to the point. This is the greater need. Once we realize this nobody can stop us. There are situations and cultures that can make it very difficult to obtain expressions of love that are at all rational; *but no one can stop you from loving*. You can love, you can look at the individual behind the pattern and love. This is an essential and an important continuing need.

There's an old story, but a good one. There was a little girl in an old-fashioned orphanage where strictness was the word and harshness was the custom, and where the children were forbidden to have any communication with anyone outside the orphanage. Someone reported seeing the little girl throwing a note over the stone wall. She was called on the carpet, very frightened, and was forced to admit she had thrown the note. When the note was brought in and read aloud it said, "If anyone finds this, I love you."

We need love. With a little theory, a little discharge, we can fill that need anytime. You couldn't stop me from loving you. We can be very sure that we have a rational, continuing need to love, a need that no one can frustrate.

ACCEPTING LOVE AS COUNSELORS

As counselors you had better get used to being loved. I don't care how embarrassing it feels. I don't care how much it restimulates and scares you, you are going to have to get your head straight and simply stand still and let people love you. This is uncomfortable for me, but I have learned. I let people love me. I have adjusted. I stand still for it.

I learned to do that because it became obvious that it was important to my clients and students to have someone to love. My uneasy feeling was, "Why me?" I'm sure many of you would feel the same way. You won't know what to do with this love. You will feel embarrassed, you will be scared, you won't know how to accept this role. Nothing in your childhood prepared you for this. Yet it is clear that for their progress, their re-emergence, it is important to your clients to love you. They work better, they move faster if they can love you, if they can believe in you, if they can have faith in you. It doesn't really hurt one in spite of the embarrassment. They need to love somebody, trust somebody, believe in somebody, have confidence in somebody. Why me?, I asked. Then I started looking around at what the choices were. Between me and Nixon I'd better let them love me, I decided.

You'll have to get accustomed to this. Don't blow your cool and think that you are in a major crisis--"Oh my God!

What will I do? My client loves me!" The first client that insisted that she tell me her love told me against my protests. She finally said, "Now shut up and listen; I'm paying for this time." At the end of two hours of heavy discharge and telling me that she loved me, she said, "I feel better. You know, kid, you are all right, but you aren't that much." My relief was enormous. That was long ago.

Face this. It is a real need. You are not violating the no-socializing rule if you allow them to love you. The no-socializing rule doesn't say, "Don't love your co-counselors." It says, "Don't mess around." Just stand still. If they start to hang other reactive demands on you, handle them. You say, "No, I have a date already." "Sorry, I don't think my wife/husband would approve." "Excuse me, I have to go to the bathroom." Any clever little dodges. You handle their reactive demands, but in terms of their loving you, just accept--that's all it takes. It really won't hurt you. It may restimulate some of your own distress. I discharged much distress over my clients' attempts to love me. Great gobs of goo came off.

The need to love is a rational need.

COMMUNICATING

We need to communicate. We need to interchange rational thought with others. This seems to be a continuing need.

(This gets stultified in some of the irrational, compulsive "clienting and counseling" that goes on. The kind of thing that happens when you try to say something meaningful and you are told, "Say that again." It's as bad as the behaviorists who try to explain everything about human beings on the basis of their patterns. This is reactive.)

THE INTERACTION OF THOUGHTS

We have a need to think in interaction with someone else's thinking--to know that another intelligence is hearing us or is trying to hear us and to think back. It is delightful, the interchange of sparkling fresh ideas from each other. This is what we see in a concentrated form in a good think-and-listen session. This is a real need. We need this interchange with other human minds.

This gets masked and frustrated to a great extent out in the world, because if anyone has any slack showing, the desperate need to be counseled turns everybody else into a client. They notice that you have a little light in your eye and begin, "Did I ever tell you about the time ------" You have the choice of changing the subject skillfully, retreating, or sitting down and taking on the burden.

Nevertheless, the other need is there, and I think all of us recognize it. We need everyday to have some rational intercommunication with the stimulus of another functioning mind.

SOLITUDE

There seems to be a rational need for *solitude*. In between the interrelation time we really need to be ourselves, by ourselves. This is going to be a powerful force for cutting population growth off at the point that there will still be the chance to be by ourselves, to take a look at our own identity. To tighten the guy wires connecting us to the general universe, as well as to the group interaction, solitude is also important and nourishing.

SLEEP, AIR, WATER, REST

What else are rational needs? Sleep. Very much so. Sleep, of course, can get spoiled and become a time when recordings are restimulated so we don't get the full benefit from our sleep. Sleep is not a time of unconsciousness. It is a time of thinking fast and hard to catch up on the information as far as we can, dealing with the things we can't easily think through because of restimulated distress, by the use of dreams, which usually allow us to at least take the sharp corners off the restimulations and throw them back in the bin.

We need sleep. We need fresh air. We need clean water. We need rest.

MEANING AND PURPOSE

We need to have meaning to our existence. We need to know a purpose for living. We need to know that we are going somewhere and that there is meaning in what we are doing.

This is one if the real rewards, of course, of becoming an RC leader, a teacher, a permeator. (Another reward is the pressure to force you into re-emergence faster. To undertake to be a model forces you to straighten out your own mind.) It is a need and a great satisfaction to be meaningful. To be a human being, to master the environment is great. It is even greater to be a human intelligence playing a key role in assisting other human intelligences to free themselves. To catalyze other human intelligences to work together to accomplish worthwhile things--this is very satisfying. If you are an RC teacher, you need never again in your life feel meaningless. There is a great satisfaction in "serving the people." This is a real reward.

There is another reward, that of being in communication with your peers. RC teachers love to be at workshops with other RC teachers and communicate with the people who have taken on the same degree of responsibility. It's just great. Reference Persons feel the same way. There was a discussion on this once at a Reference Persons' Workshop. All agreed that one of the basic reasons why they wanted to stay Reference Persons was because the association with other people who were taking equal responsibility was richly rewarding.

We each need a meaningful role individually. I think we also have a need for an *interrelationship* about a meaningful purpose--a joint purpose. We need to be associated with other people in serving humanity, in assisting the development of the universe. We need to play the role which reality has assigned us of guiding the leading edge of the great pervasive tendency of the universe toward integration, toward meaning, towards organization, towards independence, towards mastery.

(This tendency is counterposed to the one that has been given so much attention, the equally pervasive tendency towards entropy, towards disorganization, towards randomness, towards chaos. That tendency is always there and, quantitively, is larger, but the movement toward integration, toward complexity, toward meaning, toward coherence, independence, intelligence, and mastery moves faster, and human beings are right on the leading edge.)

We are the most meaningful, the most complex, independent, masterful entities in the universe that we know about. I have a hope, of course, that somewhere out in the Galaxy our older brothers and sisters who are ahead of us are on their way to some day take us by the hand and help us over the next rough spots; but we can't count on it. We don't know they exist yet. It just seems likely.

SEX?

As of now, is sex a need? We don't know. Is sex an inherent ongoing need for human beings? We don't know. There is a conjecture that if we were completely rational we would only resort to sex for reproductive purposes. There are people who say, "That's quite an interesting idea." A number of other people say, "Nonsense!" I will have to admit that if that conjecture is rational, I'm not that rational yet.

There is a reason for the conjecture, which is that, observably, the enormous pre-occupation reinforced by our culture that sex is an urgent need, a need, a need, loses almost all of its thrust as people become rational enough to separate the real needs from it. It's plain that the great "need" character of sex in the past has been because our culture has made it almost the only avenue toward closeness, toward touch, toward love, toward affection, even toward awareness; and frequently the only outlet for discharge.

I would guess that about 70% of the population thinks that a climax is largely shaking and crying. That's the only time people get close enough to feel secure enough to do a little discharging and they feel it's marvelous. They feel they have to have sex because it's the only discharge they get. As people re-emerge through co-counseling almost all the feelings that are assumed to be sexual to start with turn out to be distress feelings. *Almost* all of them, certainly.

A lot of us have gotten to the point that sexual feelings are very relaxed and voluntary. It appears that, without distress, sex feelings are under the control of the rational faculty and not in any sense a "drive". People have simply observed that as they get more rational their pre-occupation with sex goes down. This conjecture, that if we get completely rational, it will disappear entirely, except for reproduction, is completely a conjecture and not my own guess. We don't know whether sex is a rational need in the sense of this discussion or not.

REPRODUCTION

I would guess that reproduction--the emergence of new human beings--is a rational but not an individual need. Even if we solve the question of immortality, I think we are going to want to find some ways to provide for the emergence of new human beings. I can't imagine us functioning well without having new babies in our arms once in a while. As an ex-parent I feel this relief from anxiety--thank God, they are all grown--and then somebody hands me a baby to hold for a minute and I think how in the world do I get along without this? It may be, of course, that when we are rational, this precious thing that we see in a child will be in all our faces and eyes and we won't have to turn to the child to get again that fresh glimpse of what we are really like.

EXCLUSIVE RELATIONS

Do you suspect that once we reach freedom, the mating need with one special person will turn out to be irrational?

One alone to be my own?

I mean, will rational people pick someone to marry?-- 'til death do us part kind of?

Forsaking all others? I don't know. I think it would be premature for us to be very sure either way. People ask me what marriage in the future is going to be like? I suspect it's going to be of infinite variety. That in the same residential block you are going to have 27 different forms of marriage.

I'm pretty sure they are all going to have one thing in common, however. They are all going to be aware and caring, full of affection awarely expressed and received, whatever form the relationship takes. People say, "But it's so inconvenient to have more than one love." OK, that's an argument for forsaking all others under present conditions at least. I don't know about the future. I don't think any of us have any clear notion. We are still so far from being rational and free on this subject.

What we can do is to take the things that do seem to be emerging clearly and hang on to those. We can see to it that we don't have any relationships that aren't thoughtful and aware and caring, no relationships where we don't look out for each other.

AWARENESS

Awareness is the touchstone here as well as a rational need itself. I can't define or describe awareness precisely. It's more than intelligence--the fresh response to each new situation--because we do a great deal of that below awareness. We couldn't stay alive on the freeway if we didn't do a lot of intelligent thinking below awareness. We would be in a wreck immediately otherwise because we usually pay little attention to how we drive. We are often talking and listening to the radio and eating a sandwich at the same time.

I once made a conjecture that we might define awareness as thinking about thinking while thinking; but that's not a final definition. Everybody knows intuitively what awareness is. You know the difference between awareness and nonawareness. So, for now, we will say that it is an undefined term. Mathemeticians say, you either know what a point and a line are or you don't, but they're not defined. You either know what awareness is or you don't.

The thought entered my head that when you were talking about sex a minute ago, that through the centuries we kept thinking that sex was getting in the way of the worship of God, getting in the way of making money--I guess Calvinists got into that. I get the feeling that a lot of people have put sex down because it got in the way of things. What I'm suggesting is that every time that has happened, the pendulum has swung back because of the force of the need for sex--that sex needed to come back. And I'm almost hearing that same pendulum move saying that it's in the way of rationality. I'm not so sure that it can't be used as a positive force. Would you like to comment on that?

Well, you see, we are talking about distressed sex. There hasn't been any other kind. We are talking about sex as it is, loaded up with all these griefs and fears and embarrassments and shames and guilts. And I don't think that this kind of sex will make a comeback once we are rational. You are speculating that a pendulum is going to swing. Sure, it *has* swung. Every collapsing society gets very libertine about sex as the present one is doing. That doesn't have anything to do with the rational roles of sex. We have got to get the distress out of the way before we can even glimpse what that will be. Historical trends don't tell us very much because the history of sex has been the history of irrational sex.

Not all religions were repressive of sex. The traditional ones that we are familiar with in our culture were, but the Polynesians' religion was pretty good on at least this one question.

I don't think we have much to guide us in historical trends because this history has been a kind of monstrous thing.

BEAUTY AND ORDER

How about beauty and order?

Good! The need to keep our environment reflecting our own humanness. I'm sure that's a need. We pay penalties immediately when we don't. The restimulation of having the cluttered environment shout at us that we are slobs is very real.

MEETING RATIONAL NEEDS

Where will we find these relationships? A good many of the things that I have talked about we can find with our co-counselors. We can practice them with our co-counselors, practice in the Co-counseling Communities. At Gather-ins it's generally permitted to hug somebody if you do it awarely and ask permission first. You look at each other and make sure that you both want to. You don't enforce a hug on someone else in the name of RC.

You can touch. You can have think-and-listens. You can arrange solitudes.

DON'T HUDDLE

You can do a lot of things at workshops; but certainly all this would only be a warm-up for the establishment of these relationships *outside* the RC Community. It's true that many of the people we establish good relationships with will come into the RC Community; but that's not the point of doing it. The point is to have the good relationships.

We have to influence a large share of the four billion people out there *before* they ever become co-counselors, in order for our goal of a non-destructive transition of society to take place.

SKILLS TO LEARN

Tim's proposal could be the beginning of some real thought about mastering the skills of making friends. There are a few people who intuitively have these skills. Some have become mayors or heads of political machines, and they do their friend-making in a reactive way; but there are real skills involved which can be used rationally. Just because we have been conditioned to be inhibited in these skills is no reason we should settle for that state. Why shouldn't we grasp the plow handles and plow our way out to where we, too, become expert friend-makers, making friends for good purposes.

I have had some question as the RC Communities grow bigger and bigger whether, if we put our energies into growing and have more and more activities that we do together, gather-ins and area meetings and Area Reference Communities--activities where we see each other a lot--and also co-counsel, won't we get preoccupied with the RC Community and get isolated from the world as a whole?

There is a danger, but it's just a danger, it doesn't have to happen. If we organize our Communities correctly, they will not be a burden on our time, they will be springboards from which we move out into the wide world. Permeation is going to become at least as big an item in our theory and practice as recruitment has been. It's already happening.

As we develop new leadership, we are going to free some of the experienced leaders for new jobs. Experienced ex-Reference Persons, for example, are taking on jobs as directors of permeation. (Others are assuming responsibility for outreach.) When these skilled leaders start moving in this area (of permeation), when someone like this starts to think about it full time, then all kinds of good developments will start to take place. Our attention will be more on the world as a whole than ever before.

GROW ON ALL LEVELS

The growth of Re-evaluation Counseling is integral. Clienting, co-counseling, recruiting, teaching, building a community, permeating--all these activities depend on and support each other. It is to everyone's advantage to have good teachers and excellent classes, Fundamentals as well as Ongoing, to have brilliant people recruited for them and to have them successful in every way, even if you have to give a hand folding the chairs or picking up the paper cups afterwards. The effectiveness of the class feeds right back into your own session. It's all of one piece. The effectiveness of the community feeds right back into the class and into your own session.

Traveling around as I do, I can observe clearly that where the Community is well-organized and effective, everybody's sessions go better. It's just so clear. There are many excellent Communities (including the local one, of course). In Albuquerque or Palo Alto conditions are outstanding in slightly different ways. When co-counselors report on their sessions in those places, their tone is high. They give you the feeling that things are moving, things are happening, they are on top of the situation. You can get this impression from anybody there. In the business-like atmosphere of the Palo Alto Community, dramatizations stick out like a thistle in a cabbage patch and tend to quickly wilt when they do occur. People quickly go back to being responsible and business-like. The co-counseling goes well in part because of the overall organization and expectation. You can sense this.

The growth and strength of the International Community also feeds back into our individual sessions and into our classes and our Area Communities and is a source of support and strength to them all.

There are certainly other rational needs of humans. Physical work, continual contact with a fresh supply of new interesting information, an opportunity to create--all would certainly be in this category. I invite you to join me in seeing how complete a list we can assemble in the next few months.

The Application

of Theory

An Overall Perspective *

It might be a good idea to expand our perspective of the overall picture in RC, to take a long look at what we are doing. It's easy to get too narrow a view of Re-evaluation Counseling and settle for a small part of it. That small part sometimes works very, very well for a short time, but without a bigger picture co-counselors will eventually hit frustration.

There are places where beginning co-counseling has been well learned in a sort of oversimplified way. Because that oversimplified version works so well to begin with, the mistaught co-counselors assume that they already know all about RC. When they hit difficulties in re-emergence they begin to lose interest in what they think is Re-evaluation Counseling. They drift off into strange movements looking for answers that they could find in RC but that haven't been shared with them. In such situations (which are rare but do exist) teachers teach their oversimplifications over and over again to excited new students, and most of the experienced ones drift away.

The point of Re-evaluation Counseling is to completely recover our ability to think and to take charge of the world. That's quite an open-ended goal. We are in no danger of getting lost in routine if we keep that in mind. If we don't keep this in mind, it's very easy for co-counseling to become routine and one's re-emergence be frustrated. Things seem to be working well and you are meeting your co-counselor regularly. Heh, heh. The non-thinking creeps in again and real progress quits happening. It's very easy for a teacher to become bemused with how delighted her students are with

*Talk given at Madison I Workshop, Connecticut – February 18, 1975

her teaching and settle down into no progress because "every-thing is just fine". Everybody reports that "everything is just fine". The grey dust and fog that is our enemy creeps in.

EVERYONE A LEADER EVENTUALLY

Each one of us in RC, of course, is, in a basic sense, a teacher. Every co-counselor is permitted to teach another person, one-to-one, however slowly. Any co-counselor's example, from the very beginning, is going to teach people; well or poorly, but it's going to teach people.

Also, each person in RC is destined to be a leader. We have gotten a clear realization of this recently. First we had to realize the necessity of leaders. We had to think this through against the great anarchistic resentment against any leadership accumulated from bad experiences with oppressive leaders in society. Now we are getting a better perspective and it's plain that to lead is an essential function of every human being. There will be no fully-emerged intelligence which won't play this role of helping to combine and inte-grate other people's intelligences in joint, mutual effort for good goals. One hasn't quite regained all one's humanness until one does this. It's necessary for us who are presently playing the role of leading RC to realize that our goal must be for everyone in RC and eventually for all humans to be leaders. Leadership must not be the monopoly of particularly bright persons or compulsively aggressive persons or any other category, though we want them all to regain brightness and confidence as they attain leadership. Each persistent co-counselor will become a leader, however long it takes.

There are people who come into RC who need to co-counsel on the fundamentals level for a long time. Their material happens to be stacked up that way. They need only to come into a session, look at an aware counselor who asks, "what's on top?" and they discharge well. For a time they don't need any more complicated techniques than that. These aren't necessarily people who aren't functioning well. They may be functioning very well in the wide world and in that way are an example to all of us. It just happens that their distresses are stacked up in such a way that the Fundamentals of Co-Counseling is quite enough technique for a long time.

We are all going to progress at our own individual speed. This is an essential feature of RC, that we don't run people through stock yard gates en masse, we don't herd them through a set of exercises. I think you have all read the article on this. This arose out of a very real problem -- a large number of otherwise intelligent teachers were happily running their classes through a series of set exercises. That's beneath us, it's stupid, it's really ridiculous. Each person is unique as a personality, in his or her experiences, in his or her goals, in his or her humanness. Each person is also quite unique in his or her distresses. If you don't remember this you get into a position similar to that of most psychotherapists in our culture who don't know what they are doing most of the time because they are trying to lump people together.

The essence of the client's position is that as a human, and as a bundle of distresses, that client is unique. Each has a particular set of distress patterns that are the unique result of the unique distress experiences that each endured that no one else ever did. Our attitude to each client must be to pay attention to where that client is *that day*.

PERMISSIVENESS IS NOT PASSIVITY

This doesn't mean, as it has sometimes been distorted to mean, that you are passive or inactive to your client. You don't *just* say, "Well, you know what you are about. What do you want to do?" This abandons the person with the chronic. The chronic pattern infests our beloved co-counselor who is a helpless victim until we start thinking about him or her and looking hard at the pattern. I thank M——— for being such a clear example. Unless someone really looked at M———, one could easily conclude that she functions so well she must be free of patterns. One might ask who could be a more successful person than M———

operating within that pattern? But we would betray and abandon M———. Of course, her material will cry out in despair if we challenge it. Chronics always squeal when challenged; but we would be betraying and abandoning M——— if we relate to her without seeing the limitations. Most of the rest of us would be delighted if we could start functioning like M———. That would bust all kinds of *our* chronic patterns. But we have to see *her* where she is. Our responsibility is to open the next door for her and say, "Come on."

INDIVIDUAL CARING

The essence of it is that we think individually, that we care. If we care, then we care individually. Whoever enjoyed any "mass love"? Love means paying attention, giving a hand and a direction to the cared-about where the cared-about is not too clear herself or himself. We have this much clearer vision on each other's blind spot than we do on our own. The essence of a rational human relationship is caring, which means thinking, which means awarely paying attention, which means not adopting any rigid pre-conceived notions. Sure, our theory is important, our basic generalizations are very fundamental. We don't violate them. RC theory has been put together more rigorously than you could ever imagine unless you had watched the steps. It's been checked out. There aren't any serious mistakes in the logical structure of RC.

When you follow it rigorously, however, what it can do is to bring you to the spot where the job needs to be done with the tools at hand. Then you have to think about this precise, unique situation and move on it thoughtfully. Otherwise you are not doing RC.

RC IS UNIQUE

If you thought you had entered only the easiest and best human growth movement where you got hugs as well as theory, I'm sorry, you didn't. We are nothing like any human growth movement, psychology, or psychotherapy of any sort. We are a very different breed of human activity.

We start from different assumptions, we are headed toward different goals. We cannot possibly succeed in terms of what we are about unless we embrace the whole of humanity. This is the most fundamental revolution that has ever taken place in human existence.

We undoubtedly will have to mesh with and integrate with every other revolution that is taking place -- the revolutions against oppression, the economic revolutions, the political revolutions. But we are not anything else. If you want to mess up RC because your material screams so hard for us to be something else, then it's been nice to have you here, but go find something else. Don't insist that this be something else and don't allow anybody to bring in contradictory ideas and mess it up. To some timid patterns, this may sound very presumptuous and conceited, that I am saying that RC is the key development in human affairs. But it is. (laughter) There is no competition anywhere in sight.

This doesn't mean that we don't have a lot in common with and won't mesh into other drives for the liberation of the human being. We will. This is one thing that we have to think about in this period. This is what we are about -- the whole liberation of people. If you are not after complete humanness for everybody and you can't stand to have the people around you go after complete humanness for everybody, please leave RC. Find some nice human growth movement where you can huddle inside your chronic pattern.

DON'T DISTORT OR DILUTE RC

I would like you to join me in fighting for the purity of RC, the rigor of RC, the openness to every group, the long-range goals. Because it needs fighting for. Everytime we go into battle with patterns, the enemy tries to run up our necks and come out the backs of our heads and get a little toe hold there. We have to continually scrub the patterns out.

KEEP THE PATTERNS OUT OF THE PROCESS

Consider a good co-counseling relationship. It works so well. But all the time it is working so well a little fall-out from the patterns that you are taking apart is trying to sneak in. If you don't take time to scrub off identifications and other restimulations every so often, you soon have a poorly functioning co-counseling relationship. You may even be sitting there agreeing to let each other's difficult distresses alone; and that's a betrayal.

Everybody comes into RC, no matter how they act, hoping to become completely human again. They really do, whether they say it or whether they awarely know it. Of course we co-counselors don't know clearly what we are about at first. We start out from the middle of this big sack of distress and at first we move rather randomly looking for the way out; but the accumulated experience of co-counselors has punched many holes in the confusion by now. We have gotten a clear enough picture so that we roughly know where we are going. Our ongoing discussions of theory clarify the picture continually.

Few things have ever happened to people more important than RC. This isn't because we RCers are a chosen people or an elite. That we particular people are involved is purely an accident. The times are ripe. The multiplication of "seeking" movements everywhere, the revisions and reforms of all the religions everywhere, are phenomena that indicate how ripe the times are. We weren't ahead of our time. We just happen to be lucky that we are in on the leading edge of this major breakthrough in the human development.

JUST AT THE RIGHT TIME

The times are right, no question about it. The environment has been mastered to the point that it's possible to get a periscope turned around to look to the back of our heads at what is really wrong -- at the phenomenon of human irrationality, the key problem that has gone unsolved all through human existence until now. We humans have solved other problems partially but have always been tethered in terms of completely solving all the rest of them by the failure to solve this one. We who are already co-counseling are just lucky. We happened to be standing in the cornfield when the volcano came up. Those who are already involved in RC are lucky and I am the luckiest of all. This may sound to some of you as if I am saying that we are "chosen people" and we have the one "true light". We do in a sense but only because it accidentally fell into our hands. There are also much smarter, better functioning people outside RC than we have yet involved in it. Just by accident we have gotten involved in this early. Getting involved by accident, using some of our peculiarly-shaped painful emotion, including my chronic patterns, where we weren't able to be rational yet, we have put in the persistence that has gotten us to this level. At this point we have a pretty good idea of what we are about, of the probable historical role of Re-evaluation Counseling.

FACE REALITY BUT KEEP DISCHARGING

When I talk about the necessity of addressing the general population and taking charge of society, people sometimes think I am saying to forget co-counseling, that we don't need sessions, we need to go out and organize. That isn't true. Some co-counselors need to get out and organize, to quit hiding from the real world in a huddling pre-occupation with co-counseling. We all need to share our insights with people who are already organizing. But all levels of our re-emergence have to go on at the same time. We can't lose our broad perspective and just work on one level and still get where we want to go.

Our co-counseling has to be excellent and it has to persist. Our discharge has to keep rolling off. This is the key activity, the one that releases us to do all the other necessary things. The shutting off of discharge by social conditioning and the inherent tendency of a pattern to rehearse itself on the next victim has perpetuated the, until now, unsolvable problem of human irrationality all through human existence. We now have the solution; but we can't just say, "Yes, we have the solution." We have to *use* the solution.

It's similar to the simpler case of finding a good direction. In a demonstration we find a direction, the mention of which brings enormous discharge. We repeat the direction to the client and we say, "Will you say it?" And the client says, "It's a good direction, all right. Thank you very much." But he or she doesn't use the direction unless we help by insisting.

You have to *do* it. From the beginning, the discharge has to keep rolling off. If we are not moving in our co-counseling, it doesn't matter how lofty our social ideals are or how many people are out there organizing, or that we finally have contact with the working class. The discharge has to keep coming off or we will start meeting new, challenging situations with stupid responses that will bring our gains in society to a halt.

GOOD COUNSELING REQUIRES FRESH THINKING

We must as counselors, (as clients, too) keep thinking where our clients need to go. The permissive "Go ahead and do what you need to, dear" won't work past the beginning stages of co-counseling. Two pent-up beginning co-counselors can sometimes be unawarely permissive with each other and still have good sessions but it will be out of their desperate need. They are blowing the foam off the top of the glass. As they get past that stage they must learn to do things better if their co-counseling is to continue to work. Good co-counseling alternates between thoroughly cleaning up what has been started and facing new challenges. New doors have to open. This involves thinking. "What does my client need to do next?" "Where is he hung up?" "What can I ask her, how thoroughly can I be there for him, so that he or she can tell me?" If they are discharging a storm, don't interrupt them. Help them persist to clean up thoroughly what they've started but keep thinking. When the last one is scrubbed clean, help open that new door. Find the next direction. Face the new challenge.

People ask, "How do you identify a chronic pattern? You seem to spot people's chronic patterns, but I can't see them." How do you notice people's chronic patterns? Look. They are sticking out like cactus thorns. It is the nature of the chronic patterns that you can't be around the person without being stabbed by them.

RECLAIM AND USE ALL YOUR COUNSELING ABILITIES

As you and your co-counselor begin to feel some safety with each other, bring out and use your full range of tools. We need to recover the use of our facial expressions, for example. Our faces don't belong to the dumb chronic pattern. Our faces are often held hostage by the way we felt when we were beaten 20 years ago, which hasn't anything to do with how our faces ought to look now. To allow that to continue is a real drawback to your counseling effectiveness because your face is a powerful tool in counseling. It should be available to you to reach people with. It's *your* face. It belongs to *you*. Get in front of a mirror and change your expressions. Of course it will jiggle your chronic pattern. All kinds of "thoughts" will go through your head. The camouflage will be broken, the vulture will be flapping and squawking. He isn't really part of your hair piece the way he was pretending to be.

Listen to your client's tone of voice. How do all of us here talk? The same way all the time. (laughter) That's a chronic pattern operating. Your voice belongs to *you*. It doesn't belong to the chronic pattern. Reclaim it, take it back. It isn't necessary to go through life (mimics patterned voice). One of the ways to get your own back is to copy your clients' tones of voice. They will be different from your chronic tone of voice. You will have to discharge to get out of yours and they will discharge as you force them out of theirs. Reclaim your own flexible voice. It will be a very powerful tool for counseling and for communication.

I used to work a lot with married couples. Sometimes they were obviously very fond of each other back of the hurts and I might say to the husband, "Tell her you love her." And he would squirm, "Ah, I tell her that all the time." (Mimics harsh tones) We pay enough attention to words that our patterns are often armored against words. Most of us can say any words and still stay inside a chronic pattern; but change the tone of voice, change the facial expression and the pattern is disrupted. It has no armor against that. These are just two examples of being flexible.

CLEAN UP YOUR RELATIONSHIPS

The whole point is to think about each other. We are going to recover our own true natures. What all we have to do to get them back, I don't completely know, but we're finding out. We certainly have to deal with some of the oppressive things in our culture. We have to quit being sexist and racist or otherwise oppressive and victimized inside of our communities or we will load each other up faster than we can discharge. We will probably have to mesh with the great social revolutions that are about to sweep the world. (There's not going to be any stability or calm order any place in the world in the near future, in case you hadn't guessed.)

Whatever we have to do, any of us who have had very much discharge have sensed deeply that we have not as yet ever been allowed to be our real selves. We want to be our real selves completely, we want to recover our complete humanness. Enough of us are involved in our project by now that we can be confident that we are going to make it.

REVIEW THE FUNDAMENTALS FREQUENTLY

Fundamentals must be paid attention to. You can profitably go back through that manual a hundred times. Read it carefully every few weeks. It will make you yawn and you will hear some new things in it each time. Consider the introductory lectures which I do (the oral version of *The Human Side of Human Beings*) or the facsimiles of them that other people do all over the world. Often people come back and sit through that same lecture many times over a period of years. They say, "You said something last night you didn't say before." Well, I do improve it once in a while; but mainly I am saying the same things over and over each time I talk. These are the main theses of re-emergence. This body of knowledge counters the conditioning imposed by the culture. You can't expect to hear it and remember it all at once. It has to wear through the fog. When I read any of these basic writings they seem fresh to me. (I'm often startled by how well that writer expressed those truths, and I yawn and yawn and yawn as I read.) This body of important knowledge was gotten out to expression with difficulties. Mary McCabe, bless her patience and determination, extorted it from me though clouds of yawns and repetitive falling asleep on my part. She pulled it out of me from under the patterns until we got it on paper and in print. These important truths wear through the fog slowly. We need to refresh ourselves with them again and again and again. It's fundamentally important to do so.

BUT DON'T STOP WITH FUNDAMENTALS

At the same time the fundamentals theory and practice is operating and operating well, we need to be aware and make our new co-counselors be aware that all of us will eventually come up against certain chronic distresses that cannot be dismantled with permissive counseling. For these you will actually have to look and see what's going on and think and figure out what would contradict the pattern and lovingly and cleverly offer a direction and support and persist and persist and persist, while continually thinking afresh.

Now, will you make mistakes when you try to do this? Sure. If you can't stand to make a mistake, you are in a tough spot, because no one ever succeeds in doing a new and creative thing without making mistakes. You cannot predict the future, completely. Tentatively, yes, partially, yes, but not completely.

BETTER CONCEPTS OF REALITY

(Some very important work has been done in mathematical logic in the last 40 years or so. Some fundamental steps forward in humans' understanding of the universe have been taken there. Some of these theorems add up to saying that the future is unpredictable. No matter how much you know now you can't know what is going to happen exactly. This is liberating knowledge. Do you realize how boring it would be if the future was fixed ahead of time? This has been an unaware assumption by many schools of thought, that if one could just know enough of the present one could predict the future exactly. Now it has been established and proved as a fundamental, logical principle that the future cannot be completely predictable no matter how much we know. There will always be surprises.)

(It has also been established that in any given system true-or-false questions arise that cannot be decided within the system. In order to get decisions to these questions you have to place that system in a larger system and make the decisions from the viewpoint of the larger system. Those of you who read the "Cosmos" article in *Present Time* know that we are trying to use this principle to look at RC. We are trying to view RC by imbedding it in the larger situation of human affairs and in the universe so that we can get a more accurate perspective and get ourselves clearer directions than we could if we thought about things only from within RC.)

THE GROWTH OF OUR COMMUNITIES

We need to do our Fundamentals counseling well. Then we need to think about our clients where their chronics are; care about them, support them, furnish directions, persist with them. Beyond that, RC inevitably develops in the direction of recruiting. We can't get where we are going without many more co-counselors. From the beginning RCers have intuitively recruited. Everybody still does. Even if you don't intend to, your good example brings people in. (If you try to recruit without being a good example, it doesn't work. If someone acts crummy in the name of RC, such a person can turn a whole neighborhood off and RC may have to start with a whole fresh group of people when it comes in with a good model.)

RECRUITING

Inevitably we involve new people. No co-counselor can stand not to for very long. One cannot hope to regain full humanness unless one is part of a group effort in this direction. It's much easier to emerge if you are part of a class. We have certainly lost the illusion that people should take a class and then drop out and do lonely co-counseling. Participation in a group makes an enormous difference.

When the group becomes larger, when there are several classes and teachers and promising leadership, we can organize a Community. If the Community gets to functioning well, then the strength of the Community reaches right down into each individual session. Each session goes better. It's so obvious to someone who gets around as much as I do that where there is a sharp, well-organized community every session feels its thrust and support. It makes a big difference. It isn't just altruism that people reach out for more co-counselors and work to organize Communities. Each gain feeds right back into the effectiveness of their own counseling.

The existence of an International Community, the fact that in many other parts of the world there are other co-

counselors sharing your goals, taking the same direction that you are, is an enormous boost to the success of the individual Communities and to the individual's progress.

The experiences in Europe seem dramatic. People in the different countries have permanent, warm, loving relationships with co-counselors across the old national borders. The great social conditioning in Europe to be separate, nationalistic, and edgy melts. They reach each other. The old enforced barriers drop before the existence of the International Community of Co-counseling.

END OPPRESSIVE ATTITUDES

We have to be really united with every group of people in the world before the world will be safe and supportive enough for us. We are all tied to one destiny. In this country, we who are presently in RC have to get past our middle-class isolation. We have to really open the Communities to blacks and Chicanos and American Indians and young people and old people and everybody.

WELCOME WORKING CLASS CO—COUNSELORS

We can't possibly do what we need to do without a large working-class RC population. We need their competence and their sense of reality and their guts. In our present population we have a lot of openmindedness and willingness to consider new ideas; but we won't have enough freedom from chronic vacillation and timidity patterns until we have a larger proportion of working-class co-counselors. Then you will see things begin to move. Whoom! Things will happen.

We have to move in these directions. For our own counseling to go well enough, it is necessary that we challenge the sexism and the racism and the adultism toward children, the condescension toward the handicapped. We have to challenge them right here in our Counseling Communities and in the wide world.

ALL ONE REALITY

That is what I wanted to say. The co-counseling world is all one-piece. Work where you are but be aware of the whole picture. If we have perspective then we will do what we need to do so much better. We won't mill around in front of the next challenge.

We need a community of enthusiastic sceptics. Never become believers. Believing is non-thinking.

Counseling the Way It Should Have Been Done All the Time *

July 14th

I want to talk this morning about the chronic pattern and the next stage of our assault on it.

CONCEPTS ARISE FROM REALITY

In a sense all such entities as the "intermittent pattern" or the "chronic pattern" are mental concepts which we have constructed to represent reality and the names are only useful labels that we put on the concepts in order to deal with them. The concepts and names are useful; but any time we construct a concept and use a label we are abstracting from reality and oversimplifying in order to handle and communicate. It's necessary to do so but we need to remember that the reality underlying our concept and its label is very complex.

Any part of the universe is intimately connected with every other part of the universe. Each part is, itself, very complex. If we examine even one atom we must ignore a million things about it in order to examine one facet of it. (We usually ignore, for example, the fact that another atom two billion light years away is pulling at it with a small gravitational force.) To take our concepts, simplifications and labels as reality and forget that we have abstracted for the purpose of study and application is to risk drifting into a rut of oversimplification and non-thinking.

*Report on Theory at the 1975 International Reference Persons' Workshop, Buck Creek, WA, U.S.A. -- July 14 and 15, 1975

On the other hand, we have to do this concept-building and abstracting in order to deal with reality at all because its complexity is overpowering. Reality can't be studied and dealt with *en masse*. So it's useful and necessary to make up concepts like a "chronic pattern"; but while we use it we need to remember that we are talking about one segment of reality that we have artificially abstracted, separated from its matrix for study and discussion. The concept of "the brush pile" is useful to describe human distresses. Like all good analogies it clarifies some things. If the brush pile is a good analogy, then we can say that the chronic pattern is one continually-in-restimulation area of brush that we separate for examination from all the other distress with which it is tangled.

OUR PROGRESS IS REAL

The question last night--"When do you finally emerge from a chronic pattern?" reflects a confusion about this. There is no question that we are getting some place, that we are progressing, but we would like to have our progress neatly wrapped in a bundle or corked up in an urn like the ashes of our dear departed spouse so we can say, "There's Henry" or "There's the chronic pattern that I have emerged from".

It's a little more complicated than that. We don't need to get oversimple in order to reassure ourselves. The evidence of our progress is all around us in innumerable ways.

We want to get our whole selves back. The more of ourselves we get back, the keener our appetite, the greater our urgency, to recover all of our humanness. When we come into RC all shut down, our theory often begins on the basis "RC will make you feel better". It's like the song we were singing from Sesame Street--"It's all right to cry, it might make you feel better". Still, for many people in our Community, this is what the theory amounts to--"you might feel better".

It's fine to start there; but you can't stop with the over-simplification. Four years ago we had a lot of opposition to our policy on drugs. "How do you know that LSD *and* discharge isn't the answer?" people new to RC asked. Now everybody understands that drugs get in the way of thinking and install patterns and that feeling and the illusion of feeling isn't enough to guide one's progress.

Theory can't stop with "it might make you feel better". Everybody here knows that we want to be able to *think* better, not just *feel* better. We are even willing to be uncomfortable as long as it is going somewhere. The recovery of our intelligence is a far more dependable goal than feeling better because "feeling better" can lead you into numbness.

This sounds trivial to this group; but when you get back to your fundamentals class you know you will have to go through all this again many times and repeatedly clarify the concepts.

THE NEXT STEP IS UNDERSTANDING

What the leading part of our Community, including all of this group, needs is a better picture, a clearer direction, a more sustained effort at tackling and eliminating chronic patterns. We have done quite well by ourselves with permissive counseling. We have kept gaining with co-counselors who only say "what do you need to work on" and "go ahead". We haven't done badly. Still, some experienced co-counselors are wondering if their enthusiasm for RC hasn't about run out because things aren't so exciting anymore. We are milling around a little, quite unnecessarily. It isn't that we don't know how to go farther; it's that we haven't clarified and communicated and put to use what we do know.

Can a person theoretically emerge from a chronic pattern simply with enough knowledge and effort? Yes, if one were to somehow think enough, using our existing theory, one could take directions and hold them in daily living to where one would have to discharge all the time and one would have to emerge into complete rationality. *Theoretically*. In practice it turns out to be incredibly difficult.

The evidence that we have from records of the past indicates that the outstanding changes in people's lives (emergence from chronic patterns) have come about when, accidentally, enough motivation has been forced on someone. Accidental circumstances conspired to force somebody out of a chronic pattern and furnished the motivation for the change. These are the turning points of history.

CONFUSION IS THE DIFFICULTY

We are looking for a way to do this day after day, person after person, for every one of us and everyone that comes into RC. And we have the knowledge. What happens when someone wants to move decisively and exactly against a chronic pattern? He or she gets a perspective for moving. The client thinks, "I want to do this" and heads for a session. Maybe he or she explains to the co-counselor and then moves into it. But the chronic is heavy and quickly produces a fog. The direction is north, north, north, and the client heads into the fog shouting "North! north! north! north! sorth! sorth! sorth! south! south!" (laughter) That fog is very southbound. very southbound. In the nature of the struggle it's almost certain to confuse the client. We will hold to the theoretical possibility that one person alone, if necessary, will be able to do it. To assume anything less is to surrender our human mastery of the universe; but, practically, the odds go up against one enormously if one doesn't have someone standing by and reminding him or her, "North, north, north" when the confusion hits. It is impractical to count on re-emerging without this.

THE COUNSELOR IS THE KEY

We have learned in fundamental permissive counseling that it's good to have a second person there. Beginning co-counselors often get by with the counselor only saying "go ahead". The accumulated need to discharge is sufficiently great to overcome the low level of support. This is how beginning co-counselors often get started. The beginning client is so much in need of discharge that she or he pretends the other person is paying enough attention. Many religious people project the notion of God as a counselor. They talk to her so they can cry. They have her defined as someone who really cares and is really going to listen even if no one else will.

We can use such desperate measures in a crisis or for intermittent distress, but when we get up against the deep chronic fog, it takes another human intelligence with us to win out. In practice we have to have someone really thinking *about* us, really thinking *with* us.

Have we, in general, done this with each other up 'til now? No. Except in rare instances, the best of our counseling 'til now has been unaware and sloppy in this area. We have had brilliant occasional exceptions, sometimes at workshops. It's harder for a counselor running a workshop to shut down completely when 150 eager eyes are watching the demonstration. We have this phenomenon of the great parabolic reflector of the workshop's attention focusing up here. It brings in lots of light. Partly it's the effect of the group's attention on keeping the counselor thinking.

REALLY SEEING THE CLIENT AND THE PATTERN BOTH

Since almost all of our counseling is going to be two people, it's necessary that we put emphasis here on the counselor really thinking under *all* conditions. In the leaders' meeting that preceded this workshop, we talked about this and we tried an experiment and the insight began. Any conclusions that we draw are tentative, but one phenomenon got highlighted so clearly that it was impossible not to see it.

If we are going to be a good counselor for someone emerging from a chronic pattern, we need to see the chronic pattern for what it is and we need to see the person for where that person is and we need to keep seeing both antagonists in the struggle; the human, the position she or he is in, where he or she is ready to go, the strength, the course that the person intuitively maps through the thicket until she or he gets into it and gets turned around; and we need to see the kind of thickety obstacles that the chronic pattern furnishes. We need to *see* these two antagonists clearly, we need to *keep* seeing them clearly and we need to throw all our weight behind the person and against the pattern. We do not need to get confused or become indifferent.

The question I'm asked over and over is "How can you tell a chronic pattern?" Well, technically, it's not difficult. How do you notice a porcupine's quills? How do you find out if a cactus has spines? You get near them, pay attention, lean against them, notice there's a spine there. How do you see the chronic pattern? It's sticking out, like the spines on a sea urchin or porcupine or cactus. It's sticking out of the person in all directions. If you pay any attention to the person you can't help but notice it. Take facial expressions. What facial expression do you wear all the time? Not your own. You wear that loathsome creature's expression sitting up there pulling your face. When you discharge, all of you look beautiful, so human, so delightful. The minute your face goes into repose, how do you look? I just scanned the room and I will play back a few of them. (Demonstrates.) Now, are those your expressions? Of course not, no human being looks like that. Human beings look the way you do when you're laughing. Laugh for me, will you? (laughter) That's the way a human being looks. We could take the rest of the day demonstrating this obvious aspect of chronics.

What's another spine sticking out of every pattern? Tone of voice. Would you say, "I love you"? (I love you.) OK, would you say, "I hate you"? (I hate you.) (laughter) Granted this was a quick expectation; it's still certainly possible to say "I hate you" (very hatefully) or "I love you" (tenderly). Now, Linda, just like that. (I love you.) Then, (I despise you.) (Tries with Keith.) We use the same tone of voice for I love you--I hate you--Oh my God, the house is burning down--Please pass the cold mashed potatoes. (laughter) No two people use the same tone of voice, but each only uses one, in the grip of the chronic.

Parenthetically, your facial expression, your tone of voice belong to you. They don't belong to that idiot pattern. Take them back. Reclaim your marvelous tone of voice. Your voice should be able to say, "NO!" "Ah, come on." "Hey! That really is nice, isn't it?" "Oh, goody!" (All with different tones.) You have a beautiful instrument there, why not play on it? You don't have to saw on one broken G string all the time. You will be a more effective counselor, using your own voice.

(Comment: There are people who have reclaimed their faces and their tones of voice and still have chronic patterns.) That's right. (If these are the ways you recognize chronic patterns, I am saying that there are a lot more things to a chronic pattern than these. These may be in the possession of the human already and there are still chronic patterns anyway.) I absolutely agree with you. (laughter) I had not finished nor will I finish the innumerable ways that are possible to spot them. These are just two; but it is very uncommon to find anyone who isn't stuck on those two.

PAY ATTENTION

If you pay attention to your client, the chronic pattern is blinking red lights, waving orange banners (or wrinkled brown banners), is jumping up and down. All of us act out the weirdest mannerisms all the time. We tolerate them in each other and it's great that we do until we are ready to be helpful about them, because it's no use to just go up and be critical. But if you pay attention, your beloved client is a human being, beautiful, able, graceful, melodious, *acting* as if she or he is being shaken up and hung upside down by his or her heels in an iron cage with alarm bells ringing and old pieces of metal clanging all the time. This is the way they function. (That's just a little bit exaggerated.) If I go down the line with people here and just copy and act out what is actually there, it doesn't take much noticing.

Notice. Take a look. How does your client act all the time. How much of that behavior is sensible for an all-around opera singer, acrobat, scientific genius and photogenic movie star? For the person whom your client really is? How much of that behavior and appearance fits that real person? The chronic pattern is sticking out all the time.

If you want to get a clearer look at it, ask your client to appreciate himself or herself without any reservations. Use the familiar exercise, in at least four modes--posture, tone of voice, facial expression and words. "Here I am, an all-around human being, behold me, appreciate me." (Now, I'm close to doing this because I'm showing you how it should be done. If I were to try to do it for myself[shiver] I'd have difficulty, I'd start to discharge.) At this point, when this (shiver) starts, you ask, "What are you thinking" "I'm thinking bla, bla, (negative) bla, bla, (negative)." The bats fly by actively defining the chronic pattern.

ASK THE CLIENT WITH CARING AND ATTENTION

You don't even have to do that. There's a simpler, better way. You ask your client, seriously, caringly, "Where are you? Would you really tell me about you?" Then really listen, and with a certain amount of skirmishing to get some of the loose clutter out of the way, the client tells you exactly where he or she is. Exactly. If you seem like you are really interested, the client will reveal himself or herself. Then, "Where are things difficult for you and where would you like some assistance?" With possibly a certain amount of difficulty, your clients will tell you. If you are really interested, really paying attention, they will tell you exactly. They will tell you where they are ready to work and what the chronic pattern is doing to them and what kind of assistance they need to go against it. They will tell you exactly. Sometimes it will be in the first two sentences, sometimes it will be in the 120th paragraph, because everyone has his or her own unique thicket of communication difficulties to thread his or her way through; but each one will tell you. The client will always tell you.

MEANING, NOT APPEARANCES

Now, you may have to listen hard, and think and understand the difficulties of language. The client may say,."I am on the verge of becoming myself but I am afraid to make the move." What beautiful communication! However, the next one may say, "What the hell are you bugging me with that goddam question for? Bla, bla, bla."

Is the second form of communication any more difficult to understand than the first? Not really. The person is saying, "Here is a sample of my difficulty. This is how agonizing it is." They have told you a lot, if you understand. One form of communication is just as easy to decipher as the other, if we remember to understand.

We have a few difficulties getting in our way--such as our own chronics--but these have only to be overcome. It's a very real problem but it's just a problem to be solved. We are not going to overcome them because I do a good lecture. We are going to overcome them increment by increment by increment, direction by direction, section by section; but we are going to succeed.

A KEY INSIGHT

Now I would like to speak about this experience in the leaders' meeting. We asked two or three people in turn to say who they were, where they were stuck, what would be deeply satisfying and helpful to them for other people to do, for their beloved co-counselors to do. They all revealed themselves very clearly. After they spoke we asked each person in the 16 there to interact as a counselor with this person. Some good things happened. We didn't lose any ground or spoil any affinity as a result of the experiment, but the important thing that was very noticeable was that almost every counselor retreated or ran away from the topic on which the client had asked for help.

The persons, as clients, had said very clearly where they were, what the problems were, how they were hurting, what kind of assistance they needed. Counselor after counselor (and these are the best counselors in our communities) acted as if, "Oh God, I've got to find something else that I can handle," and asked a whole bunch of other questions until they had changed the subject and found something different than the client had asked help with that they could feel comfortable to work with.

The client had said, "I need such and such and such." The various counselors in turn would ask questions completely off from what the client had said. They would ask questions like "What do you feel good about, about yourself?" Of course, the cooperative client would say, "I think I tie my shoe laces neatly." "Repeat that!" said the counselor in a triumphant tone, meaning, "I have found something that I'm ready to work on."

In response to the agony that the client had revealed, the counselor said, in effect, "Thank you, I am not ready for that today. Let's work on something I'm ready for."

Revealed clearly at last, this phenomenon is one of the main difficulties we have to overcome for complete re-emergence--the habit of not really paying attention to where the client is and staying with him or her there.

Much of our counseling has become limited and inhibited by the unaware requirement that the *counselor* be comfortable. This notion must be rooted out and destroyed if we are to eliminate chronics in a reasonable period of time, if we are to completely re-emerge.

The client says, "I've got to walk through this bed of live coals"; and the counselor says, "That's not my cup of tea. Why don't we take a stroll down memory lane?" When you do this kind of poor counseling you re-define the client's problem in terms of what you feel up to or ready for or what suits your upsets, or your fears. We won't get through chronic patterns this way. We won't get to complete re-emergence this way.

THE COUNSELOR'S DISTRESS IS NOT THE ISSUE

Why do we do it? Obviously, it's a pattern of the counselor's. It's fear, lack of confidence, fear that something distressing is going to happen to us if we say to the client, "Come on, let's try walking through the bed of live coals." I think we need to raise this as a principle: *No counselor has ever yet died from the client's material.* It may sound simple but I think it is very profound because it operates at the behavior level.

The best co-counselors in the world were sitting in that circle last week taking turns backing away from and resigning from the job; not every time and not everybody, but generally enough that I don't think we should lose sight of what the phenomenon really is. It seems clear that a message was coming from the would-be counselor's own pattern that "I will die if I do that. I can't take that risk for my client." Yet the hard fact of the matter is that no counselor has died yet from any client's material or from being exposed to it.

WHAT WILL BE DIFFERENT

What does it mean to be a counselor for each other to emerge from chronic material? I think it means deciding that one cares enough about that person that one will take any risk at all. I have a little phrase that I have mumbled for years that goes, "I will do anything for a client." I almost have. I was trying to think about this this morning, thinking of what I was going to say today. I thought, "Sounds like I'll be saying, 'All you have to do is emulate me.' " That didn't sound healthy. Then the thought occurred that probably I have been able to break many trails and go past the usual reservations because of my regular chronic. (This is the one I told you about, how I gave up on myself completely and decided when I was seven and my brother had been killed that I didn't matter if I could help somebody else.) I have been able to have a sort of rigid facsimile of the attitude I am asking you to have rationally. My failures have been when my rigid facsimile didn't work well enough. Since you don't have my pattern, you will have to go against your fears and do the kind of thing I have partly done.

I think we have to decide that when we are counselor, our fears have no business in the session. Our feelings of discomfort are to be over-ridden. All the self-interests and comforts that seem so important in most situations we put by when we get to this situation. (We need to think things out clearly ahead of time. We don't launch a major assault without making preparations, without sending out scouts, getting the lay of the land and so on.) Yet we need to decide, once the battle is joined, that it is indeed joined.

A couple of years ago at the Kirkridge Reference Persons' Workshop, somebody asked me what the job was of the Alternate Reference Person. I said the job of the Alternate Reference Person is to throw herself on the grenade to protect the Reference Person. I think the job of the counselor in terms of feelings of self-preservation is to say "To hell with my feelings. My beloved client is going to make it this time." This is simple self-survival. Unless we do it for our co-counselors, how do we expect them to do it for us?

NOT JUST SPECTATORS

I think we have reached a critical point. We have come a long way in our counseling; but we have been sort of milling around waiting for somebody to take this next step. You come to workshops and Mary or I or perhaps Tim, take you through one barrier. And that is great. It's also a great spectator sport and we applaud as we watch, but we don't in general go back home from the workshop and do it yet. I think it's time that we crash this barrier.

AWAY WITH ALL TIMIDITY

I used to herd sheep. Sheep are not very human, but they are very patterny. Their resemblance to patterned humans is strong. Sometimes the band would come to an easy dip in a meadow and the head sheep would decide it was too difficult to cross the dip. All the rest would resonate with this timidity and stop. I finally had to go around and grab one of the leaders and pull him across, then the band all crossed. I think our particular band of very intelligent sheep have been milling around before a little swale, a tiny little dip in the meadow that we have been refusing to cross. I think it is time we crossed it.

When we go as counselors to help somebody out of a chronic pattern, we need to make the same kind of decisions clients make when they decide to break out of a chronic pattern. "OK, I may die but I am not going to go on living like this!" "OK, it may kill me but I'm going to stay with my beloved client until she or he makes it out!" Otherwise we start temporizing and pulling back and rewriting the script that our client has so clearly delineated for us.

The client knows where the shackles chafe. The client knows where the great thorn is piercing his heart. The client knows, and, given a chance, will give us the whole picture, but for the client to move out of it takes somebody else there, remembering and reminding him or her that she can make it, remembering that he can keep going, someone who doesn't get tired and think it's time for a break.

THE FASTER THE DISCHARGE THE BETTER

It has almost become a custom at some times in some areas, that the minute a client really starts discharging full steam, a completely wrong theoretical proposition is adduced, "You are getting in too deep. Here, look at the blue sky." If a client really gets to discharging the way she or he needs to, even just on the fundamental's level, the counselor interrupts on the grounds that she or he is "getting in too deep". This is just patterned counselor's funk. The clients are just getting into operation the way they need to.

We are simply going to have to do it. Knuckle down and do it, do it, do it. Is it going to come easy? No. Is my communicating clearly this morning going to do it? No. It's only a start. Are we going to goof? Yes. Are we going to be able to, once we back off, realize that we have goofed? Yes, if we don't pull rationalizations over our heads and defensively justify our timidity.

GREAT REWARDS

Subjectively, we are tackling a tough job. We are tackling the toughest job that anyone has ever done. We thought fundamentals counseling was tough. In a way, it was, but look at the rewards. Look at the rewards, all spread out here in this room like a table full of goodies. I sense that all of you are just delighted with each other. Isn't this true? I don't see how you could not be. Look. Look at each other. Look at where you are. Look at how much of you is showing. Everybody here. You are beautiful. Look what we have accomplished facing the discomforts of fundamentals counseling.

This is more difficult. We are tackling the hardest thing anyone ever did. Many heroisms of the past are, by comparison, trivial and unrewarding. To decide to sacrifice your life for the king and win a battle was small potatoes. It really was. Once you were in the king's army, you were probably going to get killed the next day anyway, you might as well have a little glory. Those weren't tough decisions. Here, now, we have got so much good out of living from our counseling so far that it's going to feel jeopardized to move farther. It's going to feel like moving into the jaws of death to care this much about somebody. Are we going to lose our nerve? Yes. Are we going to goof? Yes. Is the theory whose beginnings I hope I am outlining this morning going to get subverted and turned into it's exact opposite and passed around as "gospel"? Yes.

It's the nature of our enemy. The pattern can confuse, can distort, can turn a north sign around to where it points south, and it can make you forget. These are practically all its tools; but boy! is it persistent with them. A pattern is very effective at its stupid specialties. Never underestimate its effectiveness or resistance. It can functionally, for the moment, turn your brilliant mind into a big bunch of stupidness. So we are going to make all kinds of mistakes, and then we are going to correct them. We are going to forget and then we are going to remember and come back to our forgotten commitment. The only question is, will it be workable? Yes, there is no question but that it will work.

*   *   *

July 15th

When I was talking the other morning about really moving against chronic patterns in an effective way, I said many of the things I intended to but forgot one point.

Re-evaluation Counseling began as an accidental insight reaching us in the middle of the great ball of confusing distress which enveloped us. All the developments of theory and action since have proceeded by challenging and discharging these distresses and moving to a clearer picture of the universe which they previously obscured.

CHALLENGING OPPRESSION INEVITABLE

Our recent challenges against the social patterns of oppression should be seen in this light. Many of our co-counselors felt, to begin with, that we had no business "getting away from co-counseling" to challenge sexism, for example; but actually the existence of sexist attitudes was distorting and crippling the use of co-counseling because of our unawareness. To not take a stand against racism and become intelligent about it is to leave co-counseling crippled in another whole area, interfering with our individual progress as well as our outreach to humanity. The same with our oppressive attitudes toward children, to older people, to the physically handicapped. We are led inevitably by the logic of co-counseling itself to understand and participate intelligently in liberation from oppressive attitudes in order to achieve the same goals we had already begun to seek with only limited vision.

I spoke yesterday morning of challenging the assumptions that the counselor can play only a limited and somewhat comfortable role with the client. I suggested and tried to demonstrate that instead it is possible for a counselor to be an enormously more powerful force at assisting the client; by, in the first place, actually determining by really listening and paying attention and intelligent observation *where the client is* and *what the difficulty is*. The counselor can find out from the client by questioning and by observation what the client needs at this juncture and then, putting all other reservations aside, furnish what the client needs with persistence and vigor and determination.

NO LONG DELAY NECESSARY

What I forgot to challenge were the assumptions that have developed and clustered around us about the "long difficult task" that emergence must be. We have come to take it for granted (with some of my mistaken assistance) that to emerge from a chronic pattern is a "long, long difficult job".

This would be true if we expert counselors were to continue to counsel in the way we have up to now. If we were to continue to not pay too much attention to the actual situation of the client, if we were to continue to not ask the client for the client's actual situation in the serious manner that would reassure the client that it is worthwhile to try to tell us; or, if having told us, we were to continue to maneuver to change the subject to something that is more comfortable for us to counsel him or her about; or, if having succeeded in getting discharge well started, we continued to mentally dust our hands and walk away, leaving it up to the clients to continue once we have shown them, giving them less than our full assistance at remembering the directions, at repeating the phrase, or at letting them know we are there and that we care deeply for them. Then emergence will take a long, long time. To emerge from a chronic pattern with a counselor or counselors who only point at or poke at the pattern and then stand back is a long process.

I think I can say truly that the accurate description of the situation is that it takes just so much resource to melt a particular chronic pattern off a person, and that a fully committed, aware, dedicated counselor can multiply the rate of application of that resource at least a hundred times. Thus, the emergence which we have "planned" on taking months and years, looking at the speed charts which we have left behind us, can instead be possible in a handful of very stormy hours.

(I wish you would not just go home and quote these things I am saying widely. If you go home and just talk about them, they're almost certain to become one more new escapist RC fad. These are for you, among yourselves, to make operational. These are things to prove in your co-counseling -- you brilliant leaders. Then you will have something to say to the rest of the co-counselors. If you talk about them instead of doing them, we're almost certain to have once again the familiar phenomenon of the "latest word" in RC being used to disrupt and disorganize all the careful, workable knowledge that we have gotten into operation. So what I am saying should not be misused.)

SEVERAL FACTORS

There are a number of factors in a given counseling situation. One is the client. Two is the general environment. Three is the specific environment. Four is the state of the theory--the knowledge available of the process. And five is the state of the counselor.

In our ordinary patterned speech, we frequently attribute the difficulty or the slowness of emergence to what's wrong with the client. Today at least five people told me of of a difficulty with a client because "he wouldn't try", "she wouldn't make the effort", "they weren't ready", and various other ways of putting the responsibility on the client. We have known for a long while that this is nonsense, but perhaps we need to repeat it. Any difficulty that the client has is an *objective* difficulty.

Sometimes a counselor complains to me, "This client doesn't respond well. He has barbed wire wound tightly round his wrists, the despicable creature." But that is *exactly* what he is asking for help with! If his request for help comes out in offensive language, that's the way the distress is in there. That *is* the difficulty. It is not an excuse for the process not working. We have said this many times: The client is always back of those iron bars doing everything possible to assist in the process no matter what the surface appearance is.

We have sometimes attributed our difficulty or slowness in emergence to the general environment--to the fact that our culture is full of "don't discharge" phrases and attitudes. So it is, but we have demonstrated amply by now that they can be overcome. We have even demonstrated that we can begin to influence the general culture in some towns. (As you have heard hinted at, it's really not unsafe to burst into tears on a Santa Barbara street. Someone is likely to come up and hold you.)

Certainly we have found it possible to construct or find safe retreats from any such baleful influence as would prevent us from emerging. There are pillows to muffle screams when you need to scream. There are remote places you can go to, and so on.

Frequently in a session a counselor and a client will agree that the specific environment is not right. "Shall we put a check on that? I'm a little tired tonight." "I am too. Fine." Patty cake, patty cake. If there is anything not helpful in the specific environment we can usually change it very rapidly. "Come on, let's go in the bathroom and lock the door."

A real difficulty, which we have slowly overcome, is our lack of theory, our lack of knowledge.

In the beginning, one man cried for a few score hours and made a remarkable resurgence toward rationality. This caught our attention and got us started. Nine months later, I can remember sitting down with my students and saying to them, "What do we actually *know*, without kidding ourselves?" We concluded that when people cried hard they seemed to get better, whatever that meant. Maybe it worked when they shook, we weren't sure yet. That was all we knew. By now, however, we have acquired a great deal of theory, and knowledge. We have tested it out, we have checked it out, in many diverse ways. It is no longer possible to assign responsibility for difficulties to a lack of knowledge, although we certainly still have the job of assimilating and mastering and using the knowledge that is available, including, I hope, the things I am saying tonight, which are new to me.

A MORE EFFECTIVE COUNSELOR

I think what I am saying is right. Our key difficulty at this point seems to be the limited participation of the counselor in the counseling process. This is where we have been stalled and milling around. It doesn't mean we now have a magic word and everything is going to go great guns. I don't really know yet, not in any detail, what to do about this problem. Neither do you, but if we face that that's where the problem is, I'll bet we figure out how to do something about it.

Now we can still fall into patterns here. We can say, "Shame on the counselor." Or, "Shame on me, the counselor. I should have done a better job." We do a lot of that, do we not, still, but we know from our theory and experience that this is not a workable attitude. Reproaches do not improve behavior. They never have once helped in any human sense in the whole history of the world. The point is not to reproach but to improve.

THE WORKABLE WAY FOR A CHANGE

What, in general, can you do with this person to make a better counselor out of him or her? She or he needs sessions, not just any sessions, but sessions on why I'm so timid as a counselor. At first, she or he may not yet be able to work on that. You may point him or her at it and instead he or she has to work 16 or more weeks on the time the ripe banana fell on her or his head. There *is* a certain necessity of taking what's on top and what has to come off first. But we can also turn our skeptical eye on any *continued* pre-occupation with triviality. Ourselves as counselors can probably be clever enough to trick our counselor-client--our counselor who is now our client--into working on "why am I so timid about really putting myself at the disposal of the client and working on the agony that she or he has brought up under my careful listening on 'what needs to be done' "? What do I need to discharge on to keep from changing the subject when my client gets going on the really important material?

Questions like this. I think we can do this. I think we can clarify the theory of a year ago, the theory of a week ago and maybe, after we have understood it better, the theory I am trying to outline tonight in this crucial area. We can improve the general environment, we can improve the specific environment, we can get our theory up there to where we are not rejoicing in what we learned five years ago, but are integrating it with challenging questions like this, and we can share this with the counselor. We can give good sessions. We can do our best to really put ourselves at our client's disposal. I suspect that it will happen, as almost everything like this has happened so far, slowly. Any two co-counselors are each in the grips, we now realize, of enormously deep timidity still. They looked very bold and brave before by comparison with what beginning co-counselors are like, or with non-co-counselors, in terms of their daring to expose themselves to somebody else's distress, but the boldest of us have still been very timid.

We now realize how deep the timidity is. I think, however, that if first person singular over here, co-counselor A, can somehow be inspired by group spirit or whatever inspires her to say, "I'm not going to chicken out tonight. I'm going to really listen to what my client says, I'm really going to stay just with that subject, and see if the bottom of the bucket doesn't bend up and everything empty, and I'm going to stay here and glory in how wild it is." Counselor A may not do it all that night but she or he will get a little ways. And that is bound to inspire Counselor B to try a little bit of this "going beyond the pale" when counselor, which in turn is going to fan the flames some more.

I am always very hopeful when I get a new insight that a week from Tuesday it will all be over. So far nothing has ever taken less than 14 years to really develop (exaggeration), but I suspect that just this notion which I am communicating, if I communicate it well enough, may strike the spark that at least somebody in this crowd, hopefully all of you, will use to get this process going enough that we feel the movement.

When we do, as with all the other breakthroughs we have had, we will get so excited that we won't be able to forget how, no matter how much the patterns try to make us forget. (Applause) I appreciate the applause. You know what I am going to appreciate even more.

Keep in Touch with the
Basics of Counseling *

The whole complex practice and structure of Re-evaluation Counseling--its communities, its outreach, its philosophy, its theory, its creativity, its application--rests squarely on the foundation of *what the individual counselor and client do together.* Since we assume that the client is always making every effort to cooperate that his or her patterned situation permits, we seek constantly to improve our performance as counselors. The counselor is the half of the team who has freedom to be flexible, who can outwit the rigidity of the client's pattern with a correct, creative approach.

There is a great deal to be learned about being a counselor. We are constantly learning more. It is plain, in the light of experience, that all of us need to remain in ongoing classes and continually learn more for our counseling to be as successful as we would wish. Advanced knowledge of counseling is vital in the later stages of our complete re-emergence to humanness.

Yet perhaps 90% of good counseling is simply *paying attention to the client.* This is where we begin and this remains our most powerful counseling tool, the basis to which all other techniques are added.

Paying attention is more than just listening, though we must surely listen and listen awarely. Our eyes, our glance, must be available for the client to contact when his or her eyes seek it. We need to be thinking about the client, about what the client is doing and the client is feeling, *from the client's point of view*, with her or his goals in mind, not from our own viewpoint or our own restimulation. If we are in

*First printed in Present Time No. 15 – April, 1974

physical contact with the client, we note and respond to changes in muscle tone, in posture, in temperature.

We need to pay attention *with expectancy*. If we *expect* the client to have a flash answer, to begin to discharge, to take or hold a direction, it makes it much more possible for her or him to do so. Our *confident expectance* that the client will be able to make the necessary response will be of enormous assistance to him or her in doing so.

Pay attention with delight. The client is usually beset by negative feelings. Our delight in him or her, conveyed by facial expression and tone of voice, will contradict the distress and support the human. This is even more important when the client is exhibiting hostile or abusive patterns which appear to be directed at the counselor. (This is also crucial with distressed people in situations that are not overtly counseling situations.) The counselor's delight, undimmed by the hostile behavior, will throw the pattern into complete confusion.

Our delight is, of course, completely justified. Our delight is not in the pattern but in the pattern's victim, the human being, the most complex and elegant entity, within our knowledge, that the universe has evolved. We should correctly attribute any superficial offensiveness to a distress pattern and maintain our delight in the person, thus multiplying many times our effectiveness as counselors.

We furnish the *insistence* from outside that topples the tense resistance of the pattern over into dissolution--the quick, eager, insistent "Again" when the client's voice signals the imminence of discharge.

We furnish the *persistence* which enables the distress to be discharged exhaustively, to be cleaned up completely. "Let's go over it one more time," after the fifty-seventh recounting, is necessary or the client would be driven by the remaining distress to leave the scene before the battle was finally won.

With insistence and persistence, with expectancy and delight, with patience and confidence, we pay warm interested attention to that remarkable human being, our client, and see the healing, restoring processes of discharge and re-evaluation sweep her or him to that future of complete re-emergence which waits for us also.

"Let's Pull Up Our Socks And Go!" *

I want to talk this morning about expediting the upward thrust of human intelligence.

At this workshop I've been calling the intrusion of the downward tendency in the universe into our re-emergence activities, "sag". I'm defining the word "sag" in this discussion to mean the pervasive tendency for our upward-bound projects to turn around and roll down hill, to go the other way. Particularly I mean by the word, the persistent tendency for patterns to take over, subvert, and misdirect our well-intentioned upward climb.

Sag has been the outstanding *problem* at this workshop. It hasn't been the outstanding *feature* at this workshop, but it's been the outstanding problem. (laughter) This has been a good workshop and it's getting better, and I hope it will get still better in the remaining time.

Let's look at this sag, this enemy of ours.

INTRUDES AT EACH STEP

As we try to learn to be clients and to reclaim our ability to discharge, sag takes the form of rehearsing our feelings instead of discharging. The urge to dramatize feels like--"if I could just lay my feelings on somebody else, maybe I'd feel a little better." And we find instead that we have to endure the feelings past endurance and discharge them, and that gives permanent gain.

*Talk at the RC Teachers' Workshop, Kirkridge XLIV -- October, 1975

181

If we have mastered clienting and attempt to make that clienting a permanent workable process by learning to counsel someone else so that someone can counsel us back, if we try to build a co-counseling relationship so that our share of the clienting can go well, then sag takes the form of wanting to be client all of the time and not wanting to put out enough effort and thought to really help our co-counselor so that he or she can help us back. It has the lure of feeling like the chance for a quick profit. It feels that if we could just be clients all of the time, and not worry about our counselors' welfare, that we'd make it faster. Of course, this doesn't work because unless we are responsible, there comes a time when we try to be clients and our former co-counselors don't answer the door. It has to be an essentially peer relationship for it to work. So sag at this point takes the form of trying to be client all of the time.

ISOLATION BECKONS

If our co-counseling is going well, partly because we've been in a class where we've had lots of support, then when the time comes to sign up for classes again, our patterns may tell us the teacher is getting rich from the fees and we've learned enough, now all we have to do is keep co-counseling. So we drop out of class. We decide we will reduce our two evenings of co-counseling to one. One will be enough because we've done so well with our co-counseling already. Sag takes the form of isolated co-counseling. We cut ourselves off from group support and the awareness of others that keeps our co-counseling moving. Pretty soon our co-counseling has turned into patty-caking. The dust has covered it and it doesn't work well.

Suppose we've gotten past that temptation. We have a class going and it's a great group, and we have become comfortable in the class. Suppose our teacher comes up with the proposal that we join with three other classes and organize an Area Community in our territory. Now sag takes the form of "Do we need an Area? We are doing fine this way. Someone may try to tell us what to do if we get organized. We are doing alright the way we are."

THE PULL TO NOT THINK

Sag usually takes the form of giving in to the reactive pull towards "comfort" (reactive comfort), numbness, taking it easy.

The real pull at all of these levels is, of course, to not think. We are pulled to not think in any area where thinking is difficult. Thinking, of course, is fun in the free areas. Our best times have been when our thinking has been free, and we have leaped the chasms, and touched the clouds, and sparkled with the morning dew. In the area where distress is, however, there is always an addictive pull to not think. This is the key vulnerability of the human being.

When we've organized an Area, we're very proud of the accomplishments. Now we want to have our own Area workshop. How far can we cut the cost down? Perhaps we can cut it down to ––– dollars for the weekend. Of course we won't have anything for our Area Outreach Fund out of this workshop that way; we've made it to suit "our needs". Perhaps we won't need any money for outreach. Sag has sneaked up on us again.

A number of co-counselors have spoken to me in the last few months in words similar to the following: "I'm glad we've got an International Community going. I appreciate the new theoretical developments even though it's hard to keep up with them. My co-counselor and I see the point of that. That is helpful. I can see there is a point in an International Community; but this racism, sexism business! It seems like you are just trying to divide us. I thought the idea was that all people get together. If the blacks want to come into co-counseling, they are very welcome. I am sure I'm not trying to keep them out." This is a sag back into unaware racism, to staying inside oppressive patterns.

Sag can take many forms. We're always pulled to rest on our laurels, to resist progress, to coast on what we already know.

SAG IS NOT REST

There *is* a real need for physical rest, there is a real need to catch up, to have time to review the things we've learned, to sleep, (to catch up on the re-evaluation that we got behind on during the day.) This is a real need, and there are anxiety patterns that interfere with this, and we have to counter them and take care of our real needs.

However, the great overall pervasive reactive tendency is to sag, and it sends all kinds of insidious messages. Sometimes it will say, "You've been thinking, thinking, thinking, it's time to just not think for awhile." The essential nature of our intelligence, of course, is that if it isn't working it is in trouble. Awake or asleep, our intelligence should be operating, should be flashing lights all over the place. Otherwise it is picking up distress.

Did anyone here ever raise tropical fish? I used to raise tropical fish. I used to marvel at their unceasing movement, active all the time, at their brilliant, flashing flexibility. Your mind of course is far more brilliant, more complex than that, but its unceasing activity is something like that. It does not function well in quiescence. Sleep is not a time when we don't think, it is a time when we catch up on our thinking.

MINDS ALWAYS ACTIVE

If our mind slows at all we are in trouble. Yet the addictive pull, the pull of distress, is always to relapse, to go back, to sag, to coast, to take it easy, to do what is "comfortable". Reactive "comfort" is the big addictive lure. When there is distress present, new or recorded, it is uncomfortable to think. Why do humans drink alcohol? Because they don't have to "feel" their discomfort so much. By doing so, of course, they acquire more discomfort, increase the addictive pull. We'll feel all kinds of lures. This is a pervasive tendency. Sometimes we've said to co-counselors in the past, "if you're not feeling uncomfortable in a good way, you're off the track. If you're not conscious of barnacles being scraped, Y-Ahhhhh!, then your counseling is not going right.

Of course, there is the other discomfort of being freshly or repetitively hurt, which we do not seek; but *the discomfort of coming unhurt* is a live process. All of us have had experience with this, have gained from it. Yet so pervasive is the addictive tendency to sag that we must remind each other continually not to give in to it. This is one of the things we can do for one another, to remind each other to continue the upward climb. If we do there is no goal which we cannot attain.

NO STASIS

The nature of the human being is progress. The addictive pulls that pervade our culture, that claw at us in thousands of recorded messages, lie to us when they urge us to find some quiet backwater of "peace". If we give in to that, we are in deep trouble. Our real nature is to swim in the current. We are much more trout than we are clams. Sag is our enemy.

It is not that the universe should not have a downward tendency in it. A downward tendency is an essential feature of the universe, the entropy, the second law of thermodynamics, the tendency toward evenness, toward disintegration. This is very much a part of reality and it's just fine. The compost heap serves a very useful purpose in fueling next year's crop of flowers. That's the other great process at work in reality, the downward tendency of the universe. What I mean here by the word "sag" is any expression of this tendency slopping over into the area of the upward climb process, getting in the way. If rust is allowed to take over the fine machinery that should have been well-oiled, this is our enemy at work.

Sag springs in part from lack of information, in part from mis-information, in part from oppressive societies and their institutions. Overwhelmingly, though, sag springs from distress recordings which intermingle with the other sources.

DISTRESS CREATES ADDICTION

The mechanism of distress and its restimulation,. . .how can I describe it? It won't hurt to try. . .It's as if the distress invades the fine mechanisms of our mind, squirts a stream of glue or tar across the delicate machinery and jams the gears. This injury creates a heavy pull toward more injury. It is as if the hurt creates a ditch or predisposition here, which pulls for a repetition of itself. Every hurt, undischarged, in its essential behavior seeks the repetition of itself on the activity and person of the human being. Every undischarged hurt seeks to compel its own reenactment.

You can see this so clearly in the phenomenon of chemical addiction. On the addicted alcoholic, the first drink sets the elbow jerking for the rest of the evening. The poison that doesn't kill pulls the victim back to have another dose of poison. Clearly, any poison that doesn't kill you tends to addict you. There are places in the world where people eat arsenic, a little at a time at first, and then become addicted and habituated to large amounts, just the way people ingest alcohol in this culture.

OBSERVABLY SO

You can say that it is ridiculous that a reality should be like this. "Ah Love! Could you and I, with Her conspire to grasp this sorry Scheme of Things Entire, Would not we shatter it to bits, and then, Remold it nearer to the Heart's desire?" (Omar) Of course it seems ridiculous and at this point I can't give you any detailed explanation of why reality took this form. I'm sure there *is* an inevitable reason why human intelligence and its vulnerability took this form, consistent with the rest of the universe. Certainly this *is* reality. Observably it is so. The phenomenon of human intelligence is vulnerable to becoming addicted to any hurt which occurs to it and is left undischarged.

PERVASIVE PULL

This tendency of sag, the intrusion of the downward tendency of the universe into the areas of the upward climb, is universal and pervasive at any point of our distress. What we must do is resist at every point. Eternal vigilance is the price of re-emergence. Eternal vigilance, eternal vigilance. Keep an eye on ourselves, because ultimately who is it up to? First person singular is in charge of everything all the time.

To make this effective, however, we have learned, and need to continue to remind each other, that *being vigilant for one another* is especially effective. It enormously enhances our speed of re-emergence.

We have moved out these days to where we can begin to think in terms of liberation. Women have realized, for instance, that they need to be free. What form does sag take then? Women have been militant, have thrilled at the realization that life should be different for them as women than it has ever been before.

Sag pulls and pulls to take this gain and turn it into a dead round of grievancing, grievancing, grievancing. Not cleaning up the environment, but grievancing at it. This has happened a little bit at this workshop.

GET USED TO REMAINING AWARE

When we finally move to change the oppressive institutions; when all the employees of the Bank of Pottsylvania meet at lunch hour one day, (ratonality having thoroughly permeated the population of humans who keep the institution going) when a motion is passed that declares public ownership of the bank properties, which will be run collectively from now on; when the unanimous vote makes it impossible for any resistance to take place (a completely bloodless changeover--a dream but not a bad goal), what will happen? Will we have finally escaped from the influence of sag?

No. The first people's collective meeting will be full of nutty ideas for disorganizing the bank and taking personal advantage of the confusion. The Chinese say, "Remnants of the old society's thought continually seek to re-penetrate what we are doing and must be fought against." They are talking about the same thing as sag.

No matter how far we have gone, the dream of, "At last! I am getting the wheelbarrow to the top of the hill and I won't have to push anymore" takes place. We may very well be all through with that particular wheelbarrow. We may wheel it up the last incline on to the back of a big flatbed truck. We've made it through that stage, but now we need to climb into the cab of the twelve ton flatbed truck and proceed to go on uphill, facing new difficulties. To do this really is our essential nature. We must be going somewhere to be really human. It is not a tragedy that we must be vigilant against sag at every point.

PEOPLE WILL RESPOND

What has been important about this workshop? Was it that sag got a little thick around here briefly and in a few ways? Was it very hard to overcome? No, I'm very proud of this workshop. When I got out of my own confusion and called on you to do the same, did you argue with me fiercely? No. You said, "Ah, OK. We hear you. Let's go!" And you pulled up your socks and went.

In general, once we call a spade a spade, once we face reality, people everywhere are far more eager to do the right thing than they are to do the comfortable thing. Pass the word, take charge, remind others. We've just started to glimpse our own possibilities.

Nothing Less than Everything *

I once had a client who, in four hours of counseling, discharged enough so that some unpleasant chronic distresses stopped operating and he felt much better.

His relief, gratitude, and enthusiasm were boundless. He was "sold" on Re-evaluation Counseling and told everyone who would listen how wonderful it was. He came to introductory lectures and "testified" to the wonders of RC. He urged everyone else to try it.

His overall life and functioning were still very limited, however, very enclosed in patterned behavior and feelings. I urged him to join a class, learn to co-counsel, and continue to grow, but he would not agree. Offers of a scholarship made no difference. He explained to me that he "already knew all about Re-evaluation Counseling" and supported it fully (look what it had done for him) but he didn't want anything to do with "those other ideas" I had of trying to learn theory, co-counseling, and so on. I should stick to plain Re-evaluation Counseling, he said, as I had' those four hours with him, and leave that other fancy stuff alone.

Some of our leaders and teachers in the RC Community sometimes seem to be in analogous positions. They have received real benefits for themselves from the practical use of co-counseling; they have tasted of workable human companionship and cooperation in their relationships with other RCers, they have responded with excitement to being part of a "meaningful " movement of humans toward a non-distressful, "rational" future. Yet, unawarely, they have often

*First printed in Reference Point No. 4 -- December 1974

settled for a deficient and distorted version of RC. Sometimes they incorporate in it contradictory elements arising from their own unevaluated attitudes and assumptions. These, in turn, arose either from their own (often chronic) distresses, unique, or culturally imposed, or from the misinformation which the educational and communication institutions of society shower upon each person during childhood and youth.

These contradictions and deficiencies will not always be challenged immediately, even if the individual moves into a leadership position as assistant teacher, teacher, or even Reference Person. One can teach a deficient version of RC or even a distorted one (especially if the distortions tend toward "socially approved" notions) for a long time and hear only applause and appreciation from class members and workshops.

However, since growth and re-emergence to full rationality is what we are really about in RC, the discrepancies and deficiencies will eventually be challenged. The distorted theories may be carried by an individual co-counselor moving to a new area and cause consternation among the more aware co-counselors there. OR, it may be noticed that the leader who is leading workshops outside of his/her own Area has not developed any sharp new leaders at home--OR, we may see that the upcoming leaders or the ones being proposed as leaders operate on the same semi-static, trivialized, partly-patterned version of theory and policy as their mentor does. OR, it will be noticed that in spite of the popularity of the individual's classes and workshops, that the Community does not grow well, in numbers or maturity.

Somehow or other the issue will eventually be raised, the mis-functioning will be challenged. All of us who attempt to be leaders must in some sense depend on our peers to call us to account when we have lost our way or failed to grow with our responsibilities.

Such questioning should be welcomed, of course. It is obvious that our highest desire should be to function correctly, to be right in our service to humanity, to the RC Community and to ourselves, to rigorously and honestly question any possible mistakes and correct them quickly.

Many of our leaders have done just this, in such circumstances. All have grown as a result. A few, however, have defended the mistakes; concocted elaborate rationalizations purporting to show that they were "not really mistakes", or, sometimes, proposed the revision of RC theory and policy to conform to their "new position". Sometimes the person (or a friend on his/her behalf) argues that the person should be permitted his/her distortion "because he/she has been such a good leader."

Such a person often *has* done good or important work for the Community in the past. Unfortunately, there is no guarantee that past expertise or hard work will prevent a future mistake. There is no point of progress as a client (at least so far) that doesn't permit the uncovering of previously unsuspected ignorance and irrationality as new challenges spotlight and contradict deeper levels of chronic patterns.

Previous good service creates no obligation on the part of the Community to maintain someone in leadership. A teacher or leader rationally does her/his job for the satisfaction of doing it, for the opportunity of being meaningful, for the joy of serving the people, for the extra leverage against patterns that being a model for others gives. Being a good leader gives one the privilege of going on being correct, not the privilege of defending mistaken actions on the claim of past good deeds. We do have an obligation to try to help such a person as a client, of course.

What can an individual leader do who finds her/himself in a dilema of wanting to change or re-interpret policy to justify some actions or attitudes called in question by others? Well, counsel, of course, but not just unthinkingly.

Much time can be spent on "counseling", even with some discharge, to reinforce a rationalization. Perhaps a good direction might be "Can I stand to be completely honest about this?" or, "What action here would be unbearable for me? OK -- I'll do it."

The leader can step down from leadership until the issue is finally resolved. There are no really indispensable people in RC, although there are many valuable ones. If the leader has been leading well, new leadership is standing ready to have its chance. Even if some activities will slow down for awhile, or even stop, it is better so. The key need of the Re-evaluation Counseling Communities presently is not to grow fast but to grow well and soundly. Our leaders are models and they need to be clearly *good* models.

Above all, the *thinking* of oneself and others needs to be enlisted. The issues must be thought about from an RC point of view. What will be the best policy for humanity and for the RC Communities in the long run?

Re-evaluation Counseling is firmly based in logic, in the scientific method. It is *not* based on metaphysics, it is not based on unthinking beliefs, on transcendental idealism, on do-goodism, on sentiment, or on trusting or gratifying one's feelings. These things are undependable guides to action even if we "thought" they were part of RC because some actions temporarily agreed with both logic and feelings.

We counsel each other, not to "feel better", but so that we can *think better*. We want to think better so that we can function better, can make things right for ourselves.

We aim, not just for improvement and adjustment, but for regaining our *complete* selves, for *total* re-emergence. We necessarily come to seek this, not only for ourselves and those close to us, but for everybody everywhere. To have any less of a goal would be to betray our own nature to a timidity or selfishness pattern.

If we meet obstacles we seek to overcome them. If the obstacles are in our own patterns we apply all the tools of counseling to them. If they exist in the exterior world or society we apply our intelligence and enlist the intelligence of others for joint efforts to accomplish the necessary changes, no matter what resistance we meet or what difficulties must be overcome.

This is the inevitable logic of the path upon which we have begun to move. No matter how necessary the "gratification" of socializing with another RCer may seem, no matter how indignant one may feel at RC discussing social issues or seeking to reach the working class and the Third World people because our timid middle class neighbor may then be too frightened to come into RC, there is an inevitable healthy logic in all our progress.

Who could settle, once one glimpses the possibility, for any less than "making things right for everybody"?

On "Correctness" *

Often, at workshops, we have some heated protests against our use of the word "correct" in such contexts as "a correct policy" or "correct theory".

Behind these protests (as a few minutes listening and questioning will always elicit) lie distressing experiences of having some one else's version of what was "correct" enforced on the individual against or ignoring his/her own thinking, often for oppressive or exploitative uses, but always, at least, in a manner that denied the person the right to think for her/himself what was correct. It is not surprising that repeated distresses of this kind can lead to a "theoretical" position of renouncing the entire notion of "correctness".

The baby should not be lost with the bathwater, however. The notions of "right" and "wrong", of "correct" and "incorrect" are meaningful and important, no matter how much they have been misused. The distinction between what is a right thing to do and a wrong thing to do must continually be made if one is to function well at all and, particularly, if any group cooperation is to be workable.

Many people have written with enthusiasm of the reassurance they found in my statement: "There is at least one elegant solution to any real problem". Here the words "at least one" are important. In almost every situation, a number of different workable solutions can be found. Each different person, if theoretically placed in the same situation, could come up with a large number of possible solutions and even a unique best solution, best for her or him.

*First printed in RC Teacher No. 5 – November, 1974

195

One needs to remember, however, that an even larger number of poor or unworkable responses are possible, and that, though the differences between the results of using any two good solutions may be minor, the difference between the results of a good solution and a poor solution, between one of the "correct" answers and one of the "incorrect" ones, is a very decisive difference.

When we engage together in group efforts or projects an additional factor becomes important. When a group is operating together it is on the basis of an agreement, spelled out or implied, on how the activity is going to be carried out.

We need to continually improve our procedures for reaching agreement, for being more aware, more participating, more explicit. While an agreement is in effect, however, and until it is modified by agreement, (or by agreed-upon emergency procedures), the existing agreement must be treated as correct by the members of the group or the group's unity and effectiveness is undermined.

The Role of the Re-evaluation Counseling Teacher *

All our new structures and policies are, of course, tentative. We're trying to apply the intelligence we are regaining to the job at hand, the regaining of more intelligence. When unaware identifications with other groups or churches or lodges creep in, we have quit thinking, because thinking means solving the situation which is right here right now, which hasn't been met before and won't be again. The pressure to slide into old ruts, to learn and use something by rote is incessant and insistent and must be resisted.

We come together at workshops to share experiences, and this is very important. We listen to what someone else did with their class and think it was a great thing to do; but if we slip and decide we will do that same thing in our class, we're in trouble. As soon as we start taking something that worked before and applying it literally again we've already left our whole theory and the whole basis of being intelligent. It's hard to keep that in mind, with all the conditioned pressure, but it's necessary. Someone in England published a list of "things for teachers to do". That's a millstone around a teacher's neck if the teacher uses it in that way. If an RC teacher takes a list of things others have done and decides to do them, he or she has abandoned the theory. Yet, if we don't think, it can seem such a "good idea".

NO RUTS

There's no question but that you can be inspired by others; you can start from what somebody else did, and think of what you can do now. A good deal of our experience sharing is valuable that way; but we have to stay out of the

*Talk given at Buck Creek IX -- July, 1973

slippery little rut of doing the way someone else did, or what someone else did, or applying this technique to that situation. There aren't any borrowable techniques, except in the most general sense.

The levels of technique we talk about in the Spectrum of Techniques are very general. The correct technique consists of what is the new, right thing to do that moment within the general concept of that particular level of free attention.

This is a crucial thing for our teaching. RC is not encounter; RC is not primal scream; RC is not anything else. RC for you at that moment is intelligent you, with some general knowledge and experience behind you, (a little more experience than the rest of the troops you're trying to teach) and that concrete situation. The question is, "what are the elegant things I can do to allow this group of human beings to flower, to emerge as human beings, to regain their intelligence and enjoy it?" There aren't any rote answers at all to that.

I'm continually asked what to do in a certain situation, and that's a very tempting question. I think of something to do; I feel like telling it as a solution; the rut tempts me too. It doesn't hurt if I communicate in context what I or someone else has done about something similar before. People will ask how to handle a certain kind of client. The truth of the matter is that there is only one client who is that kind. The minute you start thinking otherwise you're sliding back into the old rut of all the previous psychotherapies of putting labels on people or putting them in bins or classifying their difficulties. That immediately makes the problem impossible to solve. That's one of the main reasons psychotherapy has been such an idiot pretense of a science. The minute you start classifying and putting a label on somebody or on somebody's problem, you've lost touch with reality.

That person's difficulties are his own unique difficulties, his own unique distress patterns that are the result of the unique distress experiences that happened to him and to nobody else ever in the world. There are no categories, no lumping together. So I can give some general suggestions like getting attention out, approaching fear from the haha angle, etc., but I cannot possibly tell anyone else how to handle a particular client in a particular session. The persons involved have to solve that one themselves.

A baseball coach can show you roughly how to bat, how to pitch a ball and maybe even how to slide a base, but if you ask how to win a ball game, you're on your own. You're out to win a ball game every time you move to help someone get out of a pattern.

This is basic. Yet even the good information-sharing we do is dangerously close to the rut of rote answers to categorized problems. If we slip into that at all we've thrown the baby out with the bath water.

MOTIVES

In the manual we say the only dependable motive for a counselor is helping the other person get free of a pattern. You're there for one purpose, to help the person recover her humanness. A teacher must be similarly motivated. This is why we have to be more and more aware of what RC is all about.

As many of you have heard, RC began with an accidental experience. For two weeks I tried to get a man to stop discharging but allowed him to because he was so intent on it. He moved away from psychotic collapse to elegant functioning in two weeks. Early along the line I decided it was good for him to cry. When he started to shake I told him to quit and go back to crying. A few days later when he began to laugh I became very indignant; told him we had indications that crying and shaking helped him; to quit laughing and get back to shaking. What we have learned we have learned inevitably. In spite of all the blocks, circumstances forced reality on me. Realities did impinge, and my patterns were such that I was impelled to go back and look at reality and try not to deceive myself.

We've tried all along not to deceive ourselves, to take a clear look at what's actually happening. Our theory is subject to revision all the time; (not out of somebody's recorded itch to change it. We get a lot of that, but we're smarter than that. We're not going to forget or contradict our basic assumptions which have been tested and proven valuable thousands and thousands of times.) but on the frontier where we're learning we're going to continually question any conclusions we're tempted to make.

DON'T BORROW

We're hostile to mixing in other theories for very good reasons. They're misleading. There's no question that they have good elements, and we point those out. Hurrah for Alcoholics Anonymous and Synanon, in that they establish peer relationships, but they're not good theories otherwise. The mistakes in them are sinking people who might otherwise make it, and we have every reason to be ruthless in our criticism.

I'm not hostile to psychotherapists. . .we're continually recruiting them. These are good people, often doing good things, but to a great extent in spite of their theories. We need to be ruthlessly critical with any theory that leads to poor results; not with the person but with the mistaken idea.

We have to be equally ruthless with our own growing theory. The tendency for rationalizations to creep in must be fought. "Facts are stubborn things." We should tune up our alarm circuit against kidding ourselves, listen to the bells that go off if we start rationalizing. We want to "get along", we don't like to fight; but if we don't take issue with these people who are voicing incorrect theory and policy, if we don't reject the pattern, then we're abandoning the person to the pattern. We have a real responsibility to reject patterns, and it's especially crucial that we reject them when they come pretending to be theory.

All of us have been conditioned to believe what the teacher says or what's in the book. "If it's written it must be so." I once had an English teacher do me a great service when she asked me if I could really believe the advertisements in the magazines.

WHO CAN JUDGE?

Who is smart enough to know if something is tentatively worth trying or obviously nonsense? Only the first person singular. Sure, it's uncomfortable to take the cover off your mind and blow off the dust and turn the on switch; but we should seek this kind of discomfort assiduously. This is the lovely discomfort of getting the mental wheels turning again, of questioning, of being skeptical, of making tentative judgments and trying them out.

If you tell your class something, or do something, and feel uneasy afterwards, pay attention to that uneasiness. It may turn out just to be the unaccustomed realization that you do a good job, but you can discharge on that and then know that you do a good job. If it wasn't that, then look at it. If you discover you're sweeping a rationalization under the rug or letting a little corrosion into your approach, correct it with your class. You can't afford not to.

We conjecture that it should be possible for all of us to act as if we have a limited amount of time ahead of us. We really can't afford to waste any of our time kidding ourselves, buying incorrect views of the world, rationalizing.

MOTIVES AGAIN

What are the motivations of people who ask to be teachers? A few want to be in style. They say "everyone" else is- doing it. We have safeguards against these. Others have failed at everything else, so they want to try teaching RC. We have standards that the candidate should have mastered the general environment before they hope to be a leader in RC.

We require that teachers be a model, an example, not just of accomplishment but of direction and commitment and effort. We have given permission to teach to people who were still smoking but were making a determined effort to quit. We've refused permission to teach to someone who would on no account take drugs herself but was insistent it was everyone's right to do so and that we had no business taking a position against it. This was too much confusion. Such a teacher would be abandoning people right where they needed a firm voice against the addictive pattern.

There are other poor motivations for wanting to teach. One is making a lot of money. There are a few Communities where you can make a lot of money pushing RC if you really hustle. Our teachers can make an adequate income and should, but it will never be easy money because there's a lot of work involved.

There are lots of real rewards, real motivations. I think the universal experience is that you really start applying RC to yourself when you start teaching someone else. There's the reward of attending a workshop like this and co-counseling on this advanced level. Teaching RC gives a purpose to life, one that endures. Your life no longer suffers from meaninglessness. You are through waking up and going to sleep and wondering why you bother.

You really earn what money you can get. You may have to discharge a pattern that people shouldn't be charged for something nice, that "all Quakers should do this for each other free". You have to reach people; you have to be such a magnet that people want to have what you've got; they have to gravitate to you and in intuitive ways ask you to teach them. If you can't do that yet you have to go out and hustle to assemble your classes. This takes doing and goes against all kinds of patterns. You lose a lot of patterns that feel like they were your hide.

For a teacher, I think the only *enduring* motivation can be a determination that humankind shall flower, that it shall fulfill its potential, not just you and your friends, but everybody. If we have feelings that this is something only for our gang, that all we want is to straighten out our school, or our research team, and we allow a pattern of indifference to the rest of the world to persist, we won't do a good job of teaching. As our students come out of their distresses, they're going to reach for meaning, and unless the meaning embraces the whole universe, and in particular our whole human species, they're going to be frustrated with RC. A basic assumption of ours is that we are concerned about every single human being, and in good time will get to them, and everything we do with our class and the people we work with is not only good in itself but is thought about as a step toward this cascading spreading of the word. If we aren't thinking in these terms we won't teach a good class.

STEP-BY-STEP GROWTH

Re-evaluation Counseling evolved step by step. I had no preconceived notions of RC. I began to find out about it accidentally. Co-counseling was discovered because Eddie and I were the only ones who saw what happened to Merle, were the only ones interested, and we had to try it on each other because no one else would believe what happened. We started having a staff of professional counselors in order to acquire enough experience and to pay for the research. We intuitively made the decision that these counselors had to be counseled. We noticed that students who came in because they wanted to help others would be good counselors for about three weeks and then become foggy with restimulation, so we made the decision that counselors had to be counseled.

Each step in theory and policy grew out of experience. At this point it's worth saying that we need to realize that RC is a crucial development for humankind.

Lots of other grassroot developments will mesh in with us. It's fascinating, for example, to see the similarities to RC in the self-criticism meetings in China, in which everyone participates and where they take all the time they need, if necessary shutting down the factory while they discuss.

There'll be lots of other developments elsewhere. Here in the technically most advanced society in the world, where we have most leisure and most resources, RC is the key development.

This body of ideas and practice are welded together. We pound away on theory, but it's continually related to practice. If you fail to communicate this at the proper time you will leave your students frustrated, because they want it all, and they need the whole picture. RC involves not only me, not only me and thee, not only us, but them and us and them *are* us, and there aren't are national boundaries to RC. We correctly dropped the word "national" out of our Guidelines. We have every reason to be ruthless in eliminating the taint of nationalism from our thinking and action. It's going to be as difficult to get rid of as male chauvinism is for us men, and as difficult as white racism is for us pale-faces to shed. We don't need any of them. Our communication to our students has to include all of these things.

Step by step we face the fact that if we want to get rid of our own distresses we have to be a zingy, clearheaded eager internationalist and a down-to-earth practical skilled counselor and everything in between. Nothing less will suffice.

A Fresh Look at the Fundamentals of Co-Counseling Classes *

The Fundamentals Class has been, so far, the single most effective form for mastering elementary Co-counseling, for bringing new people into the Re-evaluation Counseling Communities and for developing the Communities.

THE TEACHER OR INITIATOR RECRUITS THE CLASS

A Fundamentals Class will be initiated by at least one person. Such an initiator is usually, though not always, the person who will be teaching the class. Exceptions could be the case of an inexperienced person who is motivated to have such a class for his or her own participation, has many contacts, and is able to organize a group of people for an experienced teacher to teach, *or*, the occasion of a well-organized community having so many screened applicants for classes that it can furnish a teacher a number of applicants as a ready-made class. Another variation is the case of an existing organization asking an RC teacher to start a class for its members. These exceptions occur and are possible, but a valuable part of the teaching experience is missing here in that, in general, the teacher should, and needs the experience of, being able to recruit her or his own class.

IN A NEW POPULATION

There are two main ways of beginning such a class. The first is usual in a new area, a new locality or among a new population. Here the initiator trains several co-counselors individually to the point where at least some of them can co-counsel with each other and then they together organize

*First printed in RC Teacher No. 7 – December, 1975

the class to increase their effectiveness as co-counselors and support the individual learning process by getting together in the more efficient class.

WHEN A CLASS ALREADY EXISTS

The second main way of beginning a new Fundamentals Class operates where the teacher already has a class in existence. In this case, in addition to co-counselors that she or he trains herself or himself, she or he encourages the class members in the existing class to train one or more of the sharpest people they know to co-counsel, one-to-one, and then invites them to have an interview with the teacher, to participate in an introductory evening or one-day workshop, or attend an introductory lecture in preparation for the next series of classes.

AN INTRODUCTORY WORKSHOP

Some communities have used a one-day screening workshop to good effect, where all proposed candidates for Fundamentals Classes attend a workshop with a number of experienced co-counselors and leaders and participate with them in co-counseling and other workshop activities. Following the workshop a conference is held by the experienced co-counselors, and a consensus is reached on which of the candidates who attended are to be invited into Fundamentals Classes.

CLEAR STANDARDS

The standards for choosing candidates for a Fundamentals Class need to be clear both to the initiator or teacher and to the members of the class who are participating in recruiting. The people chosen should be people whom one can expect to become good co-counselors without an over-large investment of time and attention by other co-counselors. The amount of resource which would be required, for example, by a deeply distressed person before he or she can participate in co-counseling well can seriously hinder and delay the development of the Community.

The "need" of an individual for co-counseling can be taken into account but should by no means be the decisive element in deciding whether the person enters a Fundamentals Class. The ability to respond and participate and "carry one's own weight" in co-counseling activities is the decisive factor.

This can hardly be over-stressed. If a class is begun with the people who are "in need" or will demand great resources from the initiator or teacher or more experienced class members, then the class work will be bogged down in "taking care" of them, the essential peerness quality of co-counseling will tend to be obscured, and the class and the community will grow slowly if at all. For later classes such people are likely to bring additional people in the same straits as themselves.

EVENTUAL ACCEPTANCE OF ALL

If, on the other hand, it is clear that each co-counselor seek to find new persons who are already in fine shape, who can quickly learn co-counseling, become expert at it and move towards leadership and teaching, then the community will grow quickly, co-counseling will go well, and supplies of leadership will be adequate. In this way the resources can eventually be accumulated and the special organizational forms effectively developed to meet the needs of the persons who are "screened out" as applicants for Fundamentals Class in the current situation.

BUSINESS-LIKE ARRANGEMENTS

When candidates are accepted for a Fundamentals Class, it is important that the teacher or organizer communicate clearly to them the cost of the class, how payments are to be made, how much co-counseling practice is expected of them, and which fundamental literature is to be read early in the class.

USE ASSISTANT TEACHERS

The teacher of the class should plan on having one or two or more assistant teachers. These will be experienced co-counselors when they are available, but even in beginning a class in a new place the teacher should choose assistants. For a teacher to acquire an assistant teacher is simple. The teacher's judgment is all that is required. It requires no official permission from the Community for such appointments to be made. The teacher should choose the individuals whom she feels will quickly respond, will be helpful, and will take an interest in developing their own teaching skills to the point where they can teach classes on their own.

The assistant teacher's role should be a growing one, doing more and more actual teaching *as she or he is ready.* For example, the assistant teacher can do some of the theory presentations, handle some of the co-counseling reports, can begin to actually *teach* as she becomes ready to try. If it turns out that a person does not grow in the job, that the responsibility is premature for that particular co-counselor, embarrassment should not delay the rotation of the opportunity to another promising student.

EVERYONE HAS A FUNCTION

Besides using assistant teachers, it will be a good idea to find, early in the class, some responsible job that will suit the time and the talents of each person in the class for him or her to carry out. Interest in the class is greatly enhanced by having a role in the class. Some of the jobs that people can be asked to do are: opening the classroom and having it ready, seeing that the room is picked up and the chairs put away afterwards (this probably should be a rotating responsibility but one person can be responsible for seeing that new people are involved each week). Often finances, the collection of money and issuing of receipts, can be handled by a class member or an assistant teacher. If someone can phone people who have not shown up for a class session to make sure that they are not being left alone in some crisis or to remind them that they were missed and that the others would like to see them back, this will do a great deal for the affinity and closeness of the class and will give the person doing such a chore (which again, can be rotated) a feeling of really being a full member and full participant in the class.

OTHER FUNCTIONS

Seeing that literature is present and handling the sale of it may well be delegated to a class member, not necessarily an assistant teacher. One person can be in charge of transportation arrangements so that the class members who need a ride are gotten in touch with the class members who would be happy to offer them a ride. (Some individuals might have weary or dangerous trips home unless they had rides.)

COMMUNITY COMMITTEES

It's probably a good idea that each class choose a representative to work on the area-wide committee (when the class is in an organized Area or sub-Area) for Gather-ins of the whole community. If each class has a delegate meeting together with all the other class delegates as a committee for planning Gather-ins, not only will the needs and desires of the class members find expression in the agendas for the Gather-ins, but a much better attendance is likely to be expected at such meetings. In Areas that have delegated Area Committees because they are so spread out geographically, a member of the class will need to be chosen to officially represent the class at Area Committee Meetings (although in most instances all the members of the class will be invited to attend). Such a chosen delegated representative will make sure that the class opinions and interests are heard in the deliberations of the community. Being a correspon-

dent for the Area newsletter and for *Present Time* are one or
two more jobs that some class members may be delighted
to fill.

PRACTICE TEACHING

As the class progresses, the skillful teacher will find
ways to let, not only assistant teachers, but also other promising members of the class, conduct the class for short
periods on semi-routine activities such as News and Goods,
the closing circle, keeping time on the mini-session in the
middle of the class, etc. Even these small responsibilities
go a long way to overcome peoples' fears of taking leadership and will expedite a feeling of confidence and peerness
which will lead to more rapid participation in the community and more rapid development of teachers and leadership.

MAKING COMMUNITY MEMBERSHIP CLEAR

At the first class, or at least the first class following the
introductory lecture, it's important that the teacher outline
that the class members, if they make their co-counseling
work, will be entering a world-wide community of co-
counselors with many, many advantages accruing to them as
a result of such membership. The perspective should be
opened for them that they, probably, are entering upon a
life-long activity, picking up a tool that will not distract them
from their living or the pursuit of their own goals, but will
expedite and make possible the achievement of all their goals.

CLARIFY NO-SOCIALIZING AT THE BEGINNING

Also at this time, the no-socializing rule should be
clearly stated and the reasons for it given briefly, before the
addictive pull towards socializing or romancing with the
other members of the class has a chance to get started.

PERSISTENT ATTENTION TO LITERATURE

From the beginning the importance of reading the literature should be stressed. Every class meeting (and every meeting of any sort in the Community) should always have an ample stock of all RC literature on display. This is not difficult. Rational Island Publishers will extend credit and allow literature to be ordered on consignment by an authorized teacher. Literature goes on educating and informing in between classes. It will do a great deal of the informing which the teacher otherwise will be tempted to try to do by exhorting or talking too much.

The teacher should offer not only a selection of literature that she "thinks the students will be interested in" but should include at least samples of non-English publications and all the special newsletters. It may be, for example, that there is not a physically different person in the class itself, but the *Complete Elegance* newsletter nevertheless well may strike a real spark of interest in some members of the class. Similarly for *Pensamientos, Black Re-emergence, Asian-American Re-evaluation, Sisters, Well-Being, Seeds and Crystals, Upcoming, Classroom, The RC Teacher, Ruah Hadashah, Working for a Living, etc.*

A different piece of literature can be emphasized and featured in each session of the class. Alternately a quick review of an important piece of literature can be a feature of each session, with each student having a turn at being reviewer.

BE RATIONAL ABOUT CLASS FEES

The cost of the class should be determined rationally. Each teacher has the right to determine how much she or he charges for a class. In practice, this ranges from nothing to substantial amounts. This is guaranteed in the Guidelines-- that although teachers in a given Area may agree upon a standard fee for their classes, they are not required to, and no teacher can be required by the other teachers to charge any particular amount.

The amount of tuition for the class should be determined in part by the teachers' expertise and the teachers' usual earning capacity per hour, and should be determined in part by the students' ability to pay, by the customs of the community in which the class is held, and by the degree of commitment and appreciation of RC which the class members have prior to entering the class. This commitment can vary from deep scepticism and fear (in areas where RC is completely new) to an impassioned desire to pay almost any amount to get into a class (where the communtiy is already functioning well and the results of Re-evaluation Counseling are well-known).

Some teachers have successfully used a percentage-of-income formula. One half of one percent of yearly gross income in return for a sixteen week class is used as a starting point in some classes. Such a starting point can and needs to be modified in particular cases. The cost of the class should not be set to meet the lowest ability to pay of those present. If a sliding scale is not used, the basic fee should be set at a reasonable level and then special adjustments made for any individuals the teachers wishes in the class and who require partial scholarships.

It is important that class members contribute in some way for participation in class. Individual Third Worlders who combat feelings of isolation to attend an otherwise white class are already making a substantial effort and no request for scholarship by such a person should be denied. Organized groups of Third Worlders may have to organize and put pressure on some funding agency to pay for the class, but they should have some stake of effort invested to get the class for themselves.

People who have chosen a life style without money should not on that account have the class free but some reasonable means of barter should be worked out. All experience to date indicates that a student in a Fundamentals Class needs to have a financial investment or some other commitment to the class in order to derive the most benefit from it.

INDIVIDUAL ATTENTION BEFORE THE CLASS

Some time, as early as possible during the weeks of the class, each person in the class should have a turn in front of the class, be introduced in depth, reveal himself or herself to the other students and receive expert help of the teacher as well as the group attention of the class. This not only assists discharge and tends to eliminate any uneasiness or not-feeling-at-home in the class for the student, but it also tends to greatly assist the effectiveness of the co-counseling. New channels and new insights for discharge are often opened up by such work before the group.

LIBERATION FROM OPPRESSION PATTERNS INTEGRAL TO CO-COUNSELING

Time should be taken during the first weeks to explain why the Re-evaluation Counseling Communities are currently working to eliminate all attitudes and patterns of oppression and to explain the reasons why this is integral to the progress of co-counseling. People should know of the special groups of RCers and the special publications which have arisen to coordinate them: women's groups, young people, older people, blacks, etc.

THE ONGOING PERSPECTIVE OF CO-COUNSELING

Teachers, at some time in this period, should clearly project that there is much important work to be done beyond the important first stages of fundamentals counseling. Students should be aware that when the distresses on which they are now working are cleaned up, they will undoubtedly wish to continue on to eliminate the chronic patterns and make even more major advances toward re-emergence in their lives.

THE GOAL OF COMPLETE RE-EMERGENCE

Over and over again, the teacher needs to stress complete re-emergence as the goal of counseling and communicate to the student our concept of what the undistressed human is like so that the class member does not get confused in the details of co-counseling or lost in too limited goals or have too short-term a perspective as to what co-counseling is all about.

Policy on Set Exercises *

(The Re-evaluation Counseling teachers had been sharing teaching experiences with each other in groups and then reports from each group had been sumarized for the whole workshop.)

There were some actual experiences recounted. We need to hear more of them first-hand because the double filter of groups and reporters obviously took out a little of the life. Some of the reporters felt, apparently, that they were just to summarize conclusions, and that isn't the way we can learn from each other.

It's obvious that there's been some good teaching and some good experiences shared. If I can be succinct in what I have to say, we can hear more of these good experiences shared directly, in the time we have left.

Mary McCabe frequently says, in slightly different words each time, "What people find so hard about Re-evaluation Counseling is that they have to *think all the time,* that it won't work unless they think *all the time.*" This is so, except that it isn't that hard. You only have to resist the addictive pull to *not* think.

AN ADDICTIVE PULL

There *is* an addictive pull to not think, to find a formula, to be contented with a set routine. This has nothing in common with RC. The minute you quit thinking you are not doing RC. Any of you who are not prepared to commit

*Talk at La Scherpa XXXIV – July, 1974

yourselves to think fresh and hard in each new situation with each new student with each new session, shouldn't ask for teaching credentials. Any of you who have credentials who feel that it's too much to expect of you to think fresh and hard and come up with a new response each time should turn in your credentials because you are not doing RC, nor are you doing the RC Community any favor. If you teach this way, we're going to have to clean up all kinds of sticky messes and then start all over fresh again. Your students will have been cheated because what they have learned, thinking it was RC, will have been a lot of other really poor things. These poor things will have been taught in the name of RC and will constitute a real barrier to their relearning correctly.

Some of the things I've been listening to sound as if they have been borrowed from the junky set routines and exercises that abound in the various human growth movements. *Don't borrow.* There is a reason why we're so fierce against borrowing somebody else's cute idea or from some other "discipline". The instant you start borrowing you quit thinking. Why would you borrow? As a matter of fact, if you borrow from what you did yourself last week, you've quit thinking.

A FRESH RESPONSE EACH MOMENT

The essence of RC is that you come up with a completely fresh response at each moment that is just right to meet that situation, one you've never met before and never will again. If you are repeating something you did last week, you've already left RC. It may feel easy, everybody may discharge a little, but you've abandoned the whole theory. You're off the beam, right there. Do not borrow from what you heard someone else say at a workshop, not from yourself last week, not from any other "cute ideas" or set pieces.

NOT MANIPULATION

One mistake that seemed to be showing was an ancient manipulative notion. If the reports were accurate, (and I understand they were shorthand and the reality represented may be a lot better than it sounded) the notion was appearing here that the counselor did A and it produced B in the client. *That isn't so.* Many previous theories of dealing with human behavior assume this kind of thinking but this doesn't correspond to the reality of human beings. This is something RC theory is very clear about. . .very, very clear about. If you draw a kind of a river here, and on this side of the river are the things that the counselor can initiate with the client, and on this other side of the river are the things that the client will do as a result of the counseling, you cannot draw causal connections that you do A here and it produces B there. The old theories are full of this notion and it's completely false. It doesn't work that way. The essence of what we've come to know is that there is one important bridge across that river that leads from what the counselor can initiate to what the client does as a result. That bridge is called *discharge.* Yet, over and over again, it was implied in the reports that somebody did something with a client which caused this result for the client, and discharge wasn't mentioned, wasn't referred to. It may have occurred and been unreported, but the nature of the reports indicates some confusion at least.

All the actions you can take as a counselor on this side of the river are directed to one thing, and that's to help your clients cross the bridge of discharge. You haven't the faintest possibility of knowing accurately what they're going to do as a result over here. They are way too complex and wonderful for you to have any causal relationship like that. You can help them discharge, free their minds. They'll do an infinite variety of things over there.

Yet from the reports it sounds like some of us have been thinking, "we'll manipulate people." "Look at the keen way somebody manipulated somebody." "Why don't you try to manipulate somebody the same way?" That's rotten.

This might have been forgivable when people didn't know any better. They were grasping for solutions. Forgive Freud. He at least rebelled against the previous nonsense. Even though his theory was an oppressive theory and a reactionary theory, it was a break with the feudal stuff that went before. Now that we have knowledge, however, now that the basic mechanism of human misfunction has actually been revealed, now that we've experienced re-evaluation ourselves and seen its effects on others, any notion of going back to that kind of trivia is really unworthy of us. That's not what we're about in Re-evaluation Counseling.

What about manipulating somebody to discharge?

What about it?

I have tended to assume that if somebody's in the class, they want to discharge or should be willing to discharge and I put pressure on people. . .

You manipulate their patterns.

To make them discharge.

You're not manipulating the person, you're manipulating the pattern. I make the distinction. It's a crucial one. This is to help them cross the bridge and discharge. Not to produce this particular effect on them over there. We're not in the conditioning or manipulating business.

Harvey, could you give some examples?

Of how you manipulate patterns?

Yes, as opposed to manipulating the person, and some examples of that also.

I hope everything I've done up here in demonstrations is an example of manipulating a pattern to help the human discharge.

Well, this thinking as opposed to what you heard in the reports. What I'm asking, I guess, is if you could be specific in what the difference is.

Didn't you hear the sort of thing going on in the reports?

Yes.

OK, then you don't need any more examples there.

I'd just like you to give a specific example of that because it would be easier for me to hear the whole subject of what you're talking about. . .

OK. H-‑- is debating about continuing or abandoning his career. Now I may have an opinion that he's a good architect and ought to stick with it and become the best architect in the world. But I have access only to a tiny part of the information that he has to deal with when he makes that decision. I must not decide what he ought to do and manipulate or pressure him in that direction. If I notice, however, that his pattern is "I'm looking for help because there's something wrong with me", I can figure something to tell him to do that produces discharge. Perhaps I ask him to say, "It's time for me to realize there's nothing wrong with me and start to succeed." I crunched against his pattern in his introduction, and some dribbles of discharge came off. That's the RC action. The other is the familiar conditioning, manipulation. . . .I hate to even describe it. . . .operant conditioning, mind control, and all of those. Sara, you tell them. . . .you can stand it.

Oh, I suppose if you praised him everytime he talked about architecture and ignored him if he didn't and all the time trying to put pressure on him to make him do the thing you thought he should do.

Thank you.

What about experience sharing in general then, when we do this it can easily get into this kind of thing you are objecting to.

It can. It did slide into it. Which is why I'm trying to talk about it. . . .I'm not trying to say you are bad kids. . . .

I understand that, but I guess my question is what is the purpose of experience sharing, then? Is it just that we hear that something has worked for someone else and therefore feel the support that it has worked for someone else, or is this supposed to be a source of ideas? And if it's a source of ideas, in one sense you're already stopping thinking, when you say, "Oh, that sounds like a good idea, maybe I'll use that in my next class."

No, what somebody did successfully can inspire you to think rather than to stop thinking. It works that way in real life all the time. Data as to what *did* work before can be valuable assistance to your thinking and figuring out what *will* work now. Our experience sharing is valuable to us in a lot of ways. One way is that it has here revealed this "set-exercise" difficulty that has obviously become widespread. If we hadn't any experience sharing I wouldn't have known this kind of thing was going on. We'd have no chance to begin to speak to it and discharge on it and correct it. On the other hand, if someone has done a beautiful job, it inspires us to be creative, perhaps in a similar way, but not in the same way--information that's carried in the *RC Teacher* all the time. In still another way, I think of Beth Soley's articles on how she taught an unsuccessful class but learned from it. They have encouraged and supported more teachers than you might think.

Well, that seemed to me to be the main purpose of it. . . . the support that you get from it.

That's one purpose, but only one. I think that probably in the sections there were many other useful and beautiful things said which didn't get to us because of the filtering of the summary reports system. The summary reports were my suggestion and I think now it wasn't a good one.

One thing about what she's asking needs clarifying. . . . it's one thing to share ideas and it's another thing to just use ideas that other people have used. You can use other people's ideas to construct your own, and that's different from just borrowing.

Exactly right.

There's something else in experience-sharing for me and that is that you can hear the ideas now and later sometime when you're standing up there doing a demonstration, something will click in your mind from something you heard in the experience-sharing. You can't expect that your client is going to react in that certain way, but you have a clue, you have a hunch, an expectation that "if I do so and so, then the client will do so and so." That's how I feel.

Good. What I heard here that alarmed me were the fixed techniques and the set exercises, the words -- "this is a keen thing to do". That is completely foreign to RC. This is unworthy of you teachers, it really is. You've got fine minds, and it sounds like you've been looking for easy ways to handle the class so you don't have to think. "I will now set up an exercise and we'll all go through this routine tonight." You reported that everybody discharged. That's not enough. Once you have an RC atmosphere in operation, you can get some discharge with goodwill alone. Once the correct start has been made with people, you can get some discharge on almost anything. Once an RC workshop has been started correctly and set in motion an individual or pair can do everything wrong and still get lots of discharge. But it isn't correct to do so. You're using up your resources instead of adding to them.

THREE-QUARTER-INCH GRAVEL

Once here at La Scherpa we had a revolt in the middle of a big workshop that was going just great. A group got off in building 2 and discussed and agreed that I was completely wrong, that all this rigor was completely unnecessary, that it was just my anxiety pattern and that all that was necessary was to do what you felt like and it would still work. They tried it. They violated all the rules and they still got lots of discharge so they came to the workshop with a group report. . . . ."to hell with this anxiety of yours, Harvey, masquerading as theory. We can do what we feel like and it will still work."

The exact opposite of RC theory, but it sounded very impressive and inviting. The plain fact of course is that in a good workshop you've got a tidal wave of support and structure going for you so that no matter what you do, the workshop momentum may carry you along.

That time I was able to demonstrate this by pointing out that any phrase can produce substantial discharge at a good workshop because of the workshop situation. I asked people to repeat the phrase, "three-quarter-inch gravel". (laughter) Exactly. No one was able to say it without discharge.

TREASURE CORRECTNESS

Out in the world with sparser resources you need all the care and accuracy of theory you can manage. And you really need to apply it or you will wind up in trouble. Here at the workshop you've got 77 supporting factors, with perhaps 25 of them in the open, all moving together. There's been a lot of hard thinking and planning experience plus a lot of intuitive cooperation that goes into a good RC workshop which makes the workshop such an effective experience. This carefully prepared luxury of support has nothing to do with the rigor necessary for continued growth outside, in ordinary living.

Any set piece, any formula for the whole class, any routine for everybody, is a violation of the dignity and self-respect of your students and your clients. Where is the particular student and the particular client? That's the question. He's where he is. She's where she is. Who knows unless you find out? You fix up a little exercise and run them all through it and they get some discharge and you feel very happy. -- You've missed the whole essence of the relationship. This essence is for you as a teacher, as a counselor, to say, "where are *you*, what do *you* need to do?" and from the reply you get construct a series of experimental responses until you find one that works effectively for discharge.

The reply you get may be direct communication or it may be the backward communication of a dramatization that's thrown at you. Each dramatization is, of course, a communication which in effect says, "Look, I have this problem. Help me with it." The problem is defined by the dramatization. If you come back with a thoughtful response, and it doesn't work, try another one quickly. You can try 22 things in the first minute and a half. This is the way you can find the correct new technique. You just keep trying new approaches until one of them clicks. You can't possibly know ahead of time which it will be. For certain, no one approach will be just right for a whole class or group.

You haven't heard me talk about this business of trying 22 things? All right, I'll say it again. I'm speaking as counselor, but the analogy as teacher-counselor is plain. Sometimes it happens I do lectures and demonstrations in the presence of experienced therapists. When I do demonstrations and things go well, they have saucer eyes. Afterwards they come thronging up, "My God, that was amazing. I've never known anybody could be so perceptive. You knew exactly what to do. How did you know that this was what he needed? How could you possibly know that this was it? Such amazing perceptivity!" I, of course, respond with appropriate modesty by saying well, you know. . .(polishes fingernails -- laughter). The secret, of course, is simply that I didn't know any such thing. No one could possibly know. The situation is too complex.

What happened? They felt that the first thing I tried landed square on target, because without consulting any psychological tests I had the client discharging. The plain fact of the matter is that it wasn't the first thing I tried, it was the 23rd thing I tried. You don't have to wait a week for the report on whether or not what you're trying works. Immediately when you try something, you get feedback and you know within a tenth of a second if it's working. You try. You make your first approach and it goes clunk. You try something else and it goes clunk. . .something else. . .clunk, clunk, clunk, clunk, clunk. If you stay aware you know right away when you try a fresh approach that it either goes clunk or it goes sproing! You can tell the difference if you're awake at all. So you try 22 different new things and they all go clunk. It's taken a minute and a half. The traditional therapist in the audience doesn't realize you've begun working yet. Then you try number 23 and it goes sproing! and you say "again!" There's tremendous discharge. You're an instant genius.

You can't know what to do ahead of time. You're always testing and paying attention to the feedback, staying aware. This is what makes you an effective counselor, staying aware. If you go in there commited to any preconceived notion, they might as well have a psychiatrist working with them.

Sometimes at workshops you'll have a situation where it's pretty obvious that everybody's been conditioned in a similar way, say on sex material. A teacher will suggest that everybody do the same exercise.

And they shouldn't. This happens, but it shouldn't happen. We need to have more discussion with the people who are doing it. No two people have been conditioned in the *same* distress experiences as anyone else. The fact that you *can* handle people as if you were running sheep through a chute and get them all to discharge a little, doesn't have anything to do with whether you should or not. People have so much good will and such desire to discharge, they will often manage to somehow produce some, no matter how clumsy you are.

Well, why is. . .I mean, I think what you're saying is right. I'm not disagreeing. I see that on the one hand, but on the other hand you say what a counselor does is fire some approximately right direction at the client and it doesn't even have to be dead on target, because the client will move under it to a certain extent. . .

They'll do their darndest.

In the instance of, say, something like being awarely touched, there's a pretty good chance that you've been fairly starved for touch if you've grown up in this country. So to be awarely touched, say, in a group exercise. . .there's a fairly good chance that that is going to bring discharge, even though each person. . .

Yes, but you see you're not in the business to bring a little discharge, nor to prove that you're a jim dandy teacher, because with one direction everybody discharged a little. You're in business to be at the service of each particular person, to help each find his/her particular way out of a particular morass to where he/she wants to go. This is what's wrong. You've got to care about them individually. Otherwise you are back to some kind of sheep herding.

Now I really herded sheep when I was a kid, and the two situations have nothing in common. Human beings are not sheep, even in their patterns they are not sheep. (Sheep will frustrate you to death. If you try to take a band across a little dip in the ground about two inches deep and if the head one comes up to the dip and gets suspicious, then the rest will do the same. They really will jam up and you can't move them for love nor money. They *won't* cross that two-inch dip. On the other hand, if there's a cliff, and one of them runs up to the edge of it, three of them will run up behind and push the head one over trying to see. . .they will! It's really a problem keeping sheep alive.)

But human beings aren't like that, they really aren't.

What about the idea of having themes for work shops or gather-ins where something like sex is the theme. I tend to resent that and wondered what you thought of it.

I think you're right. This is something we're debating. There's this demand or pressure for sexuality workshops. We realized that they were so touchy that we haven't let anybody but Annette do them. Annette works hard to do them right, and she's an outstanding person. Yet, more and more I question whether or not we should be doing that sort of thing. The conjecture right now is that we should have workshops perhaps on common projects, achievements, or interests but not on common problems.

I think my problem has been the idea that tonight we're all going to work on our mothers, and next Monday we're going to work on our fathers, that kind of thing.

Yes, that's the sheep herding business. Let's eliminate it.

The thought occurred to me when you talked about sheep herding, what about discharge games and even the song fest. Is that sheep herding?

Well, many of the routines that were mentioned tonight possibly have their place as discharge games. One of them that was mentioned with great enthusiasm . . ."I love you, honey, but I just can't smile" was originally used by Carol Willis purely as a recreation. Here it was presented as a great counseling technique. We do have everyone in a group tell about 'my loveliest love', but look at the latitude, the room for being specifically unique. It isn't the same as, "You will now each grab your partner by the ears and kiss her on the nose." If we're going to do things as groups there's going to be an element of commonality, but it has to be open-ended, allowing each to find their specific place. In our closing circles we always have some kind of validation, and it works, it's helpful, everybody's tone lifts and people go out feeling loved even if it's been turbulent. But we try to have them open ended so people can come up with their own creative, thoughtful validation. "If you wished just one wish, what would it be?" There's a lot of latitude in that question.

No one's being herded through a stockyard gate. My loveliest love has enormous variability but even there, I think you're right to be suspicious and question, because otherwise the best intentions can slide back into a rut. The whole idea of common routines or set exercises should be expelled from RC, or set pieces of any kind.

Well, at a couple of workshops, one was the men's workshop, Mary had us in a circle facing the other men and saying at different times, "you love me" or "I love you". I think we did it twice and did it different. Would this come under the same category that you're talking about?

I would be a little uneasy about it. Mary and I haven't had a chance to discuss it. I don't know exactly what she did. In general, I've got no business second-guessing Mary. She's a leader in her own right.

So, what I hear you say in essence, it's all right to establish different formats for exchanging information and for pursuing discharge in a counseling class such as a mini-session, lectures, think and listens, what not. But one, you shouldn't define any of the content within such a format and two, you should always be thinking about whether the format's working or not.

If you define at all, be sure that it's very open ended, that the person is free to work where he/she is. We only do the song fest and the loveliest love in order to have a group activity. This is what it amounts to. This isn't the essence of our counseling. Our work is concerned with reaching the individual right where he or she is and encouraging her or him to follow her or his own particular path out of her or his own particular thicket. This is crucial. There was a lot of evidence in experience sharing tonight that we've been off playing games and not thinking.

We did a whole series in Bobby's class on relation-ships. I'm trying to figure out whether this fits in or not. There was a lot of freedom in that and yet, in a sense there was a real movement during the eight weeks to work on relationships and to work on it in a lot of different ways starting off with just the relationships in class between people, between co-counselors.

This is possible. If you have a positive goal, if you want to establish good relationships or work on establishing them, for people to join the class who are interested in that is OK. We have *similar interest* classes that work very well. . .people need to write dissertations or articles, they get together and they organize a class. To get a class or workshop together around *common problems* or around set exercises, however, is beginning to miss the point of RC.

I just wondered what your thinking was about workshops on common problems.

Well, I think that on a common project, it's going to work fine, but not on common problems. If people do something together, it should not be because they are forced to but because they want to. If people come to clear brush at Ben Lomond, knowing ahead of time that that's what the workshop is about and they want to clear brush as well as co-counsel, I think they'll probably have a good time. How did it work by the way?

It worked fine.

It got really restimulative. People got sunk quite a bit.

They got sunk quite a bit. Just from the hard work?

Yes.

229

"People don't know what hard work is anymore," said the old man.

I'd like to ask you about when you're working on simple things like just the discharge process. Some people will maybe say, "Now we'll all have a mini and see if you can get in touch with times when you felt angry."

I wouldn't do that, ever. Who are you to decide that that's what they need to do? Everybody is at her or his own unique place. They've got their own unique thickets to find their way out of, and that's what we are here for, to assist them where they are instead of lumping them together. See, to do this involves, "I don't have to think about them all, I'll just give them one formula. I am a teacher." If you intend to go on doing that, I wish you'd turn in your letter, because that isn't RC. It's fundamentally in violation of what we're doing. To do real RC, of course, is much more work. It involves actually using our heads, that most painful of processes. No formulas. No rigid techniques. We call what we do techniques, our spectrum of techniques, our arrangement; but these are the most general things. The specific technique is the one you invent at that moment, for that client, that day. If you're not doing that, you're not doing RC. This is one of the huge differences between what we do and what everybody else does.

Then, for instance, in a class, a beginning class, people who have never counseled. . .the idea of a mini-session on pleasant memories is something they might do in their first session?.

Oh, yes. Pleasant memories is open-ended.

Anger is not open? In the sense of they might have a multitude of. . .totally different reactions.

Yes, but the person who needs to do that will get to it without it being suggested. What should our beginning counselors do? They should perhaps tell the story of their lives for a year. Now we try to speed it up because we get impatient, but everybody needs to tell the story of his/her life for one year without any-more direction than that. We mostly don't have the slack to do that. We will have it someday.

I'm really confused, because if you say the love-liest love is accepted and you say pleasant memories is accepted, I don't see why the most painful experi-ences in school would not be accepted.

Well, why do you say *in school*? What was the most painful thing that happened to *you* in school? Why should the counselor or teacher choose school? That may not be what's concerning them, the student or client.

Well, we find out that some of the most painful experiences did happen at school. That just is a fact.

Some people have never been to school.

Alright, I've never met anybody who has never really been to school. People have really been turned off in school. We found that there was a lot of discharge.

There are a lot of commonalities, but how do you know that the particular person you ask has that as a crucial problem at that point?

Well, I'm just saying that was used and it was successful.

All of these routines that we've talked about. . they were all reported with great satisfaction that everybody discharged.

OK. Here's another one you're saying is not acceptable. One night the teacher asked us to write to a parent that we had a problem with and validate that parent. That was one of the best sessions we've ever had. Everybody just . . . When we read the letters, everybody stood up and discharged. Now what do you think of that?

It's not terrible, but I think it's already sneaking back into this set piece business a little, and I think it's a beginning of a substitute for good teaching of RC. Just the agreement that discharge is alright that is implicit in using RC theory, just the notion that the teacher is concerned, is enough anti-pattern resource so that many people can discharge a lot -- just because of that, regardless of what pretext you offer them. They'll twist themselves into pretzels in order to get some discharge through your formula. Their effort will make it work.

The whole notion of herding people like they were sheep is fundamentally false still, even if it works for awhile, even if you are getting by with it. That's what I want to say loud and clear tonight. Some of you hear me, don't you? ("Yeah" in unison from the group, or most of the group.)

Could you put that in Present Time?

Write me a letter reminding me, OK?

What I want to say is that I'm really relieved to hear you say that because I've been at sex workshops where I felt really uneasy with having to go through some charade of having to say a sexy hi to somebody for five minutes when I'm not really at that place and wondering why we were doing it. I don't want to see the baby thrown out with the bath water, though, because I think there's really a lot of re-evaluation and good information that comes out of some of the creative things that go on at the sex workshops, where people are dealing in ideas and input and each person is being asked from where they are, and I think the same thing happened with the racism workshop. For me, both times there was a lot of re-evaluation that went on as being part of a specific theme workshop. I really agree with the point that we don't have to go through these set, rigid things.

We've been getting a lot of benefit even out of the set pieces. It's working, sort of, but if we start going in that direction, pretty quickly we'll sour. This is where you've got to look ahead. It's analagous to the business of holding a direction against a chronic pattern; you're not getting too much discharge, but you're creeping out of it, the discharge comes hard at first. If you turn around and just slide back in the pattern, oh my, how hard you can discharge temporarily. You get a big glop of discharge coming off easily, but then you get sunk, and you have to climb out again slowly, slowly, slowly. We've learned the hard way that this business of turning and using up your capital in order to get quick discharge isn't the way to get rid of a chronic pattern. It's much slower than going all the way out there against the pattern until the rubber band snaps, when you really get discharge.

We can get some discharge in all these distortions of RC because we've got so many other things going for us. We've got our own caring attitude and the community around us and the notion that it's going to work and validation and a confident teacher, but if we don't correct this, and I think the distortion is very evident, then the whole thing is going to sour on us and we won't get to complete re-emergence.

One sort of distortion that I've seen coming out of the specialized workshops and classes is that people are accepting the little bits of new insights that appear at different stages like in the sex workshops and classes as part of the theory. It's been really disturbing to me to have to clean that up with my own students or with someone who hears something and comes to me and says, "What's this new theory from the sex workshop?" It's being passed out in such a way that a lot of people think this is policy or it's theory. It's coming out of workshops, and they assume that since the workshop was a recognized thing this is now part of theory or policy.

People sometimes come from the sex workshops, they come home to the areas, quoting Annette as saying this or that. I get hold of Annette when I hear this and she didn't say anything of the sort, but the person had a reactive need to claim he or she heard it. They come home with the most outrageous statements, quoting Annette as authority for them.

On a more local level though, even things I've heard her personally say have been accepted as theory and almost parenthesis policy, when in fact, it was her own thinking, speculating out loud. Just because she's been doing so many of these workshops. Some of the things that have been quoted have been things that she'll back up in terms of that's where she's thinking now, but it has been accepted more as an authoritative statement because she's in the position of doing the workshops. I think that can be very misleading. There's had to be some cleaning up of that, and it's getting confusing to people, locally, particularly when it goes unchallenged by anyone else.

Yes, there is a real question whether we should have this kind of workshop. I don't think anybody could have done better with them than Annette has done. I think she's just worked superbly, yet over and over again you hear these funny phoney results. The only way I can figure it out is that for people in a sex class or in a sex workshop, what's usually available is their embarrassment about sex. Everybody's got enormous embarrassment about sex. You poke at them and say, "Sex", and they say, 'Ha Ha Ha Ha Ha". Tremendous discharge, they feel a great relief, and the workshop or class is over, and they conclude that what they now feel is rational. All kinds of really heavy distress material, really messy, is accepted as being rational because they are now free of the embarrassment. Where the embarrassment used to inhibit them from coming out with the nutty stuff, now they're very proud of it, you see.

(A request to put the above in *Present Time*.)

I think I'm hearing that general topics of theory, established theory, for instance, dependency patterns, that's open-ended and a person can plug into that wherever she/he needs to.

Yes, but you wouldn't even set up your class and say, "Tonight we're going to work on dependency patterns."

Even in a fundamentals class where you're. . .

Tonight we're going to work on where you are. Where are you tonight? Where are you tonight, Robert? That's RC, not -- Tonight we're going to jump this particular stile, all in line. Let me take a gross example. You say, tonight we're going to work on dependency patterns. What's your worst dependency pattern? The person sits there and tries to think, and it turns out her father died yesterday, and she's been waiting to tell somebody, but she's trying to think of dependency, because she's shut down and she wants to cooperate. That's a gross example, but on a light level it's the same thing. You don't know where they are, and your first job is to find out. Then you've played the role of assistant. If you do this other, you're playing the role of manipulator. "I'll give him a truck and I'll steer." That's not RC.

What about a situation where supposing you've just discussed the blue pages, presented the idea of the blue pages, and everybody comes with massive questions, and everybody seems to be restimulated by the subject. Is it legitimate to have a mini-session about this area?

On what's restimulating? Sure. Real life comes in, you have mini-sessions on restimulation.

But you just have a mini-session, you don't need to say what it's for? People will work on whatever they need to?

Yes, they have a mini-session and work on whatever they need to. Somebody may say, "Ha, Hurray! At last the blue pages have been established," and work on their Aunt Petunia.

New Doors, New Perspectives,
New Challenges*

Basic communication is one-to-one. Every person who knows RC is encouraged to teach at least one other person to co-counsel. No one needs permission for that. It is true that to teach Re-evaluation Counseling as such to the public we ask people to have permission, letters of accreditation; but no one needs permission to teach one individual.

The best jobs of building new communities have always been done on the one-to-one basis. Margot Janeway always trained several co-counselors before she started a class. She always had a group of people to support her who were enthusiastic about the benefits of co-counseling.

How do human beings apply intelligence to reality? They look at the actual situation they confront, think about it, and come up with the best answer they can for that precise situation. In building an RC Community, there'll be lots of situations in which training one co-counselor is exactly the thing to do. If you haven't trained one co-counselor, that's exactly the thing to do.

We've had enough experience in Seattle to know that no one who has ever had one good session is lost to co-counseling. They may become angry at their co-counselor and even slander RC, but seven or eight years later they'll drop by to see if you've improved. Our numbers will become large.

In newer communities people are beginning to learn that it's possible to cry hard for an extended period of time, or shake or laugh, and think better as a result. In these

*Talk at Buck Creek IX -- July, 1973

situations, that's exactly what we do--learn to discharge well. In communities where many people have discharged their intermittent patterns and are working on their chronics, activities should expand. More of those people have taken charge of the environment, have regained the initiative. In these more mature communities we need newer, more advanced perspectives.

In this RC Teachers' Workshop we are concerned with communicating theory, and with intensive outreach. As teachers we need to realize that every human being *needs to be going somewhere.* Happiness has been well defined as the process of overcoming obstacles on the way to a goal of one's own choosing. If people become restless with limited activities in RC, then teachers need to offer some higher perspectives. If you have people who co-counsel extremely well and you'd ask them to teach except that you can't give them part of your class, you need to think about encouraging them to reach new sections of the population. Even Santa Barbara has 98,000 people who aren't co-counseling yet.

We'll never have too many teachers. It's a matter of using imagination, letting people find their own students, helping them do so. The person who is waiting for a list of students in order to teach isn't ready to teach. The role of the teacher is to be a model of handling the environment.

Not everyone wants to teach; but all of our developing co-counselors, the ones who stand tall and think clearly and are aware of what goes on, who have re-learned to love and be loved, are surrounded by all kinds of challenges and they need to be tackling them. We need to be continually raising, to our sharp co-counselors, the question of what they want to do with the rest of their lives.

We're already doing this pretty well in terms of individual goals. Your client may have wanted to make $75,000 a year. If you didn't quibble over his goal, and have worked with him for a while, he is probably by now making $75,000 a year. That person needs a new goal. An attained goal can be a millstone around his neck; he needs a fresh one. Otherwise boredom starts to set in.

We have this responsibiltiy to continually challenge each other's perspectives. This is because the cultural patterns which have been laid on us continually limit our perspectives, tell us to get into our slot and shut up. "You've got a pigeon-hole that fits, be satisfied" We all feel this conditioning, whether we're esteemed as successful by the culture or not. As teachers we need to keep raising the perspectives. "You've got your last goal, what next?"

We need to ask, "What needs doing in the world?" "If you had all kinds of resources, what would you do?" A surprising number of people would tell you that they'd declare universal peace, or something that important. The question is, how do we go about it? Help them figure out how to attain the lofty goals too. "How could universal peace be brought about? What would have to happen before that could happen?" Work back to "What could you do today to start the process?" The familiar way with goal setting: Set the farthest goal and work back to what can be done now.

In addition to such goals as universal peace, I think we have to offer people goals in RC. We tend to underestimate the prestige and affection RC holds for the people who have had even a limited experience with it. I hear echoes of this from many places, and in many ways. Our theories and communities are held in esteem even by people who are apparently opposed to us.

Actually these people are fighting their own discouragements. When people come to you and insist that the world is hopeless and we might as well give up, you tend to feel you're a lonely positive person in a sea of discouragement and unreason; but these persons are always trying somehow to find enough sturdiness and confidence in you to contradict and stand up against these patterns that are sinking them.

If you say, "Oh, go on, it isn't that bad. Feel that way if you want, but it isn't true," he or she may argue fiercely but will also find some way to burst into tears or throw a tantrum. He or she has to have that much contradiction and this is what people are depending on you to furnish.

I think we need to ask our growing, maturing co-counselors to do more jobs and more difficult jobs. Don't let anyone in the RC Community be idle from neglect. How are you going to feel a part of the family if you don't have anything to do in the family? I think our teachers need to see that everyone is asked to find a way to contribute to RC growth. This means a great deal. When everything else is discouraging you can hold on to the thought that more and more people are co-counseling every day, and maybe this will eventually end war. All our students, once they have enough skill in co-counseling under their belt, need to be assisted to find jobs to do, to find goals, in RC as well as in general living.

I raised this because I find a sense in our stable communities that have grown well, that we're letting good people be frustrated by not involving them, not giving them enough to do.

On Teaching and Leadership *

Much of the dream of women's liberation has been for a just society where women could take their rightful place and assume leadership on the basis of ability. I would like to commend to you an institution which is growing in influence very rapidly, where you might wish to participate in just this way--the Re-evaluation Counseling Community. In the Re-evaluation Counseling Community, key positions of leadership are the Area Reference Person and the teacher, and of the 56 Area and sub-Area Reference Persons at present, 44 are women. Of the 500 teachers, probably 400 are women. Re-evaluation Counseling is a women-led movement. It has been since the beginning. The leadership is now almost entirely women; men are working to clear themselves enough to assume their share of the leadership. In most Areas the women leaders are taking special steps to assist and encourage men so they can share in the leadership. This is the reality of the situation in Re-evaluation Counseling.

Patterns come into the Community with the people. We have to deal with them inside the Community as well as outside, all kinds of patterns, including sexist patterns, but the tools are at hand and there are no obstacles except the patterns themselves.

THE GUIDELINES

I recommend you study the Guidelines. They are revised once a year. This is the best policy we've been able to evolve for relating to each other in the meaningful activity of Re-evaluation Counseling and all the things that spread out from it.

*Talk at the First All-Women's International Workshop – November, 1973
First presented in RC Teacher No. 5

People new to Re-evaluation Counseling sometimes unthinkingly try to use their garden club or their Sunday school class or their trade union as an organizational model. The Guidelines have sometimes been ignored or distorted. There's lots of room for improvement in the functioning of the Re-evaluation Counseling Community, and your ideas and thinking are welcome; the Guidelines are subject to revision every year at the Reference Persons' International Workshop; but a lot of hard thinking and experience has gone into the Guidelines. These are workable ways to keep us successfully relating and growing and doing things. The relationships spelled out in the Guidelines should be thoroughly understood and read by everyone, and *then* improvements proposed. The Guidelines are a collective job. Our Community grows and changes. Each revision is an aware attempt to update just exactly what is sensible to agree on, what rules and principles now make sense in relating to each other. We follow them until we change them by agreement.

THE COMMUNITY

What is our Community? It's an association of people who agree to use Re-evaluation Counseling to recover their intelligence and help others do the same. Everyone who agrees to this and is able to do it, is welcome. In a sense our Communities are already an elite, the people who are able to do it. Through no fault of their own, a lot of people in the world are not able to do this yet. We think of ourselves as average, but we are a very fortunate group of people. Most of the population of the world is leading lives of quiet despair.

We're not taking into our Communities (which are leading bodies in a sense) people who can't handle the relationship. We're learning to screen, to take only the people who can contribute quite rapidly, given a little help. It isn't that we're abandoning the rest of humanity. We'll never do that. It's that we first have to accumulate some resource and set up structures that can reach them. We have plans for this.

To enter the Community is to take a position of trust and responsibility. Everyone is a peer. If you have just joined and I'm a long-time international leader, we're absolutely on the same level. It takes work to make this peerness operate, but we're determined to do it.

The requirement for membership in the Community is to participate in co-counseling and the things that support it and to help others to do the same. This doesn't mean that anyone has permission to rehearse their patterns in the Community and attack others or violate the blue pages or use alcohol or drugs or defend their patterns as rational. It's a great privilege to be a member of the Community and we accept the responsibility of trying to leave our patterns outside. Certainly we are responsible to not let them disrupt the Community. People in the Community can have all kinds of patterns operating as long as they're trying to get rid of them. We don't put each other down for still having patterns, but we expect of each other that we will not defend or impose them.

THE RC TEACHER

To be a teacher of RC is more demanding. To desire to be a teacher or have a reactive conviction that you're ready to be a teacher isn't enough. It requires the judgment of the Community that you are competently representing the theory and practice of Re-evaluation Counseling. This judgment is expressed through consultation of the Area Reference Committee and the approval of the Area Reference Person and the International Reference Person.

Your letter of permission to teach carries both signatures. It is permission to be an active teacher; it lapses after six months if you don't teach. You usually get a one-time permission first and your work with your first class is reviewed before you get a regular letter of permission.

If you have patterns that will hold a false picture of RC up to the people you teach, then you shouldn't be teaching. It's that simple. It's not your fault you've got these difficulties, but if you're still defending distress patterns, if your example will speak to your students in a poor way, drowning out the good words you may be using, then you shouldn't be teaching. It's a position of great honor and responsibility.

There are teachers who make a living out of teaching. It's a hard way to make a living, and that isn't the main purpose of teaching. The main purpose is to carry on and spread the humanness. Teachers should, of course, be paid for the work they do, because it is hard work, but that's not basically what it's about. It's questionable when someone wants to teach for honor or the reward of money.

THE REFERENCE PERSON

The other main post of responsibility in RC is that of Reference Person in an organized Area. This position is unpaid, deliberately so, to keep economic considerations from influencing this post of judgment. The principle job of the Reference Person is to think about the Community and to exercise judgment. All activities which are done in the name of RC should be cleared with the Reference Person before they're undertaken. It's a simple requirement and it saves all kinds of trouble.

Many of you should plan on becoming teachers. You're needed. There's no end to the numbers of teacher who will be needed, if they are able to do the job.

People are waiting desperately for this word. At last something makes sense; at last there's a way to get going like you always knew there should be. People are waiting like this everywhere for teachers. Please be encouraged. The conditions for getting approved as a teacher will get tougher and tougher; standards are going up and up, but you can meet them. Fine human beings, scramble up here, get your head up high enough so other people can see what RC is about from looking at you. Please get in shape to teach.

At the first workshop we held, Buck Creek I, 38 people attended. I think 32 of the 38 are now teaching.

What steps do you take if you want to teach someday?

If you are in an organized Area you need to have had extended class work. The requirements are different in a new place than they are in an established place. In Santa Barbara you practically have to have a PhD in RC. In a brand new locality, if you are an intelligent, interested person whose patterns will not 'offend other people or create a scandal in the name of RC, we will say "go ahead". A lot of RC teachers started out when they were not yet very competent, and many of them who are today fine teachers taught weak classes the first few times. By their own current standards, they were terrible. Persisting against their fears, they finally got enough discharge that they were able to think and then taught good classes. The students in their first ones, who were sometimes turned off and disappointed, still came around periodically to see if things had improved, and when they got better signals they came back in class.

We've taken lots of chances wth new teachers in new places, and nearly all have worked out fine. In an Area like yours, however, you should undoubtedly have extended class work, should get permission from a teacher to be an assistant, and then finally get the recommendation of your Area Reference Committee and Person, and write a letter of application to your Area Reference Person with a copy to me.

See the requirements in the Guidelines.

It is hard to become a teacher and it is easy to stop. Your letter of permission to teach RC is not a lifetime degree. It is permission from the Community and to keep it in force requires that you keep growing, discharging, improving, that you keep up-to-date on RC theory, policy, and practice and on teaching skills. RC Teachers' Workshops will help you do this.

Pretending Is Not a Substitute For Thinking *

As co-counseling moves against patterns the patterns will resist and attempt to persist against the impact of the counseling in any possible way that they can. A familiar way is for the pattern to adopt the camouflage of Re-evaluation Counseling language. Thus it continues to dominate the human with its same patterned, reactive content but conceals itself, using "counseling" phrases to do so.

A clear goal of our counseling is to be in better and better touch with reality. Even when we use fantasy as a technique, we do so with an understanding of the process at work. We use fantasy as a special technique to enable us to get to *reality* by thus handling fear that would otherwise be difficult to handle. Our goal is always to be real in our communication, real in our picture of the world, real in our interaction with the environment.

In the name of "being positive", or "holding a positive direction", or "validation", a patterned phenomenon has crept into some Re-evaluation Counseling practice. It has aroused protests and questions from many co-counselors throughout the world. This phenomenon is the resort to pretense in the name of being positive.

An example is, in attempting to appreciate another person, the use of trite, banal phrases or generalities which can be uttered without really paying attention to, or thinking about, the person whom we are supposed to be appreciating. "You're just wonderful" muttered with a vacant grin and an unaware tone will be accepted as validation only by the most desperate of clients.

*First printed in Present Time No. 16 – July, 1974

It takes hard, hard work to make the Present and Future Reality technique work, it takes thinking in the area where it's the hardest to think and commiting oneself to act in this same area. This has nothing in common with announcing, "there are no patterns, ha, ha, ha."

Any positive-sounding words or phrases or well-intentioned acts which become a *substitute for thinking clearly* about the present situation and the best possible way of handling it, fall into this category of pretense. To make positive sounds is not in itself Re-evaluation Counseling.

We endeavor to be positive and validating at all times; we endeavor to see the reassurance of reality and the basically favorable-to-our-survival nature of the universe, but this requires thinking clearly at all times and achieving meaningful communication, a meaningful appreciation of reality, a meaningful commitment to the kind of change that our most elegant thinking would provide.

Don't Stop at the Permissive
Counseling Level *

I would like to raise one question with you for your consideration in this workshop. This question is the quality of co-counseling.

Anyone who has had even one good session becomes permanently interested in co-counseling and excited about the process. This initial enthusiasm for the fundamental portions of counseling is usually very motivating. We learn to counsel permissively. We learn to keep our mouths shut and quit interjecting our material into our clients' sessions. We learn to let people discharge. The process works well.

This is a big step forward. If we can go through fundamental classes and learn to really listen -- to really pay attention, to care, to be supportive, to permit discharge, to help the clients get started crying when their chins begin to tremble, to start them over again and repeat when they are sure, because they feel so relieved, that they must be through, to coax them to go back and go over the distress 50 or 60 times if necessary to really clean it up -- this is a great deal to learn. To learn this much in fundamental co-counseling is an achievement. Sometimes we have to sit through many classes and co-counsel many sessions before we feel relaxedly pleased when our clients discharge.

If you are new to counseling, don't think I am saying you can skip this Fundamentals stage. There is a great deal to learn at this level. We have to throw off a lot of conditioning from the culture to master Fundamental Co-counseling, to absorb it, to have it become second nature for us to act in this human way.

*Lecture at Buck Creek XVII -- March, 1975

The initial relief at shedding an intermittent pattern, at discovering that it is *possible* to re-emerge, possible to reverse this slow attrition which has weighted down our lives, can mislead us. We need to realize that there is more to the process than that.

It's a mistake to assume that being permissive and allowing our client to bring up what he or she needs to and helping them to find their way to discharge is all there is to counseling. There is a great deal more to the re-emergence process than you can attain with just being permissive.

Intermittent patterns discharge well with simple, permissive counseling. Each of us has many such intermittent patterns. The bulk of our distress is, however, in chronic distress patterns. The great distortion of our lives comes from these big chronics that we have grown accustomed to, that we tend to identify with. We "can't remember" that there is any other way to live. We've "grown accustomed to" them. Our lives will stay very limited unless we successfully attack the chronic patterns and emerge from them.

There is more to human beings than we generally allow ourselves to face. There is much more to each of us. I know each of you knows this, if you dare to admit it. I used to think it was just I that had a secret knowledge of my vast potential. Now I know that everybody knows. Each of us knows that he or she, personally, first person singular, is much more a person than other people realize. All of us treasure this secret knowledge that we are better than we have been able to act, that we are smarter than we have been able to show, that we have worlds of ability that we haven't used yet. Each of us has this secret, treasured knowledge about ourselves. We tend not to think about it very much. We are too busy being discouraged and restimulated. In practice, we will tend to not credit this about other people, either, although we may accept its existence theoretically.

Marvelous as we are, we have just begun to use our abilities and capacities. This is true of even our best functioning co-counselors. Some of them are now living well. Their incomes have doubled and tripled and their families are happy and good things are happening; but we have reason to think that this is just the beginning of what we have in store for us.

Human beings are naturally so good, so smart, so warm and loving and so at ease in the universe as the loving masters and mistresses of the environment that we musn't settle for less. We don't want to take long vacations from progress. This requires that we get to work at emerging from our chronic patterns. The need to do this will come, at the very most, a year or two or three after we begin counseling.

When our client works on chronic patterns it isn't enough to be permissive. Now really caring and thinking clearly about people comes into play. At the heart of our theory and practice is the distinction we make between the human being and the pattern. Theoretically, and practically, we make this distinction between the person -- the real human being -- and the distress pattern. This distinction is at the heart of our accuracy and leads to all the other theory.

To make this distinction when working with each other on chronic patterns, we have to at the same time -- in fact it is the same process -- really care about the human being and really reject the distress pattern. We have to really love her or him and at the same time think and act to destroy the chronic pattern.

Though they have been so separated in our culture, there is reason to conclude that thinking and caring are really two aspects of the same process. Our culture tells us that one only loves if one is blindly sentimental and one only thinks if one is cold and hard. We have confidence instead that they are just two sides of the same process -- that one is not really loving someone unless one is thinking hard about them, and one is not really thinking about someone unless one is loving them. If one is really being smart about persons, of course one loves them. Love and intelligence are the same process. So when we come to thinking about our clients and ourselves in terms of chronic patterns, we have to at the same time be completely warm and loving and supportive of the person and deftly, skillfully murderous toward the chronic pattern.

Sometimes the effective way of murdering a chronic pattern is to deluge its victim with affection until the pattern drowns. You don't go after chronic patterns with a knife and gun. Nevertheless, what you are after is the destruction of the chronic pattern. You want to peel this parasite off the beloved human. You want to completely get rid of this squawk box that sits at the back of the human's head and goes awk, awk, in its dumb, destructive way. You are out to destroy this monstrous thing with all the ingenious techniques that you can learn and invent.

We have to learn to go beyond permissive counseling. Co-counselors who have learned permissive co-counseling tend to go on being permissive to chronic patterns. They blindly, unawarely, let their beloved co-counselor go on struggling without assistance, let dumb, stupid chronic behavior continue while they, the counselors, smile and say, "that's all right, you know what you need to do."

Undoubtedly as clients we *are* thinking at some level way down in the underground vault where our intelligence has retreated to preserve itself, but we are functioning and behaving in terms of the chronic pattern. On the functioning level (almost by definition) if the pattern is chronic we are *not* thinking. The client alone is not likely to be able to notice, to be able to see this as a chronic pattern.

I have a little misunderstanding about that because my understanding was that a chronic pattern was something you weren't aware of, that you can't think about. So I am con-

fused when I hear you say that we have to make a commit-ment to work on chronic patterns.

That's what good counseling on this level can do, get the chronic pattern exposed where the client can see it, can take a direction against it.

If you are aware of it, it can't be chronic any longer.

You become aware of it with a little help. This is what I am talking about. The teacher who simply says "you have got to be aware of your chronics and work against them" and doesn't help to hang the chronic up on the wall where you can see it or paste up the direction against it in foot-high letters is just talking. This is insufficient. As a client you need help from your friend the counselor. Being a responsible counselor at this level means holding the pattern up to the light for your clients, helping them to commit themselves to a direction against it that will bring discharge. This is what we have to do for each other.

Permissiveness towards chronics is still widespread. We are working to change this. This is something we cannot accept. The urge to not think, to simply follow a routine will pull at everyone. If we've learned the routine of being permissive, we will "feel like" going on being permissive to chronic patterns. It will be a reactive pull, but it mustn't be yielded to.

To really help each other flower, to find our real selves, we have got to go beyond permissiveness. We have got to make a commitment to each other to not let each other stay within the chronic patterns.

This is what makes an ongoing class sparkle: a) the continual study of theory; b) the commitment to support each other as human beings completely, to really openly love each other and be at each other's disposal; c) the commitment that the group as a whole will turn its individual aware intelligences on each person's chronic pattern, hold it up to the light and persist in its removal.

The continual improvement of co-counseling, the challenge of faster re-emergence is always our choice and our delight.

Ongoing Classes *

All experience to date indicates that co-counseling proceeds much more effectively if co-counselors continue to be members of a class. Group support, increasing knowledge of theory, the opportunities for problem-solving, the variety of co-counselors available; all expedite individual co-counseling greatly. The most effective co-counseling over any long period of time requires ongoing participation in a class.

It is also clear that "cooperative" classes or groups in which no one assumes the responsibility of a teacher run into trouble. The best of intentions are not enough. Leadership is necessary for any group human activity to work well and this is especially true of an activity so beset by the resistance of patterns as co-counseling. An ongoing class should always have *a* teacher. The responsibility for particular class sessions or parts of sessions can, in fact should be, rotated so that everyone participates in leadership; but individual overall leadership is necessary. A regularly accredited teacher of co-counseling should be in charge of each ongoing class. Otherwise, patterns will eventually take over in some form or other.

The cost of ongoing classes can vary to suit the circumstances of people involved, the culture, and the skill of the teacher. The teacher can set the fee or it can be set by negotiation of the class members with the teacher.

It seems essential that the successful ongoing class engage in continued ongoing study of and mastery of theory. There is far more known about co-counseling than has been mastered by any group of co-counselors. There is already

*First printed in Present Time No. 17 -- October, 1974

more in print and on tapes than most co-counselors know, and new developments in theory are occuring all the time.

The essence of the relationship in an ongoing class should be a compact between the members that each will give warm, loving support to each other in the achievements of goals in living and in co-counseling, AND that each will be continually alert that no class members collude unawarely with any chronic pattern. As soon as any class member has the attention free from the last struggle to tackle a new layer of distress, the class members, thinking carefully, awarely and lovingly about *that particular person* will be ready with directions, assistance, and support to help the class member make the next move.

Continual re-emergence should be the theme of every ongoing class. This re-emergence should be decisive. There should never be any settling for counseling being used to make an individual's continued existence within a chronic pattern more comfortable.

When a co-counselor has mastered the group of theorems and practices which constitute the Fundamentals Class (and this may take a very long time in some cases, not because of any backwardness on the part of the person but because of the great amount of material that needs to be discharged at this level) he or she should move directly into an ongoing class, where the continual study of theory and the continued vigilance of the class members on behalf of each other and against each other's patterns can operate at increasing efficiency.

Combating Distortions
of Theory and Policy *

Sometimes a new co-counselor (or even a whole group of new co-counselors) become entranced with RC, delighted with the results of their co-counseling, and even acquire a superficial grasp of some parts of the theory and at the same time begin to put forward revisions or contradictions of RC as "improvements" in the theory and policy which will make it "even better".

The patterned motivations operating are often obvious. Sometimes it is the insecurity of participating in something as non-conforming as RC that leads the insecure one to try to tack on something from orthodox psychologies or the more glamorized "human growth movements". Sometimes it is the reactive itch to be a "discoverer" that smuggles unthought-out contradictions into a "personal" brand of RC. Often patterns of rebellion against "authority figures" find "safe" targets in RC teachers and leaders and their commitment to not attack back, so that the pattern-gripped person proclaims "independence" and "disagreement" by tampering with RC theory and policy.

It is often a difficult lesson for an RC teacher or Reference Person to learn to not be permissive toward such dilutions and distortions of theory and policy. Our leaders necessarily come mostly from those who always hope for and expect humanness from others, and it is usually only after seeing the handicaps which poor theory and policy impose on the co-counselors influenced by them that we learn to be flexibly intransigent about our theory and our Guidelines.

*First printed in Present Time No. 14 -- January, 1974

257

Re-evaluation Counseling is by now a very rich, complex, and integrated set of ideas. The basic theory of RC is a never-failing fountain of fresh, effective, particular techniques for human beings to create to help each other recover their intelligence and humanness.

Re-evaluation Counseling encompasses a profound philosophy, carefully thought-out and tested in its basics, still growing on its periphery. Re-evaluation Counseling as a movement has a policy, summarized in the Guidelines, carefully worked out from the experiences of thousands of people and dozens of communities, for we re-emerging humans to use to effectively relate to each other and to the population at large. This policy is still growing, still changing. Its formal expression, the Guidelines, are opened to revision by representatives of the communities every year, and freedom to arrange temporary adjustments is placed in the hands of the International leadership between yearly revisions.

Re-evaluation Counseling *is not* a vehicle for careerist patterns to use for personal ends. It is not a subject to be parasitized by anyone's desperate need to publish a paper, either for academic, prestige, or other reactive pressure reasons, by distorting or "interpreting" Re-evaluation Counseling as a substitute for doing the independent creative work which their situation rationally demands.

Re-evaluation Counseling as such must not be abused by having modifications and distortions, which are proposed by thoughtless and inexperienced co-counselors, attached to it. If these distortions and hybrid mixtures really had the merits claimed for them by their sponsors, they could certainly succeed under their sponsor's names. They would not need, nor may they use, the names of Re-evaluation Counseling or Co-Counseling to describe these "creations".

We have a very real need in the present period for accurate *translations* of existing Re-evaluation Counseling literature into other languages. We have a real and growing need for thoughtful writing about the *application* of RC theory to special fields, special communities, and various cultures.

We do not need "new interpretations" of Re-evaluation Counseling theory, either in English or in any other language, at the present time. (People who have actually understood RC theory well and have actually used it enough to move out of chronic distresses are, in general, quite agreed that existing theory does not presently need revision or interpretation but rather personal application by the would-be interpreters or revisers.)

The Guidelines require submission of articles about RC that are intended for general publication to the International Reference Person for review, before publication, in order to reduce the misrepresentation of RC to the public. Many writers have done this, but I now plead for relief from the mass of words. Many of these articles have simply been re-writing of existing literature (like a high school book report re-written out of the encyclopedia). Others have been "hack" writing, obviously responding to "publish or perish" academic pressures, which have borrowed some RC ideas to mask a failure by the person to do his or her own creative thinking. Some have embodied the grossest presentations of the person's own chronic distresses, with "revisions" of RC theory to protect the chronic distress from contradiction.

I do not propose any relaxation of the Guidelines requirement for review prior to publication, but I would appeal to would-be writers to either write about their own ideas (rational or distressed) and leave RC out of it (in which case I don't need to review the article), or turn their writing talents to concrete experiences of the application of RC in particular circumstances. If they write in another language, please consider the difficult but rewarding task of accomplishing translations, that are at once accurate and literary, of existing literature.

259

Our Communities and classes, as they grow, will continually absorb many, many chronic patterns along with the lovely human co-counselors who are their victims. These patterns will try, through the voices and actions of their victims, to "take over" and distort RC theory and policy and dilute the safe, pro-human, anti-pattern atmosphere of our Communities. These patterns must be rejected from our Communities (generally, but perhaps not always, keeping the human with us by freeing him or her from the pattern.) Intransigent commitment to basic theory and policy, coupled with completely flexible application of it, is the principal means for accomplishing this.

Occasionally a person joins our RC Communities who has already thought and worked profoundly in this direction so that finding RC is like "coming home" for that person, and in a few months study and practice the person has integrated the theory and policy deeply.

For most of us, it takes a long time to really assimilate the theory, philosophy, practice, and policy (it has taken me over twenty-three years). The "instant expert", the "revision-proposer" who is an "authority" on less than prolonged experience in contact with expert co-counselors, will usually turn out to be a chronic pattern in a "new" camouflage suit, and needs to be met with the flexible intransigence we turn on any pattern, while we reach lovingly to make effective contact with the human being it has victimized.

Wider Use of
One-to-One Teaching *

It has always been an essential feature of our Communities that all co-counselors are permitted and encouraged to teach other people to co-counsel on a one-to-one basis. This is in contradistinction to our care and rigor about giving out credentials to teach official classes.

At this point I think some of our Communities should put greater emphasis on this one-to-one activity. Where our communities are new, where knowledge and practice of the theory is still a little shaky, and where we do not have a strong core of excellent model co-counselors who understand and use the theory in daily life and can serve as a check on any mistakes which arise and tend to be perpetuated, it is probably important to continue with our emphasis on *classes* by the very strongest people we have.

We have some strong Communities, however, where a sizeable body of very united co-counselors understand the theory well. These co-counselors are not, out of insecurity, mixing their patterns, or congealed distresses from other "systems" which they have heard about, into RC. In these Communities at least a half-dozen or a dozen co-counselors are really functioning so well that they are models to everyone in the general society as well as to the people in RC. In such places I would propose that we begin putting much greater emphasis on the each-one-teach-one program.

In such strong Communities and strong classes I would propose that even beginning co-counselors be told at the end of their first class session, "Tonight you have learned something about co-counseling. This week, besides your co-coun-

*First printed in RC Teacher No. 8 – May, 1976

seling with a class member, try to find one individual who is not now in co-counseling and teach that person what you have learned in class tonight. Come back to class next week and report on how it went." Similar emphasis, of course, should be given to experienced co-counselors.

In the U.S. today, a customary greeting is "How are you?" In China thirty years ago, peasants greeted each other with the very pertinent concern, "Have you eaten?" I would propose that we establish a greeting in our strong communities something like, "How is your one-to-one teaching going?"

I think certain real benefits will accrue from such a program. First, I think even the beginning student, having tried to teach someone else between class sessions, will return to the next class with a host of eager questions and be very ready to learn the theory and practice. His or her real attention will be turned on by what he or she discovered in trying to teach another person.

Second, I think that we will accumulate a back-log of people ready to join regular classes, and our formal RC Community who will be much more thoroughly checked-out through their one-to-one experience than we have usually been able to do with new people in the past. Those people whom we do invite will come in much better prepared for good classwork and will progress much more rapidly. It should be made plain that being taught to counsel one-to-one is not an automatic entrance-pass to our Community but is of benefit *in itself.* This should allow our screening on actual entrance to classes to be done more intelligently.

Third, I think that some of the knowledge of RC which is valuable even in fragments to wide circles of the population, will come to be disseminated more quickly and more widely. I often meet people who attended only an introductory lecture and heard only one or two points years ago yet tell me with great enthusiasm that their lives and those of their family have been changed completely, sometimes simply by the idea that people should be validated or other times by hearing that children should not be punished but should be allowed to discharge. In the strong communities we can maintain our care and rigor on the composition and practice of our community members without inhibiting the wide spread of basic RC knowledge that people everywhere are ready for and use eagerly.

An incidental advantage would be ending the embarrassment of dealing with co-counselors who are eager to teach but of whom it is difficult to decide if they are really prepared or operating on a frozen need for prestige. In cases where there is doubt, I think our leadership and teachers can simply say to such a person, "Of course, go ahead and teach one-to-one. When you've taught one, teach another; when you have taught six people and encouraged them to co-counsel with each other, then let us know and one of the teachers will be glad to meet with you and your six trained co-counselors for an evening. If they have indeed learned co-counseling well from you, then there will be no question -- you will be recommended to be certified to teach immediately."

I think this approach is valid, since the best of our teachers have always taught a number of people to counsel one-to-one before they organized a class. In the process of actually teaching as many as half a dozen people, any person is likely to realize whether he or she is actually ready to teach a class or is operating on patterned motivations.

In summary, where we have strong models and dependable group leadership to furnish examples for new co-counselors, I propose a much broader encouraging emphasis on the teaching of people to co-counsel one-to-one *prior* to their being accepted into the R.C. Community.

Touch *

All humans need physical contact with other human beings in a regular and continuing way.

This need has been confused by our culture with sexual or erotic activity and feelings. Certainly the two needs can occur together, but they are completely separate phenomena.

We have recognized this need to some extent in our literature and theory with our slogan of "four hugs a day", but the need goes beyond this. We find some members of our Communities exploring various theories of massage and body manipulation and saying to us that they feel these are needed in addition to co-counseling. I think that such rubbing, massaging, body manipulation theories and practices are probably embarrassed attempts to get to the real need, the need to be touched. I suggest that we begin thinking in our RC Communities about the use of touch.

We've known for a long time that most clients discharge better if they can hold on to the counselor or be held, that the child discharges much better with warm arms holding him or her. An arm around the shoulders or a hand to hold is a very reassuring thing when one takes one's turn before a group or at a workshop introduction.

I think that the key word in description of the touching that is a rational need is *awareness*. I don't think that we need to be rubbed or pummelled or squeezed or manipulated or massaged as much as we need to be *touched awarely*. If we have tension or pain or discomfort in any part of our body, the loving touch of fingers or hands or arms helps put

*First printed in Present Time No. 13 – October, 1973

our own attention on it *from the outside* so that the distress can discharge and the natural healing processes can bring ease and well-being to the area. To touch awarely, keeping it completely separate from any erotic activity and not letting it go over into pressure or violence or manipulation of any sort, should rapidly bring us better knowledge of this phenomenon.

I'd like to hear from people on what they learn, and we'll attempt to summarize their experiences in a later article.

Scholarships *

Scholarships to Re-evaluation Counseling classes and workshops are never given on the basis of "need" or "worthiness". Everyone is worthy and everyone, or almost everyone, feels "needy" when it comes to paying for anything.

Our Communities are not institutions of the existing society and should not be confused or identified with colleges, universities, etc. What money we have to assist anyone to attend classes or workshops comes out of our own co-counselors' pockets, collected as outreach from class and workshop tuitions.

This means that scholarships are restricted to outreach to new populations. This is the criterion for judging when to give scholarships (providing, of course, that we have any money to use at a particular time.)

If the "new" population (new to RC, that is) is an ethnic group that has had special difficulties saddled on it by social oppression, then we will try very hard to assist individuals of that group to secure training in RC. If an American black or a French Arab wish to learn RC to transmit it to their communities, for example, we will make every effort to provide a scholarship.

This will also be true, with perhaps less urgency, for geographically "new" populations and for occupational groups. We need, for our own benefit and theirs, to include larger numbers of factory workers of both sexes in RC. We need to find future teachers of RC in Asia, Latin America, and Africa.

*First printed in RC Teacher No. 3 – February, 1974

Our outreach collections will always be limited, and quickly spent. We need to use logic, not sentiment, in spending them effectively.

Relationship Counseling *

In the development of co-counseling our major concern to date has been with solving individual problems of each co-counselor. Each of us comes to counseling with an accumulation of distresses that interfere with our own individual functioning. It is an important step forward to realize this, to stop blaming the environment or other people for our distresses and to conclude that it is our own patterns that must be tackled first, the ones that are interfering with our individual performances. It has become a guiding principle that where two people become distressed with each other each one should first look to his or her own patterns, co-counsel on them and in general, resolve the difficulty which otherwise might be blamed upon the other person and left intact.

WE HAVE BEGUN TO LOOK AT SOCIAL DISTRESSES

With substantial gains in our individual progress, we have begun to take a challenging look at some of the patterns which are embalmed in our society. Discussions of liberation theory, the liberation workshops, and interaction with groups of people who oppose racism, oppression, agism, sexism, etc. have taken place. (There is much that we have not mastered in this field, but our progress is hopeful and encouraging.)

DISTRESSES IN RELATIONSHIPS AND FAMILIES

Between individual distresses and the distresses of the whole society, there is an intermediate area. More and more of our co-counselors are requesting theory for dealing with

*First printed in Present Time No. 20 – July, 1975

relationships between individuals, in small groups of individuals, and in families. People intuitively seek to be of assistance to each other with "relationship counseling". There are many requests for workshops and classes on these themes.

TIME TO ADDRESS THIS AREA

To play the role of one-way counselor to people with relationship problems is not, I think, the best way for our co-counselors and Communities to address this area. It is important that "instant professional" patterns and cooperating dependency patterns not creep into and distort the basic co-counseling channels of our Community. If we do some aware thinking about it, it is certainly possible and better for good relationship counseling to develop and take place within the framework of *co-counseling,* of *peer relationships.*

SOME KNOWLEDGE HAS BEEN ACCUMULATED

What is different about relationship counseling?

The distress here takes the form of two or more patterns being entangled. The components of the difficulty are individual distresses. The problem, however, is more complex than with an individual distress because of the interaction between the patterns themselves.

(It has been a maxim in RC that it requires at least two irrationalities for difficulties between two individual human beings to persist. Each party must be contributing some irrationality. If even one person were rational the difficulty could not persist because the rational person would resort to counseling tools and thus begin the resolution.)

We have the complex situation of a pattern being restimulated by and interacting with another pattern. This means that some destimulation, some effective separation of the interaction is a preliminary requirement. As long as two patterns continue to push each other's buttons, it is difficult to begin the discharge process, difficult to get enough attention outside the self-restimulating tangle to allow re-evaluation to begin.

(In the following reprint of an initial interview with a married couple, you will find certain rules often used to begin the separation. One of these is that the participants in relationship counseling not talk to each other during the initial interview with the counselor, but only with the counselor.)

In a joint session it is helpful if any strong feelings which insist on being expressed shall be expressed to the counselor *as a stand-in for the other party* rather than directly to the other party. Other safeguards are a commitment made in advance by each party to hear the other person out, and a flat commitment that neither person will refer later to anything that the other said during the interview.

To resolve a tangle between two people may be four times as difficult as the untangling of an individual distress pattern. It is, however, probably eight times as profitable in terms of the immediate benefits accruing to the parties.

In the beginning the counselors need techniques to interrupt the compulsive restimulation between the individuals involved in the relationship. After this, the individual patterns can be addressed with the familiar techniques of individual counseling. To begin with it is usually simpler to do this with someone other than the partner in restimulation. Long range, however, the goal of relationship counseling is to get the parties to the point where they can (with great care and enhanced skills) be effective co-counselors *for each other.*

This should always be the goal of any relationship counseling. With marriage counseling, for example, the third party counselor never concludes for the parties that their marriage must be preserved (that is up to them to decide), but does insist they should continue with their work until they can co-counsel with each other, until they have a friendly, open, viable relationship. At that time it is up to them to decide whether they continue in a cleaned-up version of the older relationship, build a new relationship afresh between each other, or part on the friendliest of terms.

Relationship counseling generally will involve a third party to begin with. Its goal should always be, however, to bring or restore the people involved to two-way co-counseling with each other.

Counseling on relationships has been part of RC from the beginning. What we have at the present is not something new but an upsurge of interest and the attainment of favorable conditions. I think our whole Community should master these skills. I propose that the leadership of our Communities, our Reference Persons and teachers, take the lead, that they begin to do local and area workshops on these topics so that everyone present at the workshops will acquire the tools for helping each other with relationships.

Relationship counseling should not become another "newest fad" in our Communities. Individual co-counseling remains the basis of everything we do. Our beginnings at reaching Third World and working class people and understanding the issues of liberation must go forward.

As with everything that we've learned to do well in RC, however, we can think in many areas at once. Relationship counseling is simply an area that needs addressing at this time for the rounding out of our approach.

"Additional Activities" Rather Than "Additional Relationships" *

In the continuing discussions of the basic principle which underlies the no-socializing rules of our Communities (the "Blue Pages") many new insights continue to occur.

I now realize that I have contributed in the past to confusion in this area by saying at workshops that, with increased intelligence and awareness, RCers might someday be able to successfully handle other, additional, relationships with a co-counselor as well as the co-counseling relationship. What I was thinking of was the successes people have been having in workshop activities together, in working on Community committees, planning Gather-Ins, etc. These remarks have apparently encouraged the addictive pull on some co-counselors to try to satisfy frozen needs by drifting into additional relationships with a co-counselor and rationalizing to themselves that they were now "advanced enough" or "out of enough chronic patterns" that they could do this with success.

A general consensus among thoughtful leaders of RC is that even with quite experienced co-counselors such efforts are based on escapism and frozen-need-filling and that such experiments have led to the slowing of the progress and growth of the participants as well as many other complications for themselves and others.

I now realize that what I was trying to say and what I should have said is that *as one becomes more rational one can apparently add more activities to the list of things one can do with co-counselors and still have the activities have a co-counseling content.*

*First printed in RC Teacher No. 5 – November, 1974

273

To work together on a community committee, to plan a gather-in together, to attend a workshop together involves many joint activities besides formal sessions. In practice these activities have worked toward emergence. They have had, in effect, *a co-counseling content.* This has been the difference, that these are *additional activities*, broadening out the co-counseling relationship rather than *additional relationships.* It is these last which, when attempted, seem to create difficulties for the co-counseling and slow down the growth of the partners.

I am sorry to have been unclear in speaking about this in the past. I am especially sorry about encouragement I thus gave to co-counselors getting into difficulties.

To re-formulate the question in the above way helps to keep the issue straight in my own mind. I think it may be helpful to other co-counselors as well.

An Initial Marriage
Counseling Interview
by a Re-evaluation Counselor *

(This type of initial interview, with slight modifications, works well for any pair or group of people in a relationship that has become restimulative and distressing. Married couples with a troubled relationship are a prototype for such difficulties, and the interview structure is here presented for such a couple.)

The counselor asks an agreement by each spouse to abide by three rules:

First, that each spouse agree to speak only to the counselor during the interview and not to the other spouse directly.

Second, that each spouse do his/her best to listen without offense to what the other says; that each try not to hold anything that is said against the other person; in other words, that each resist being restimulated as far as possible.

Third, that each spouse make a firm commitment not to discuss outside of the interview anything the other spouse says during the interview, neither with each other, nor with any other person, except the counselor. The interview is a privileged conversation and a confidential one for both partners, and is not to be shared with anyone else, nor referred to with each other. Failure to follow this procedure can lead to intense restimulation. The counselor does not proceed with the interview until each party has agreed to this last condition.

*First printed in Present Time No. 20 – July, 1975

The counselor then turns her attention to and questions the partner who appears most reluctant to take part in the interview. This is usually both reassuring and disarming to her/him. It results in greater cooperation and openness if the reluctant one is given the counselor's full attention and allowed to speak first.

(If there is a second marriage, ask a few questions about the previous marriage. The roots of the present difficulty may lie there, and this may become apparent as it is talked about.)

The counselor directs a series of questions to the first spouse, explaining that the other spouse will get her (or his) turn later. (The other partner should refrain from commenting on what the first says until that time.)

Ask, "How long did you know (spouse) before you were married?"

Then, "Before you got married, what did you like about her (or him)?" Persist with this, and ask further questions, if necessary, such as, "Did you think she was attractive? intelligent? competent?" etc. until positive attitudes from this earlier period have been expressed.

With this perspective of desirable qualities firmly established, ask, "If you had a magic wand (or some other light wording) at that time and could have made some little changes in (your prospective spouse) in order to make her (or him) perfect, what changes would you have made?" Be sure the answer is in terms of the changes that would have been wished for before the marriage and not in view of subsequent events.

Next ask, "How long was it a good marriage from your point of view?"; then "Was sex good for you in the beginning?" The second question may or may not be important, but a couple coming in for marriage counseling generally expects to be asked that question, and once the tension about its being asked is gone they can relax about this.

After dealing with this, ask, "What happened when the relationship began to go bad?"

After this is answered, bring the questioning up to the present situation by asking, "What do you like about her (or him) now?" If there is little or no positive response, say, "Take a fresh look at her (or him) now." Further questions might be, "Is she still intelligent? Is he handsome? Is she still competent? Is he thoughtful?", etc.

With these answered ask, "If you had a magic wand now and could change some things about her (or him), what would you change?" or "What bothers you about her (or him) now?"

This is the crucial part of the interview. The answers to these questions reveal the structure of the patterns which have become tangled in the relationship and which need to be counseled on. If necessary, take notes on these responses.

Then turn to the other spouse and ask the same questions.

Next, give each spouse a chance to comment on the remarks made by the other, keeping in mind throughout that both parties should continue to address their comments to the counselor and not to each other.

In the course of the interview discharge may occur from either spouse. It should be listened to attentively and encouraged. This will help the counselor to spot those patterns which are causing the difficulties in the relationship. It is these patterns in particular which are becoming entangled and which must be worked on to ease the relationship.

Having given the couple a full chance for expression, the counselor might then restate the point of view of Re-evaluation Counseling regarding marriage problems: Both spouses are basically good people. They have acquired rigid patterns of behaving, thinking and feeling which become entangled and result in poor relationships. With counseling, these patterns can be eliminated and the relationship improved.

If the couple is not familiar with Re-evaluation Counseling theory, this will need to be explained. Since this usually takes an hour or more, couples are often asked to attend an introductory lecture before coming in for a marriage counseling inteview.

The counselor can point out that theoretically, at least, both partners still love each other, even though it may not feel that way. People never stop loving those they once loved. The love becomes hidden by feelings of distress which can be cleared away.

Neither partner can simply walk out of the present relationship without taking along into other relationships the patterns which are spoiling the present relationship. Until they are at least on friendly terms with each other, they will carry their distress with them wherever they go. They need to get free of their distress feelings and they will then be able to decide rationally whether the marriage should be continued or terminated.

The counselor should make clear that this decision must be theirs, not the counselor's. When they have discharged some of the tense feelings about each other, they will be in a better position to make the right decision.

Finally, the counselor should make a firm recommendation to both partners regarding the next steps. She might recommend one-way counseling for one or both. She might suggest that they join a class. In any case, the counseling directions which contradict the patterns which came to light in the course of the interview should be communicated to the couple and their counselors or co-counselors.

The counselor doing the interview might try these directions out with the couple then and there, to sharpen them and find out in which form a particular direction works best.

If the couple has severely tangled patterns, they should be cautioned against attempting to co-counsel with each other at this point.

The couple is, at parting, reassured, individually and as a couple, that they are good people and that problems can be solved. If they have not yet decided to accept individual or class help they are reassured that the counselor will be glad to hear from them.

The above sample interview will be useful if used flexibly. It is not a set of rules; it is a possible sample approach. The counselor's caring for the couple will determine the usefulness of the interview more than any set of procedures.

Originally collected by Inge Snipes from conversations with Harvey Jackins, and revised.

Aware Thinking, Not Repetition
of Jargon *

Distress recordings or patterns are not only rigid but are persistent. Until they are dissolved completely by enough discharge and cease to be distress recordings (when the frozen input is converted into ordinary information and the tied-up intelligence is free to function once more) they persist. Until any remaining portion of the pattern is completely discharged, it continues to persist and use any captive intelligence to rationalize and justify the irrational attitudes and behavior associated with the pattern.

Re-evaluation Counseling is a powerful weapon for dissolving patterns, but patterns will persist in the face of counseling until completely discharged and will camouflage themselves with counseling phrases or jargon if one unawarely permits them to. Some things currently being said and done in the name of Re-evaluation Counseling are simply old patterns, now decorated with counseling phrases. Only "thinking all the time" is an effective antidote to the stupid (but sneaky) persistence of patterned behavior on ourselves and our groups. Only critical awareness operating from a sound grasp of theory can keep our own selves, our groups, and our communities progressing the way we wish them to.

I sometimes hear pretense and denial of reality being offered as ways of being "positive". It's true that one needs to not accept negative attitudes as reality, but pretending unawarely is not the antidote. We seek to be in accurate appraisal of present time reality, because only with such an accurate appraisal can we really take charge of the environment. We act on a basic assumption that actual

*First printed in Present Time No. 14 – January, 1974

reality is handleable (any other assumption would leave us at the mercy of despair patterns) and that we will handle it better if we observe it accurately and apply our intelligence fully.

Sometimes the patterned use of counseling jargon becomes obvious and ridiculous. Most of us have run into at least one "counseling nut" who responds to a rational greeting of "Hello" with "Again!"

Sometimes a client's voice, caught up in a self-reproach pattern, will detail past behavior (caused by the pattern) to support the pattern's conclusion of self-reproach. Then the counselor's reminder, "That's not you, the person, who does those things. That's the distress pattern" is a helpful separation of person from pattern and contradiction of the pattern (which can lead to discharge).

How very different the invalidating pattern which seeks to win arguments with people or establish reactive "superiority" by announcing "That's your pattern!" in a mocking voice to every difference of opinion.

In a similar way, I sometimes hear the most thoughtless and irresponsible behavior being justified, by the perpetrator's patterns, with counseling phrases. "If he got restimulated by what I did, he can go discharge on it. That's not my responsibility."

It is true that we may have to take a firm stand at times against "blame" patterns looking for a victim, that we refuse to cooperate with such a pattern even though it may be groping at some rational (or irrational) act of ours as pretext for going into action. We would take such a stand, however, only after very careful examination of the possibility that our own distresses had been doing the mischief and after appropriate apologies and corrections had been undertaken.

The co-counselor must take full responsibility for all relationships. That includes the results, in those relationships, of any rehearsals of his own distresses.

The use of counseling jargon can never be a substitute for continual aware thinking about everything, to the best of our growing abilities.

Comments on Learning Situations *

CURIOSITY

The basic attitude of human intelligence is certainly one of curiosity. You can count on this enormous drive to learn something new. There is a thirst for new information that one can evaluate and relate to what one already knows. It's a fundamental human characteristic to want to know, to desire more information, more, more, more. Haven't you known people to say, "I learned something new today" "That's something I didn't know". This certainly exists in all of us. To remember this, to know it theoretically will save your bacon often when you have to communicate while under restimulation yourself.

HOW INTELLIGENCE FUNCTIONS

We have learned that intelligence functions well in relationship to the environment only within certain information limits. Intelligence cannot keep operating when too much new information is coming at it. Only a certain proportion of new material can be assimilated. We can only handle a certain percentage, maybe five percent, of new items, at least with the load of distress we carry. We may do a lot better than that as we unload our distresses. There's a certain proportion of new information one can handle, and if the new information coming in from the environment exceeds that amount fear takes over. You may call it confusion but the discharge is in trembling and laughter. It appears to be fear.

* Talk at Calvinwood I, The First Classroom Teachers Workshop -- Feb. 26-28, 1971

You know this. When people try to tell you too much you ask them to "back up". "Give it to me one at a time." Some of the most frightening science fiction is about people who awake in a completely alien environment; they can't relate to anything. Haven't you awakened and not known where you were for a moment and panicked? Probably being born is like that.

(Someone asks about his public lecture, where he gives a great deal of new information.) If the public lecture is as effective as we think it is, then it's because we have assembled a whole lot of reassuring, discharging, communicating, techniques to make it possible to communicate that much. Of course, we still overwhelm some people. (Someone says that under that situation there is no obligation to remember the information, whereas in a classroom the student is obliged to remember and feed it back, Martha comments that most people basically know what Harvey is telling them; that what they hear they always knew was true.) People respond and take it in, but you can feel the strain build up until the discharge part of the lecture comes. I try to throw in my little witticisms early, but there's a certain point where they all start laughing together and then you can feel the situation relax and the evaluation open up.

Someone asks if information taken in by the bored child can be evaluated later.) Yes, all the information that goes in can be evaluated. It's either understandable at the time or it goes in the brushpile and becomes available on complete discharge. This is true of even the most terrifying experiences. Most of us haven't had the opportunity to clean something up with complete discharge all the way up the spectrum, but when this happens even the most distressing experiences become all information. People can remember and recite the fine print in the notice on the wall in the undertaker's parlor.

(Someone asks about the possibility of being shut down by boredom in a lecture but then freeing the information in the discussion afterwards.) Yes, this even happens with the hallowed institution of tests, and discussing the results of tests. It's the worst way to get at meaning, but it's been continued partly because anything that allows the children to talk about it allows them to learn from each other what they couldn't hear from the teacher.

(Someone asks about the recall reached under hypnosis.) The recall which comes after discharge puts it over here in the memory where it's useful; recall under hypnosis digs it up over here and puts it back in the brushpile of distress coated with the harmful agreed-upon shutdown of the hypnotic trance. This recall doesn't have anything to do with really remembering in a flexible sense. You have new distresses from the hypnotic shutdown. Hypnosis is always injurious, never helpful. If you were ready to evaluate that material you would recall it spontaneously. To force it out with hypnotic recall is to do new injury, usually setting up some new recorded contradictions.

Too high a proportion of new information is one limit under which intelligence operates. It triggers fear and shutdown. (Barbara wants to know if it wouldn't trigger frustration in a child who felt safe because he would want to use the new information.) Yes, if they are in better shape they'll throw a tantrum at you.

The other limit that intelligence has to operate within is a requirement for some new information. If you don't have something new coming in, something new you can make sense out of, boredom sets in. It's called "light" and it discharges in talk, but in a way it's the most terrible of painful emotions. Clients who keep bouncing away from feeling their heavy fear and can't be pushed to feel it, if you give them a choice between feeling it and boredom will always eventually choose to feel the heavy fear in preference. Human beings will eventually face anything else rather than stay bored. Not having any new information for a long time is the most grisly of prospects.

If you have clients who avoid feeling heavy fear, just set up a phrase and ask them to stay with it. Settle back, and no matter how they object say pleasantly, "let's keep on with it." They'll keep on with saying, "I can't face it, it's too frightening," and you keep saying "again," 5000 times. Finally they'll say, "all right, brr!" and begin shaking.

Boredom is unbearable to the human intelligence. The Limelighters put it very nicely in their song about the lady bullfighter. They had a line about "why did she become a bullfighter? Because she'd rather be gored than bored."

The other limit we have seen clearly. On this end there must be *some* new information. People will commit suicide out of fear occasionally, but I'm sure they'll commit suicide much more often out of boredom.

Key Insights for Teaching And Learning *

1. Any shut-down of the person prevents learning.

2. Validation combats shut-down.

3. Learning operates only between the limits of too much new information too fast (confusion, frustration) and too little new information (boredom).

4. New information should be offered accompanied by its relationship to information already assimilated.

5. New information can only be absorbed in small, ordered increments.

6. "It is the nature of humans to desire to know" -- Aristotle.

7. It is difficult to accept important new knowledge except from someone one loves.

8. It is easier to learn from peers.

9. Most learning must be one-to-one transfer of information. This requires that learners teach each other.

10. All successful new structures grow within the old structures before they overthrow and replace the old.

11. Loving self-confidence on the part of the teacher *and* correct policies will overcome all obstacles.

---

*Calvinwood I, Classroom Teachers' Workshop -- February 27 - 29, 1971

Always Two Distinct Viewpoints

The counseling relationship must always be viewed differently by the counselor and by the client, and the two viewpoints cannot correctly be combined into one.

The client needs to assume full responsibility, in his or her viewpoint, for the results of the counseling relationship, for mastering and applying the theory fully, for deducing the directions and decisions, and for taking the actions, which will contradict distress and bring discharge and re-emergence.

The client needs to determine to achieve full re-emergence even if there were no more helpful counselor present than a tree or a rock. The client needs to try to state clearly what she or he needs from the counselor at a particular time, to patiently and courteously correct any mistakes the counselor makes, and, if necessary, to "counsel the counselor on what is getting in the way of the counselor counseling the client".

The counselor, on the other hand, must assume that the client, regardless of appearances, is at all times doing the very best that she or he can do to make the counseling work, and that any freedom for improvement lies solely with the counselor.

The counselor must remain aware to pick up and understand the flood of signals which the client is continually giving off, signals both of rational thinking and of "cries to be noticed" rehearsals of distress, and be guided in her or his actions by this information from the client.

*First printed in Present Time No. 27 – April, 1977

The counselor needs to offer profound and thoughtful attentiveness to everything the client is doing or saying, but also take repeated, changing initiatives to try to help begin and support discharge on the part of the client, and must furnish insistence and persistence once an initiative has been successful.

The counselor must not be intimidated by the client's distress nor by his or her own discomfort, but needs to act boldly to precipitate discharge, needs to provide confidence enough for both client and counselor, and needs to furnish the persistence which will discharge the distresss completely.

The counselor's attitude needs to be that each session is a golden opportunity for the client's decisive re-emergence and a chance for the counselor to make an elegant difference in the success of the counseling.

In their separate viewpoints both client and counselor must assume full in-chargeness, power, and confidence. To do otherwise is to open the door to allow such familiar patterns as "assigning responsibility to someone else", reproach, blame, powerlessness, confusion, and discouragement to take over.

Liberation from

Patterns of

Oppression

The Role of Re-evaluation
Counseling in Liberation

1. Re-evaluation Counseling is not a program for social liberation. The Re-evaluation Counseling Communities have a one-point program only, that is, the use of Re-evaluation Counseling to recover one's occluded intelligence and to help others do the same.

2. Re-evaluation Counseling Communities do encourage and support rational attitudes on the part of all co-counselors on all questions, including the questions of resisting oppression and achieving liberation.

3. Re-evaluation Counseling is a program for individual liberation.

4. Re-evaluation Counseling is a tool for assisting individuals to struggle more effectively for liberation by eliminating acting on distress or painful emotion and assisting them to act intelligently and successfully.

5. The Re-evaluation Counseling Communities are ready to support and assist all liberation movements and the individuals within them to be more effective in their struggle for liberation.

The Elements of Oppression and The Struggle for Liberation *

1. Oppression of one group of people by another group of people originates in, and is perpetuated by economic exploitation, by the organized taking (often in a concealed way) of the value produced by the work of one person or group of persons by another person or group of persons. Thus, the slaveowner takes the value produced by the slave and returns only the minimum necessary to keep the slave alive. Similarly, the baron takes the produce of the serf, the capitalist that of the wage worker.

2. An oppressive society has many ways of maintaining oppression and exploitation. Control of communication, mis-education, lies, false propaganda, habits, culture, and religion are used and are re-inforced by force in the form of laws, courts, police, prisons, armies, etc.

3. The crucial social means for the perpetuation of oppression is dividing the oppressed and pitting them against each other, so that different groups of oppressed people co-operate in oppressing each other to the benefit of the oppressing people.

4. The principal individual means for the perpetuation of oppression is the feeling of wanting to switch roles in a distress recording of mistreatment, to accept the more "comfortable" role, in a re-enactment of a mistreatment recording, of being the mistreator rather than being the mistreated, and to settle for co-operating in oppressing someone else rather than ending all oppression.

---

* First printed in Pensamientos No. 1 -- September, 1975

5. To end the oppression of any one group of people completely it is necessary to end all oppression.

6. The oppressed peoples always have the strength to end oppression and exploitation. The difficulty lies in confusion, lack of cooperation, and fear, as well as in old habits of thought.

7. It is in the real interests of all human beings to end oppression.

8. The oppressed and exploited groups of the population are the ones who can be counted on to realize this in a majority and to struggle consistently for liberation once they are aware of the true situation.

9. Individuals from among the exploiting group and their supporters can be won over for liberation on an intellectual basis, but only a minority of these groups can be won over for liberation until liberation is achieved.

10. Each group of oppressed must realize their oppression, must proclaim their own worth, must forge unity around a common program, must seek and win allies among the other oppressed, and must act.

11. Oppressed people must evolve leadership in order to struggle successfully for liberation. This leadership must have a rational theory to guide them, must constitute a dedicated, informed, united group and must seek and achieve unity with leaders of all other oppressed groups.

Propositions About Human Liberation *

1. All presently existing human beings are very closely related. All are members, not only of the same species, *Homo Sapiens,* but of the same sub-species, *Homo Sapiens Sapiens,* an even closer relationship.

2. The most important physical variations that do exist among humans, e.g., blood types, body structures, and brain sizes, all vary more widely *within* each ethnic or skin-color group usually described as a *race* than they do between such groups.

3. Each human being whose forebrain has not been grossly damaged begins life with a far greater capacity to be intelligent than the best functioning adult has ever been able to demonstrate.

4. The differences which do exist in the behaviors and functioning of groups of humans are *cultural*, are learned and acquired characteristics. Any human being, given the opportunity, can acquire and master the same culture and skills which any other human being has been able to do.

5. There is no human culture which is superior or inferior to any other human culture in any *overall* human sense, though there may be, and are, particular outstanding richnesses in any culture. Some cultures have developed farther *technically* in the mastery of the environment than others, enabling them to be misused to oppress members of other cultures as well as their own people. This does not imply any human superiority of such a culture.

*Presented to the Liberation Workshops I & II and revised. -- March, 1975

6. Class societies evolved as tools to master the environment more effectively, and functioned to that end through allowing some members of the society time and leisure to think, to accumulate knowledge and to plan the activities of the society.

7. All class societies which we and our ancestors have experienced and participated in to date have been *oppressive* societies, in which the results of the work of most of the people was taken from them by the ruling people by a kind of legal robbery. All such societies to date have operated primarily to organize this exploitation of the majority of the people by a ruling minority.

8. The principal forms of class societies which have existed to date are, in order of their evolution, and in their basic relationships:

A. SLAVE SOCIETIES. In these the ruling slave-owners own the slaves outright and their production as well. (e.g. Pre-Civil War southern United States.)

B. FEUDAL SOCIETIES. In these the baron or landlord owns the land or workshop. The serf is tied to his plot of land or job and receives part of what he produces with the rest going to the baron. (e.g. Post-Civil War sharecropping in the southern United States.)

C. CAPITALIST SOCIETIES. In these the capitalist owns the factory, railroad, bank or farm. The wage-worker is "free" to work or starve but what he produces belongs to the capitalist who returns a variable portion of it as wages. (Present Industrial United States.)

9. Societies which will be cooperative, and in which no one is exploited or oppressed have been imagined and described. Some attempts have been made to establish them. (The Paris Commune, the Soviet Union in the 1920's and 1930's, China currently.)

10. The oppressive societies of slavery, feudalism, and capitalism each inevitably arose in turn because of a human need for change. Each contained within itself a built-in long-range unworkability which, in the case of the slave system eventually led to its collapse and replacement by feudalism (e.g., Fall of the Roman Empire), and in the case of feudalism to its collapse ·and replacement by capitalism (e.g., European Rennaissance).

11. There are many indications that capitalist society is now in the late stages of collapsing because of its own built-in, long range unworkability.

12. Slave and Feudal societies were able to be openly oppressive, using naked force openly against the slaves and less openly against the serfs.

Since wage-workers are more independent and better informed, capitalist societies have had to be more subtle in concealing and enforcing the exploitation and oppression.

13. One of the principal means used by capitalist societies to maintain their oppression and exploitation of people has been to secure the cooperation of different groups of people in oppressing each other.

This has been done by installing and maintaining attitudes of racism, prejudice, discrimination, sexism, and adultism between the different sections of the oppressed population.

14. The basic mechanism for keeping any person in an oppressed condition is the installation upon the person of a distress pattern or recording by hurting him or her in an oppressive and invalidating way.

This leads to one or both of two results when the distress pattern is restimulated.

The first result is to be forced again into the role the person filled in the original hurt experience. In this case the person is pushed to "accept" or "agree" to be oppressed, to accept the invalidating feelings, to be defeated in the attempt to remain human. The slave "agrees" to be a slave, the serf picks up his hoe and bows his head, the wage-worker feels inferior and "lucky to have a job".

The second result occurs when, in an attempt to escape the role described in the first result above, the victim of the restimulation seeks relief by "occupying" a different role in the restimulated distress recording, the role of the oppressor. In this case the male victim may turn the abuse and invalidation originally turned on him on a woman (the basis of sexism) or a white victim may turn it upon a black or other non-white (the basis of racism) etc., etc.

15. An oppressive society actively reinforces both of the results described above with false "theories", propaganda, discriminatory treatment of all kinds, religious pronouncements, secret societies, etc., etc.

In this way each group's attempts to resist oppression are discouraged and their confidence sapped, and each group is mobilized to cooperate in the invalidation and defeat of every other group.

16. When any oppressed group begins to awarely organize to achieve its liberation there will be a reactive attraction towards blaming and attacking the other oppressed groups who have mistreated it, fighting with them as if they were the source of oppression and leaving the real (and more threatening) oppressor forces unchallenged. (Thus women will at first be pulled to see "men" as the source of the oppression, black and Chicano high school students will be urged into gang wars against each other, etc.) Needless to say, this tendency will be encouraged by the real oppressors in every possible way.

17. To attain complete liberation two processes are *both* necessary:

one: effective organized social action and struggle

two: discharge and re-evaluation to free each individual from his or her individual distress patterns.

The two processes are complementary and each enhances the other. To fight intelligently against social oppression is to contradict one's individual distress patterns and expedite discharge and re-evaluation *provided one pursues one's co-counseling systematically.*

To emerge from one's individual painful emotion enhances one's effectiveness in social struggle and helps avoid mistaken strategy and tactics based on feelings, *provided that one really engages in activity and doesn't just settle for talking about it.*

18. To be successful, any oppressed group seeking liberation must move in two directions:

A. It must consistently strive for unity within its own group *around a clear-cut program of goals and actions.*

B. It must consistently seek unity and mutual support *with every other oppressed group*, no matter how difficult this task may seem at first.

19. Reform of an oppressive society cannot bring liberation from oppression. Replacement is necessary. Since the sole reason for the oppressive society is oppression and exploitation, such oppression and exploitation is bound to be re-introduced after the reform in some other form as long as the oppressive society exists.

20. The great liberation theoreticians of the past are useful inspirations and models to liberation workers today in many ways, but cannot be applied except in the most general ways to a current situation. Of most use is their

method of concretely examining the real situation they were confronting, making sure they had the facts, and then thinking fresh and hard for new solutions to that particular situation. All our situations are new.

21. It may be true that "right" in a political sense is irrational, but it by no means follows that "left" is necessarily rational. The numerous movements and theories that call themselves "left" and "revolutionary" abound in rigidities and can by no means be accepted as guides. Fresh, intelligent thinking is required.

22. People can only be effectively organized to participate in liberation on an individual basis. Calling mass meetings, distributing leaflets, and other "mass" activities are an almost complete waste of time *unless* they are peripheral to a systematic making of individual friends, who will consider a liberation program if you offer it because they trust you.

23. Every group of oppressed people can be reached to participate in the struggle for liberation if we reach correctly.

The first job is to counter the fears, suspicions, antagonisms and resentments that have been installed between us. This means a sharp stand against all sexist, racist, condescending, or invalidating statements and language of all kinds.

We all begin afraid of each other. We have been conditioned to fear anyone who is "different". We can learn to love and trust each other but we must begin with an attitude of *respect*, of complete respect for every human being in the world. The love and trust can come later.

24. Every group of people is important to the unity of the liberation forces. Even individuals from the oppressing classes are welcome if they really "throw in their lot with the people".

There is one group of oppressed people, however, who overlap and include parts of nearly every other group and who are centrally important to liberation because of their great power in relation to the oppressive structure.

This is the group of *wage workers*, especially the industrial wage workers, in particular the wage workers in the *basic* industries.

The entire social structure of capitalism is dependent on their continuing cooperation in production. No profits are produced without them. If they refuse to work the whole capitalist system comes to a grinding halt.

Liberation cannot hope to succeed without them. It cannot help but succeed with them.

25. The *trade unions* are and will remain the basic organizations of the wage workers. To win the trade union members to a liberation policy, to recover the trade union leadership posts from the employers' agents and the criminal elements who have been smuggled into many of them is the most crucial organizational job facing the liberation forces.

There can be no avoidance of, or substitute for, doing this.

26. Farmers are oppressed as a class and are being forced off the farms by the spread of large-scale capitalist production methods into farming. Many of them become agricultural wage workers.

The preservation of the smaller farmers in this period is important, however, because they possess a vast treasure of knowledge of how to produce food for good nutrition, while the newer, larger, capitalist operations in agriculture operate only on the motives of profit.

27. People cannot be organized successfully for liberation around programs of distress or painful emotion. To

appeal to their fear, guilt, shame, is to paralyze them by restimulation in the long run.

They must be organized by appealing to reason, logic, and confidence. All programs and policies should be rational. The tone of communication should always be one of confidence in the inevitiability of success.

28. Liberation of any group will only be complete when all oppressed groups are liberated.

The Productive Majority *

Those of us coming into RC who are accustomed to "work for a living", can sometimes feel a little uneasy at first. As RC has spread around the U.S. and into some other countries it has usually been picked up first by college professors, students, lawyers, and other people who think of themselves as "middle class" or "intellectuals". It may be a real question whether they are any more "intellectual" than those of us who drive trucks or hold down factory jobs, but they have been taught to think of themselves as intelligent and sometimes to feel superior to working people because they have been "better educated".

On our part, if we or our folks were working people, we have usually picked up a message that we are not truly "successful" if we didn't get to college and become some kind of professional. We often suspect that people who finished college must have a lot of information that we missed. We are likely to feel that if we open our mouths and speak out somebody will think we're "dumb" because we may mis-pronounce a word. We've been pretty thoroughly trained to be "modest" about ourselves and to avoid ever acting "conceited" (that is, we've been trained to put ourselves down continually).

COUNSELING HAS BEEN GOOD

Our experiences with counseling have generally been good. It may have seemed strange to be encouraged to cry or openly admit that we are afraid or shake or laugh for a long time while our counselor makes us try to say a phrase over and over, but the effect of doing it has obviously been good or we wouldn't have stayed with it. Most of us have

*First printed in Working For A Living No. 1 -- June, 1976

307

confidence enough in our own sense to know when something is working for us and have kept on with co-counseling. We may not have played a leading role, not tried very hard to become teachers or Reference People, not spoken up about some of the nonsensical things that go on in the RC communities.

Some of us, of course, have become RC teachers and Reference people. Most of us who have done that so far have pretended that we were middle class, have acted as if we were on our way to being professionals just as soon as we can get more time in the community college. It has been a surprise and a pleasure to many of us to discover as we "came out of the closet" that there are other working people playing leading roles in RC who have been pretending to be "intellectuals" also.

CONFUSION FROM OUTSIDE

It is, of course, hard to draw the line between someone who is a worker or whose family were working people, and intellectuals or middle class people. In the U.S. every poor child is told that he or she has the right to become president if she or he works hard enough and studies hard enough. They're told if they get far enough in school they can be a "success", meaning that they can wear a suit to work or take long vacations and live in a "good" neighborhood instead of the ordinary people's section of town. It used to be said that if you were born on the "wrong side of the tracks" that you could cross the tracks if you were determined and worked hard enough. This was supposed to be the great thing about the U.S., that it was the "land of opportunity" where working people could rise from the "unfortunate positions" they were born into to become, if not wealthy, at least professionals.

It is important that many of us in RC at the present time are beginning to challenge these attitudes that were put on us that we should be ashamed of being working people or that our failure to get beyond a factory or mining job was "our fault".

WHO ARE WE?

Just who are we? Sociologists are likely to speak of us as "working class". We're likely to talk of ourselves as working people. What is different about us? How are we like each other?

First of all we should say that each of us is unique and different. Just like all other humans, each one of us is a completely unique individual with his or her own special interests, own special experiences, and own unique distresses because the exact bad things that happened to each one of us never happened to anyone else. We're very different in our personalities, our interests, our physical makeup, our appearance, our names, our racial and ethnic backgrounds, our cultures. We have great variety. Any two of us are likely to be quite as different from each other as any one of us is different from any professional or wealthy person, any scientist or factory worker.

What we have in common is simply that we work for a living, that we produce almost all the wealth on which the entire population lives.

THE MAJORITY

We are the great majority of the population. Probably at least 65% of the people in the U.S. belong to the "Working Class", even by the narrowest definitions. If we include with us the very large numbers of people who are workers but have been fooled into thinking that they are not, by being given management jobs or a key to the executives' washroom, or allowed to keep their hands clean by working for less wages, then our proportion of the population is higher than 85%.

We live by selling our ability to do work, whether it's unskilled, semi-skilled, or very skilled work, to someone else and being paid back a small amount of the wealth we've produced in the form of wages. We, in general, do not own any means of production, we do not own any factories or banks, or railroads, or mines. These are owned by other people who "hire" us. They allow us to produce wealth with their factories, mines, etc., and then keep most of it for themselves, giving us a small portion of what we produce as wages.

We have nothing to say about the way the factories, etc., in which we spend most of our lives are run. The decisions are made by someone else. At the most we can make a suggestion for the suggestion box.

We have no security beyond what we have been able to battle for through union pension funds, or such reforms such as Social Security and Unemployment Compensation that we have forced the people that own the country to put into law.

THE OWNERS

The wealthy, owning group of people is a very small part of the population. About 1% of the people own or control a great majority of the country's means of production; that is, the factories, mines, railroads, banks, etc. These have security through the very possession of their wealth. The people who do professional jobs for these wealthy people, the college professors, accountants, lawyers, etc., are often either paid well enough or are allowed to set up retirement funds and special securities so that some of them have some security in their lives. For us, bad times mean we live on our unemployment compensation until we can find another job.

WE'VE BEEN BRAINWASHED

We have been made to feel (and have often "accepted" the notion) that we are not as smart as the people who own the wealth or their "intellectual" assistants. We've accepted tremendous invalidations of ourselves and are in the habit of perpetuating it. The familiar statement, "If I was smart I wouldn't still be working for a living" is a succinct expression of the way we've been made to feel over and over again during our lives until we've come to accept it and act like we believed it.

REALITY IS OTHERWISE

We are the absolutely essential part of the population. If the country were composed only of workers (including, of course, the farmers who work on the farm) then we could exist very well producing for our needs. We would miss some of the "finer things of life" if there were no artists, musicians, college professors, professionals, etc. -- these people have valuable things to contribute -- but we could function and live without them and they could *not* function and live without us. The wealthy people who rule society are absolutely dependent upon us to make their wealth for them. They produce nothing themselves, but simply take it from us by a kind of legalized robbery which is called the wage system. All wealth is produced by us and oftentimes we produce a great deal of it. A worker in a modern factory, running a piece of complex equipment, for example, will frequently produce as much as $100,000 worth of wealth in one day for which he is at best likely to get $50 wages in return as his "share".

We are actually very smart, very intelligent and very knowledgeable. We know how to do things. We know how to do the most important things in life. Civilization could not function without our detailed knowledge of our various trades and jobs. Even very knowledgeable "intellectuals" such as professors of mechanical engineering, whose information is respectable and useful, would not know how to run, say, a turret lathe and thus could not produce the actual articles which our society depends upon for use. The professor is dependent upon the work of a skilled turret lathe operator for his ideas and inventions to come to fruition. The turret lathe operator, on the other hand, could get along, not as well, but satisfactorily enough, without the professor of mechanical engineering.

WE KNOW THE SCORE

We are in much closer touch with reality than the rest of the population. For wealthy people, prolonging their control of the country and of the wealth is dependent on their lying to working people through all their newspapers, magazines, radio stations, television stations, churches and so on. They come to believe their own lies so that they are quite out of touch with the reality of existence. This is also true, to a great extent, for the professional and intellectual people who do their special jobs for the owners, who organize their universities and teach in them, who handle their law businesses, etc. We, on the other hand, though we've been trained not to trust our own judgment, generally know the score about what's going on. We have a fairly accurate picture of the world (we view it from the seamy side, too) and on the average have a greater ability to differentiate between sense and nonsense.

Does this mean that working people in RC (or outside) should glory in physical labor and disparage information, intellectual achievement or being smart? Not at all. A good education and accurate knowledge of the world on all levels, including all the good things about science, literature, music, and art should be in the possession of every working person. Undoubtedly in the future when we have a decent society people will work with their hands and also be well-educated and will lead much happier and more balanced lives as a result. Certainly it's very worthwhile for any of us from working people's background to get all the education we can, to become skilled, proficient, to take jobs as college professors, physicians and lawyers if it suits our purposes.

KEEP OUR PRIDE

But we do not have to buy the usual delusions of these people. We do not have to become ashamed of our working-class background or origins. We do not have to give up our contact with reality. It is in fact most unfortunate when some of us do, when we feel ashamed of the fact that our folks had calloused hands or that we held a long succession of dirty and difficult jobs to put ourselves through college or when we try not to let on to the neighbors that we "came up the hard way".

In the future, in a just society people will be extremely proud of the work which they do and they will study and understand philosophy at the same time they're working with their hands. Now, at least we can keep our pride in productive work while at the same time acquiring the knowledge which our opportunities allow us to grasp.

WE ARE ALMOST EVERYBODY

We are the biggest family of people in the whole population. People who work for a living are men and women, are black and white, are young and old, are composed of every ethnic group, every race. Even though a lot of us have bought the propaganda of the powers-that-be, and are divided by prejudices against women, against blacks, etc., etc., any interruption of this propaganda, any real contact between us, always shows that our real nature is to cooperate with all other people and that our actual working interests cut across all lines of race, sex, or other petty differences.

SIMILAR DISTRESSES

The distresses which we are freeing ourselves from in RC are, of course, unique to each one of us but there are some common tendencies because of the similar ways we have been treated. It's well for us working people to encourage each other to work on these. One is any feeling of being inadequate. This is not our individual problem, this is what's

313

been put on us by the society. We need to act proud against any feelings of shame at our poverty or the kind of jobs that we hold. We need to thoroughly contradict the pressure that's been put on us to "feel dumb". We need to assert our intelligence, to aggressively insist on our opinions and thinking being considered, both within the RC community and outside. We need to assume leadership roles.

It will seem hard, at first, for many working class RC'ers to believe that people with college and professional backgrounds aren't really smarter than we are. Let me say to you from my own practical experience (I came from a poor farm family and was working for wages until I was 34 years old, when RC began) that intimate association with large numbers of the doctors, lawyers, college professors, teachers, ministers, priests, and artists who have dominated the early populations of the RC communities (and who are very splendid, enlightened people) makes it very plain that there is no one any smarter than working people. You have fine minds, your thinking is clear and close to reality. If you have contrary feelings, these feelings need to be contradicted and discharged thoroughly.

NOT HELPLESS

All of us who are workers or come from a worker's background need to flatly contradict any feelings of helplessness or of powerlessness, any feeling that no matter what we do, someone else will always decide the important questions. The actual present condition in our oppressive society re-inforces these, of course. At present, people of wealth *do* decide all important questions. About the most choice we ever have in a supposedly democratic election is to decide between two equally reactionary or equally puppet-like representatives of the wealthy people as to which one will win a particular office. This powerlessness could not continue to exist, however, except as we continue to cooperate with it, continue to "agree" and act as if we were powerless because of our distress.

The entire economy cannot function for very long, nor can any wealth be produced if even a substantial number of working people refuse to cooperate. Unless workers agree to continue working, nothing productive can happen and the whole structure will come to a crunching stop.

NOT JUST POOR

It's important that we not confuse being poor with being working class. Many intellectuals are poor and lead terribly pinched lives. There are also poor people who have been so destroyed that they cannot work anymore -- large numbers of sick people, alcoholics, old people, people forced into lives of petty crime. These people are poor but they are not necessarily working class.

It's important that in insisting on full respect and a full role in RC that we not slide into any "emotional" attitude that we're more virtuous because our folks were working people or that we can look down on and deride people from middle class backgrounds. We're just exactly as virtuous or as "sinful" on the average as anyone else. What makes us different is our position in respect to the economy and in respect to the population (we are the majority and we produce the wealth). We have great power to require that society change in a positive direction.

Some few wage workers who have built strong unions, actually have adequate incomes. A very few have better incomes than most professionals, but nevertheless they are producing the wealth. They have the power because of their economic position, where the professional is a supernumary, an addition, a luxury. Unless we and the workers on the farms keep working, no one eats, no one gets a new television, the trains don't run, the trucks don't haul, the airplanes don't fly.

THE FUTURE

In the society of the future, of course, we will not only do all these things, but, we will become intellectuals as well as workers. We will teach the intellectuals to work with their hands as well. We will eliminate the drudgery, the monotony and the danger from jobs. We will use tools to the fullest to free people from drudgery instead of for super profits. We will lead informed, fulfilled lives. All of us will be workers, all of us will be intellectuals, all of us will be leaders, all of us will be in charge of our society.

Re-evaluation Counseling
And Latinos/as *

Re-evaluation Counseling is a program for individual liberation. The Re-evaluation Counseling Communities have a one-point program to use Re-evaluation Counseling to recover each one's occluded intelligence and to help others to do the same.

Re-evaluation Counseling is not, in itself, a program for social liberation. However, in our effort to achieve rationality in all ways, Re-evaluation Counselors cannot but seek to be rational about society and about the social relations of human beings. This leads inevitably to questioning the irrational relationships in existing society and to noting their effects on individuals in the installation and maintenance of distress patterns. If one is intelligent or aware, one must notice that in our present society wage workers are exploited and are treated callously, children are treated condescendingly by adults, physically handicapped people are treated condescendingly by the non-handicapped, females are treated less than fully human by males, and most vividly, people of a different skin color, race, or ethnic background are subjected to discrimination and oppression by the majority groups of the population.

The Re-evaluation Counseling Communities intend to integrate with and include people from every group of human beings in the world within the co-counseling program. In order to do this, we must come to new communities with awareness and understanding, must learn the actual conditions of life in each culture, and must apply Re-evaluation Counseling with insight and understanding. It is crucial that we develop leaders and teachers of Re-evaluation Counseling *from within each group.*

* First printed in Pensamientos No. 1 -- September, 1975

The Latino Communities in the United States are people with a rich culture and heritage. Their art, literature, music, skills, productivity, and culture have deep roots in Latin America, in the pre-Columbian cultures, in Spain, and in the territory in which they live. They have endured and survived oppression even though their lands were taken from them by force of arms and even though they have suffered discrimination, indignities, exploitation and oppression ever since.

Re-evaluation Counseling comes to the Latino Communities with respect, inviting Latinos to participate in Re-evaluation Counseling for the benefit of the whole Community as well as for the individual.

The Latino Communities will necessarily be involving themselves more and more in a struggle for their full rights, for respect, and for freedom from discrimination and persecution. Not all members of the Latino Communities are as yet agreed on programs for achievement of these goals. Many are as yet opposed to militant struggle. Others have adopted a militant program and seek to engage in organized struggle for liberation.

Progress requires the widest unity of the Mexican-American people, of the Puerto Rican people, of all Spanish language peoples. It requires that broad programs can be agreed upon that will unite all members of the group, that more militant programs be available for those who support them, but always in cooperation and communication with all members of the Community.

Re-evaluation Counseling can be useful to all people and to every individual. It enables each person to free his or her individual intelligence and bring it to bear on whatever problems the individual is facing. Whatever position one is in, whatever one's goals are, any situation will be handled better if one co-counsels regularly.

Re-evaluation Counseling can be of use to the person who militantly seeks to end oppression because it can help him or her distinguish between acting on painful emotion and distress and acting, with commitment, but intelligently, flexibly.

Re-evaluation Counseling can pinpoint the basic individual mechanism for the continuing of oppression, which is the addictive pull to invalidate someone else once one has been invalidated and hurt.

Re-evaluation Counseling highlights the importance of using validation to enable people to discharge and achieve appreciation of themselves.

The Re-evaluation Counseling Communities, as a policy, are commited to eliminating all racism from their attitudes. They are commited to including within the Communities members of all classes and all groups, including all Latino communities.

The Re-evaluation Counseling Communities stand ready to assist with all the means at their disposal with any rational projects for assisting in the liberation of the Latino Communities and in making Re-evaluation Counseling more available for their use.

As Re-evaluation Counseling becomes established in the countries of Latin America and in Spain, we will have much to learn from each other. RCers in the different countries will be encouraged in our liberation, both of our people and of ourselves as individuals.

Re-evaluation Belongs
To Young People, Too *

Children and young people are the single most important section of our population. They constitute the future of
humankind as a whole. They are, as a group, less distressed,
more reachable, quicker to grasp and use RC theory, and
more in touch with the reality of human nature. If the Re-
evaluation Counseling Communities are to attain their goals,
they must include and involve children and young people
in large numbers.

Young people who have been able to sample RC have
concluded that this must be done. They have asked to be in
classes and workshops, even though most of our present
classes and workhsops are unwieldy and too slow--moving
for them. They have worked out co-counseling with parents,
written appeals for information, participated in the few
children's and teenagers' classes that have been offered, and
in family workshops.

Still children and young people are, as yet, almost
absent and, de facto, excluded from our Communities.

This is partly and superficially because of financial
considerations. Children in general have little money and
unless their parents agree to finance their participation
require subsidy from the Community. Beyond that, the
question is raised whether we are not putting the young
person into an impossible situation if we do not see to it
that their parents are also functioning in RC so that they
have some support from their environment for their attempts
to discharge and re-evaluate.

* First printed in Upcoming No. 1 -- May, 1976

It seems to me that this must be looked at from two different viewpoints. Our experience with one-way counseling in Seattle in the '50's and '60's led us to a very firm attitude toward parents whose children we were asked to counsel. Some parents would bring a distressed child to the staff counselors expecting them to solve the "problem". Sometimes they would pay for the counseling, sometimes they would evade even that responsibility.

We found that, though the children would almost always respond to counseling, to let them go back into an atmosphere created by the parents' patterns of uncaring and attack left them in a very ambiguous position.

We learned after a number of experiences to take a very firm attitude toward parents who asked that their children be counseled. This attitude was that we would refuse to work with the child unless we had commitment from the parent to also be counseled and to attend classes and learn Re-evaluation Counseling theory and apply it. Otherwise the child could make some gains, have great hopes raised and then be sent back into a crushing, invalidating environment to despair and lose confidence in counseling as well as in hope for the future. The only exceptions that we made in that policy were times that the survival of the child required some emergency help. Even then we tried to do it without relieving the parents of responsibility. This is the attitude toward the parent, as parent.

Towards the child, apart from the parent, it seems to me we must take the attitude that they are full-fledged human beings in every way -- that they are the people of the future and so very important to the survival of all of us and to the future of the Re-evaluation Counseling Community. We must understand that they are an especially oppressed group in that adultism or parentism patterns pervade the culture, make their lives very difficult, and that this phenomenon is the principle means for the perpetuation of distress patterns in the population as a whole.

Part of the special oppression of children and young people consists, of course, of enforced dependency, the lack of resources, the lack of finances, the organized interference in their being in charge of their own lives, their not being allowed to set their own goals.

It seems to me that we have a need to carefully and thoughtfully find avenues which will open our Communities to large numbers of children and young people, including those whose parents are not participating in Re-evaluation Counseling. Rather than limit participation in RC to those whose parents are active, we can use the participation of the children as a means of reaching the parents, as has been so successfully done in the Roxbury, Massachusetts situation.

Children and young people are quick to understand RC theory, are quick to put it into practice and use it with great flexibility and deftness. Over and over again, we have had experiences with children or young people in quite desperate situations surrounded by parental patterns, who, given the support and even a minimum of theory have been able to apply this to maneuver the patterns around them sufficiently to achieve their own survival or sometimes escape from an impossible environment.

They must be given the *whole* theory, however, in language they can understand, but *complete*. Condescendingly giving them only part of the theory, or oversimplifying it will deny them the overall consistency of understanding they need. They are more ready to grasp the whole picture, in general, than are adults.

Growing Older Rationally*

In the 1950's, when RC first started and began to work well between co-counselors and with our one-way clients in Seattle, I was curious to learn what the differences in response to the co-counseling process would be from people of different ages and conditions. I had many naive negative expectations from our cultural conditioning. I thought that children would have to be of a certain age before they could think well enough to use Counseling. I supposed that deeply distressed people would be "impossible to reach". I expected that most elderly people would be too preoccupied with "being old" to take an interest in and engage in the process.

These expectations all proved ridiculous. As co-counseling and one-way counseling began to be attempted with a wider and wider spectrum of people it became clear, for example, that on the average, the younger the child was, the more functioning intelligence was at the child's disposal. Contrary appearances clearly came only from the patterned initiatives that adults extended toward children and expected them to respond to, or from the child's lack of information, resulting from the short span of experience.

Counseling "deeply disturbed" clients it became clear that, except for those whose forebrains had been physically damaged (by surgery, disease, alcohol, etc.), the most deeply distressed person was quite able to respond and use the re-emergence process of discharge and re-evaluation just to the extent that she or he had the opportunity. The real limitation here was the amount of free attention, skill, resource, and resistance-to-restimulation which the counselor could contribute to the relationship.

*First printed in Growing Older No. 1 – April, 1976

ALL OF US CONTEMPORARIES

When older clients, (in their 70's, 80's and 90's) came to classes and for one-way counseling, there was often an appearance of less free attention at first; but with very little assistance and only short-time use of the discharge process, this superficial appearance gave way to the reality of keen, aware, intelligence which could not only think, discharge, and re-evaluate well, but whose larger store of knowledge gave valuable perspective and stability in taking up and using the RC process.

As RC experience accumulated, it became evident that, from the time the forebrain functions in a developing infant till the moment of death, "We are all contemporaries". Experiences in co-counseling classes led to the discovery of this reality over and over again, to the delight of the participants. Co-counselors often came into RC feeling estranged and isolated from people of other ages, but found that their co-counseling achieved a unity and a contemporaneity with all different chronological ages.

AN INTEGRAL PART OF THE COMMUNITIES

Many older people have, by now, participated in RC over sustained periods of time. There is no question of their solid place in RC and in the RC Communities.

Their participation has not always, however, been easy or without difficulties. Many of them have dropped out for shorter or longer periods of time because of a feeling of isolation, or of facing distress which they did not find easy to work on with younger co-counselors. Health and financial problems have inhibited some older co-counselors' activity. Some of the attitudes of an oppressive society toward older people have crept into and persisted in the RC Communities.

SOME PROBLEMS

It seems to me that growing older poses some special problems that need to be faced. These fall roughly within two sets. One set is special cases of the problems which everyone in RC faces. The other set is problems which become acute in later years. Neither set concerns us only when we "pass 60", but are fears and worries for people at all ages, but which we tend to ignore or hide from until conditions force us to face them.

All of us endure the misfunctioning caused by our unique, individual distresses. As with all present human beings, considerable portions of our intelligence, awareness, zest, and ability to have good relationships, are occluded and interfered with by the accumulation of distress recordings. Here, the older person's difficulty is just like everyone else's, with perhaps the slight difference that we have had more time to accumulate distress in the larger number of years that we have lived (and there is no question that the accumulation of distress tends to snowball, that it increases in a non-linear fashion.) This difference makes it perhaps a little more urgent for us to get started (if we are new to co-counseling) and persist with our discharge and re-evaluation to lower the level of our general distress below the dangerous part of the curve, the rapid "snowballing" portion which tempts to passivity and surrender to distress. "Senility", except in the rare instances where it has a basis in the physical deterioration of the brain from disease, is simply the piling up of distress patterns to a "topple-over" or chronic point. Senility can be recovered from by discharge and re-evaluation just as any other distress.

Another group of distresses which all co-counselors are learning to face, are the distresses which are placed upon us and reinforced and restimulated by our societal institutions. These are the patterns which we have called oppression. All sections of our population in our present societies suffer from these oppressive patterns; even the people in the position of oppressors do, since their role in that relationship dehumanizes them and fills them with guilt and self-hatred. The victims of oppression endure much greater distress.

In our present socities, almost everyone is a victim of oppression in one or several ways. Children are treated very badly, just for being children, even in the best of homes. Women are invalidated, exploited and relegated to second-class citizenship. All ethnic minorities (blacks, Jews, Asians, Spanish-speaking people, etc.) are mistreated and oppressed. The handicapped, the sick, the deeply distressed, all are treated in ways which install and perpetuate distress.

Older persons are certainly victims of such special oppression. They are barred from employment. They are forced or encouraged into inactivity and uselessness. They are isolated from the life-giving contact with their families and people of other ages. They are stacked up in nursing and retirement homes. They are treated like "useless baggage" by a money-centered, profit-motivated society.

WE CAN FIGHT BACK

In these respects it is plain that older people need to begin to fight back. They need to fight back with confidence and hope. In particular, our older RCers can be leaders and initiators in this and can greatly expedite the process by their contribution of the special tools of co-counseling, tools which can lead to more effectiveness in activity, more rational programs, and to wider unity within the older persons' groups and between them and their natural allies in the other groups who are oppressed.

I think our experience in doing this will probably parallel in most respects the beginning efforts of women RCers, of black RCers, of Asian-American RCers, and so on. It will be necessary to participate fully in the general RC Community, but at the same time to meet together with other older RCers for co-counseling and consultation on the issues that people of other ages tend not to understand well.

In such older persons' caucuses, classes, and workshops we can lay out programs for ending "ageism", (that is, discrimination against, exploitation of, and oppression of, older persons in our society) both within the RC Community and outside. Many allies will be waiting for us in this struggle. Older people everywhere are beginning to organize to defend their interests and insist on humane and human treatment for themselves. The programs of the groups which are arising spontaneously are often confused or tied to the profit-making attitudes of society. RCers have a special contribution to make in helping these organizations achieve more rational programs, and seek for greater unity with other groups in the population.

NEWSLETTER A START

The appearance of *Growing Older* is an encouraging development. The efforts of Clemmie Barry and her presently small but growing groups of supporters deserve the congratulations and the assistance of all members of the RC Community.

Older people are not by any means helpless, though they can be conditioned into such an attitude by the imposition of distress if they do not have the tools to throw it off. Older people have rich resources. They are not always without economic strength. They have vast reservoirs of experience and can swing great political clout when it is needed.

I think the beginning of older persons' caucuses, support groups, and classes in RC is an excellent development. We need to be clear here, as we need to be with all other groups, that these "drawings apart" to work with each other on our common problems is not in any sense a segregation or an isolation from the other human beings in the RC Communities or outside, but is a necessary step, alternating with the fullest unity and participation in the Community and society as a whole. All groups seem to be able to think well and communicate well to other groups only if they can first meet by themselves, and in the safety of common interests and an atmosphere of commonality, work out their thinking and their approaches to the solutions to their problems, before they begin communication as a group with the larger Community and the other groups. I think we should plan on special workshops and classes as well as the continued publication and expansion of our Newsletter.

TWO REAL DIFFERENCES

In perhaps two respects older people have special problems or sharply accentuated problems different from the rest of the Community. These are: 1) The physical deterioration involved in aging; 2) The relative imminence of death (now postponed for most people for at least a score of years more than a generation ago.)

It seems to me that these are real problems to be faced and not hidden from behind euphemisms or hollow rationalizations. Up to the present moment human beings have inevitably deteriorated physically as they become older, and have eventually died. The existence of these phenomena must be taken into account if we are to devise, on the one hand, ameliorating processes that will spare us most or all of the distress involved in these occurrences, and on the other hand, allow us to go beyond the present frontiers of thinking and find ways to prevent or reverse the aging process, and perhaps eventually to postpone death indefinitely.

In the article *Is Death Necessary?* I have conjectured that physical immortality should be possible to attain by examining the processes which lead to aging and to death, and devising means for interrupting these. When I first conjectured this there was great emotional resistance to the idea. Apparently the chronic fear of death which has been installed on all of the population led my listeners to feel intensely afraid to consider that what they had always assumed to be true (that "everyone must die") is not necessarily true. This is the familiar upset of any person who steps outside of a chronic pattern. They feel distress on "leaving the pattern", while inside it they are numb and "resigned".

NO ROOM FOR GLOOM

It seems to me that to take a positive attitude toward these conjectures is important. To do otherwise would disarm ourselves and invite us to be swamped in hopelessness, discouragement, and other kinds of negative patterns. It is true that there is not a workable way of preventing the aging process yet. It is also true that we do not have in hand any concrete way of postponing death indefinitely. But to simply accept that as "final" is to lose the fight ahead of time, a fight that perhaps could be won by a consistent attempt to explore alternatives to the "weary acceptance".

It is not that we should delude ourselves about the reality. The reality may very well be that most of us who are reading the Newsletter will inevitably deteriorate physically through the aging process and die, before the necessary research can take place and changes be made. (I, in particular, must be realistic about this, since I am almost 60 years old and have had one severe heart attack and three experiences of surgery in the past year.) However, to keep open the possibility that aging and death, which seem so obviously wrong and unproductive for beings possessed of rational intelligence, can be prevented, will encourage the research and the positive search for a solution to go much faster than it would otherwise. In the words of a familiar religious sect in this country: "Millions now living may never die."

I think, however, that the main need of us older RCers in this period is to get together, discuss with each other, work out good programs, insist on our full place in the general RC Community, and take a full share of the responsibility for the progress of all humanity toward re-emergence, toward complete mastery of the environment and the full flowering of our human potential.

I have no doubt in my mind at all that "There is at least one elegant solution to any real problem."

An Important Clarification*

One of the incidental, but important, results of the
Liberation Workshops was the clarification of co-counseling
between people coming from different sides of relationships
which are oppressive in our society; co-counseling between
blacks and whites, between women and men, between
Latinos and Anglos, between adults and children.

We have understood for some time that it is correct for
an RCer to stay in the role of "counselor" in any situation
involving distress or restimulation, that this is the responsible,
human attitude. We have agreed to try not to approach
situations as "clients" in everyday life, to not put other
people in the role of listeners to or handlers of our distresses.
We try not to act on our distresses or restimulations or bring
them up to others.

The only times we allow ourselves to be clients are when
it is our turn in a co-counseling session to be counseled, when
the second person has clearly agreed to be our counselor.
Even then, it is part of our commitment that we not work on
material that is distressing or invalidating to the particular
person that is our counselor. When we plan to introduce
a new person to co-counseling, for example, we plan to give
him or her a session and then invite the person to be counselor to us, but we choose carefully what we bring up and
how we discharge on it when we are client so that the new-
comer will not be frightened or invalidated by our performance.

Yet Third World RCers at workshops or in classes with
white RCers often find themselves asked to listen to a wide

*First printed in Present Time No. 19 – April, 1975

gamut of restimulations from the whites, both as client and as counselor, both in and out of sessions. These range from the blatant "You frighten me! (shudder, shudder). You won't rape me, will you?" kind of insult to the "subtle" "I've always admired black people's appearance. You're so exotic"; from the "I feel so guilty for the handicaps you people have endured. I eat Mexican food every chance I get" to the "I'm so glad, glad, glad, you're here! *We've* needed *you!*" to the "There was a Japanese girl in our class in Junior High."

All these behaviors have in common the exhibition of the white's restimulation to the Third World person, the treating of the Third World person as a stereotype, the failure to see him or her as the distinctive human individual he or she is. They are clear indications of the depth of racism that has been imposed on whites in our culture and of the unawareness which our guilt and other distress continues to use to hide it from us.

Usually, the white RCer who has been offensive in this way but has managed to discharge somewhat at the expense of restimulating the Third World RCer, will feel relieved and a little triumphant at having "worked on" his or her racism. He or she may even expect the Third World RCer to be grateful or appreciative for his or her having done this "difficult thing" in the interests of eliminating racism and achieving unity. Needless to say, the Third World RCer at this point is feeling pretty hopeless about whites in general and white RCers in particular, and is probably considering dropping out of RC.

"But", says the white RCer, when this is explained, "I couldn't help being restimulated, and I needed to work on what was on top." This, of course, is *not* so. The restimulation may be unavoidable, but to give in to it and exhibit it in this situation is pure irresponsibility and not co-counseling. This view of co-counseling is a caricature of real RC theory and policy, not only in these special cases, and leads to low-level counseling under any conditions.

"But, but, but. . ." continues the white RCer's pattern, "If we don't co-counsel on these things, how can we get rid of our racism, how can we break down the barriers between us?" The answer, of course, is for white RCers to be clients on the subject of racism *with a white counselor*, preferably with a very sharp, determined white counselor who will lead the client from an incident of being oppressed himself or herself in some way to an incident of opposing or refusing to collude with white racism and, only then, to an incident of colluding with, or remaining silent in the face of, white racism. We have learned that the safety of the first two steps by-passes and contradicts the occluding guilt sufficiently for the white client to reach and discharge the basic content of racism distress, which turns out to be terror or deep grief at being forced by society to accept such inhumanness.

Similarly, a woman should not have to listen to a man work on his sexism. He can do this with male counselors.

Adults should not "dump" their distreses about children on children when children and adults co-counsel (or any other time). Physically handicapped RCers should not have to counsel unhandicapped RCers on their "feelings" or "attitudes" about handicaps. This is a general rule for co-counseling between members of any groups in our society which play opposite roles in oppressive or discriminatory relationships enforced by the society.

Should white RCers, on the other hand, undertake to be respectful, permissive counselors to Third World RCers as they exhibit and discharge their distress and feelings about whites (including their stereotyping of that particular counselor) and about racism, and never insist on a turn back on the same material? Should male RCers listen respectfully and indefinitely with full counseling skills and support to the grievances and distress of women clients about men, the particular male counselor, and sexism, without ever turning the tables? Should adult and parent RCers listen with respect and attention to all the complaints of a child about grownups, including the counselor, without feedback then or later?

Yes. Yes. Yes.

A white co-counselor at the Liberation Workshop said that co-counselors from the oppressing groups should do this because they are "beholden" to them, that they owed this to Third World, women, or child RCers. This is an expression of guilt, however, and is not a good enough reason.

Yes. Yes. Yes. For one good, overwhelming reason.

Because it works. For a member of an oppressing group (white, male, adult, etc.) to listen with respect and without reaction to, and to counsel well, a member of the oppressed group of the relationship *is to contradict all distresses in this area* and will lead to discharge (then sometimes, but, hopefully, usually later) and re-emergence. For a member of an oppressed group (Third World, female, child, etc.) to be listened to and counseled well and with respect and no feedback by a member of the oppressing group *is to contradict all distresses in this area* and will lead to discharge (later sometimes, but hopefully, right in the session) and to re-emergence.

Is this "fair" asks the cornered pattern? There should be nothing "fair" in our treatment of patterns. It is fair and positively helpful to the humans involved and begins to undo the enormous unfairness of the past.

Some co-counselors from oppressor groups may not yet be able to hold this correct attitude toward Third World persons, women, or children, but they should not attempt to relate in RC to these people until they can.

These are concrete guidelines toward the wonderful warmth and unity between all RCers of every group which we saw beginning to emerge at the Liberation Workshops.

An Essential Part
Of Re-emergence *

   The Re-evaluation Counseling Communities have come to realize that our efforts to go against the patterns of discrimination and oppression in the culture are really fundamental and essential parts of the process of re-emergence for all of us. In addition to discharging old distresses left on us by bad experiences in infancy and childhood, we must interrupt the social processes with which we inflict new hurts and invalidations upon each other daily if we wish to progress toward full re-emergence.

   Each step in interrupting oppressive patterns has revealed more oppressiveness in our usual relationships and behavior than we suspected in the beginning. Insistent criticism by women RCers of male sexist attitudes in classes, workshops and literature led to critical inquiry into why black RC students tended to drop out of classes. The unaware racism thus exposed led to realizations that other non-white groups were also being treated less than well within our Community, not often with open, invalidating racism, but very often with stereotyping that failed to accept them as the unique, individual humans that we all are. Our "usual" attitudes toward older people, toward children, etc. began to be seen to all suffer from the same warping. We are coming to realize that   our society and culture seek to divide us in every possible way that we can be divided and have each group cooperate in oppressing each other group.

   I would like to say to all Asians and Asian-Americans on behalf of the entire International RC Community, that you are most wholeheartedly welcome in Re-evaluation Counseling. The Community apologizes for the lingering

* First printed in Asian-American No. 2 -- October, 1975

remnants of stereotyping and other expressions of racism which you may still meet on occasion from the remaining distresses of other RCers. There is no excuse for it, but we do apologize and have determined to free ourselves from it in the shortest possible time. The Communities as a whole, as an official policy, are committed to wiping out racism and oppressive attitudes, not only inside the Re-evaluation Counseling Communities, but in society at large as well. We are only just beginning to think effectively about how to solve this problem both in RC and out, but we are committed to doing it and we will continue to progress in that direction.

The Community expresses appreciation to all the present Asian-American co-counselors for their persistence in using and leading Re-evaluation Counseling to the extent they have.

We realize that separate caucuses, separate workshops, and co-counseling with other Asian and Asian-American co-counselors are necessary to have the safety with each other to think through some of these questions and work out the necessary programs. These will be supported in every possible way, including financial, by the Communities as a whole. All Asian-American RCers are also welcome in every activity of Re-evaluation Counseling. We look forward to their growing participation in and leadership of, not only the Asian-American groups, but the entire RC Community.

Acting Against Racist Attitudes
In the RC Communities *

The Liberation workshops, of course, were an outstanding event. We used up a lot of our outreach resources but we managed to get together a very significant group of blacks, who are black and who are RCers also, led by people who are RC leaders as well as black leaders; a very significant group of Puerto Ricans who are RCers as well as Puerto Ricans and are leaders of RC as well; of Chicanos who are leaders in Chicano movements as well as in RC; four Asian-Americans; two American Indians (they were a very important ingredient). For the first time we held a Jewish Caucus, which began a very important process of examination and emergence of the issues of Jewish oppression and liberation, a caucus which has had many repercussions since.

There is no question that once we start tackling it, once we get something workable going, eliminating racism is an integral part of co-counseling, even if our efforts were purely intuitive to begin with. Everybody's eyes are brighter once we have actually *done* something about racism. Third World people feel that RC just may belong to them too, they see some possible hope in RC, once they have seen a serious attempt to confront racism in RC.

Whites lift their heads a little higher, beginning to realize that racism was something that was forced on them when they were young, that they can get rid of it instead of sulking and hiding their feelings from themselves because they don't know what to do with them. Whites often haven't realized that they have been broadcasting racism.

*Excerpts from the Pacific Palisades Workshop -- September 13, 1975

Once the issue has been confronted and some work done the Third Worlders can talk to the white RCers and point out that there are other ways to greet a Third Worlder than the typical ways they have run into at workshops, that they can be looked at as individual human beings instead of as stereotypes. We have a collection of some of this stereotyping that Third Worlders run into: "How do you do? I am *so glad* that you are here", "We need *you* at this workshop" (both in condescending tones) (Laughter), "We're friends!" (said with nauseous sentiment), "I eat Mexican food every time I get a chance!", "We had a Japanese girl in our class in Junior High School!" (both said in eager, self-congratulatory tones).

This stereotyping business hits our Third World RCers in the face all the time. We can begin to cut through that, begin to see it for what it is.

White RCers are asking, "Well, until we get rid of it, what can we do? It will take a long time."

We don't need to wait. It is going to take some work to get the racism all out of our pink skins because it was put in there very heavily; awful things were forced upon us and they hurt deeply, but we don't have to act upon them any more. We don't have to go on sounding like either a racist or a chintzy apologetic.

There are guides for how to act. How do you treat a Third Worlder? How? Like a person! How do you treat a person? You love her or him.

Y—, come on up front. Let us show them how to treat a Third Worlder. (She comes to the front.)

Hi! (Said very warmly and lovingly--he holds out his arms.)

(Laughing) *You are doing this because I am a Third Worlder.*

I wouldn't do it just because I'm delighted with you, would I?

Besides I am exotic looking--I know.

Tell the rest of it.

(Laughter) Eccch! (Laughter)

You thought of something else. What?

(Laughter) You think Asian women make good wives because they're very subservient. That's not true! (Much laughter)

More.

I remind you of obedient maids and housekeepers. Wah! (She cries a long time.) You like me just because I am a nurse. I've been told by whites that only the nurses among Orientals are good. (Cries.)

What are you thinking?

(Cries a long time) I was thinking about my experience with the whole restimulation of people in RC being afraid to be affectionate to me. One person in particular. That time had a very restimulative influence.

What happened that time?

You want me to talk about it?

Please do.

I feel like I am gossiping.

Just say some nameless co-counselor.

I came by to talk about starting an Asian RC class. I didn't feel like I should have to beg for it. It's something that the Community needs--something to have so that a lot of Asian people will not drop out of counseling. (Cries)

I have often felt discouraged that I am the only Asian person in the class, or in the Community of 300 or 400 people, or the only Third World person at a workshop. I didn't think that I should have to tell these things again. These things are just so obvious. (Cries) I didn't think that I would have to argue for everything, to give reasons why it is important to have an Asian class or a Third World class, or even to have to ask permission to do it. It's not fair to have to ask permission to do what is right and what's needed. The restimulation was heavy, and the fear. When I started to go, all of the somewhat supportive verbal statements that I had heard were totally invalidated by a very abrupt goodbye. (Shiver)

Again. (He copies the shiver.) Let it come. (Y— cries a long time.) You are doing fine.

(Stamps her foot and shouts loudly) It's not enough just to give workshops on racism. It's not enough to talk about it. It's not enough to give a day long workshop on racism to all the experienced, very strong co-counselors who are able to move through that material, and yet at the same time, in a very basic, loving and caring way (Cries) NOT BE THERE! All the workshops in the world wouldn't solve it. Not being there as a human is so basic a disillusion--it's so basic!

Talk about it. Spell it out.

(Shiver) The physical warmth is the sign of being supportive. Even in hugs it is easy to detect someone who is scared of you--it's hugging in a very distant way--

Like, "I never hugged an Asian before"? (Laughter)

The physical contact is the most important way of communicating that persons really love and care and are working against their racist material. The tension is going to be there, and the physical contact is going to bring it up, but discharge on it right then. It's much easier to take your discharge than to just be approached and given one quick hug while hearing "It's nice to see you again" (said in a drooping voice) or having you avoid eye contact even in appreciation of what the Asian person looks like. It's very basic RC theory to give aware *hugs to anybody. It's not even especially for Third World people, it's to anybody in the Community or out of the Community, friends and family and acquaintances even. That's one guideline for you.*

(To the workshop) If you are busy really being loving you can't act racist.

That's right.

So if you want to know how to stop acting racist, start being really loving and that will guide you on to how to act until you can get rid of the racism distress.

Yes. It's okay to discharge while you are hugging, too. That is much more human than not discharging and going through the motions of caring and affection. It's easy to detect that kind of pretense. The facial expression and the eyes give a lot of information as to what that person is thinking behind the actual words. To just say all these polite things and to not really feel them is to cover up a lot of the racist patterns. If you care about people you can mean what you say. All these other ways of talking communicate to us that we are not good enough, or "you remind me of a maid" or "you give me an idea of the exotic east" or any other kind of racist pattern.

Saying polite things without really feeling what you are saying (or discharging on the feelings that you can't help) is sort of putting sticky sweet icing on top of all the bad material that's really there.

Thank you. That's a lecture that I couldn't have delivered. Is there more you want to say before you sit down?

Yes. The other thing is that right now with the growth of the Third World Community I see a need for enough Third World classes to provide enough safety within the RC Community. What's happened is that several people here entered different classes and have been the only Third Worlder there. In those classes a lot of the very subtle racism should have been worked through first. From my experience I know that a lot of Asian and other Third World people have left such classes because the work hadn't been done.

It's not overtly said that "we don't like you in this class" but the actions give that impression. Or maybe not that "we don't like you in this class" but "you're different and we are scared of you". It's hard to function then. It's hard to discharge or to work through a lot of distress when you don't feel safe. Safety is one of the things that anybody in a class needs and particularly so a Third World person who is the only one there. That's just some more of what it is like in the society already. We are vastly outnumbered and the need to survive is so great. When you go into a class and everybody else in that class is white, there it is again. You face the added need to survive in that class, wanting to allow the feelings of fear, but feeling that one's identity of being an Asian-American is going to be totally obliterated in the class or in the community.

Again, I think basic warmth and attention and affection and being very careful of what's being said is crucial. In a class I was in, (I was feeling very vulnerable,

344

and hadn't worked through a lot of my material about being told heavily distressed things) there was a discussion about minority races and it was just enough to trigger a restimulation. If I hadn't been clear on what was happening, and hadn't worked through some distress already, that would have been enough for me to leave the class.

I am saying that you don't have to be so guarded that you become unaware of what's happening. There are certain things that need to be checked into, you know, like actually having the class and really picking out the people with racist patterns and working on them, in the class. (Shiver)

May I say something here?

Yes.

(To the workshop) Unless we say something it's bound to happen. The question has now been raised, white people are trying to think about it. The first thing they'll feel like doing is to rush up to one of the Third Worlders and start apologizing.

Yes. (Laughter)

Well, that's just some more stereotyping, it's just some more of the same thing in another guise. Do not lean your feelings on the Third Worlder. Go grab another pink-skinned person and have a session out of the Third Worlders. earshot. You can make all kinds of mistakes there, in a session with another white, but don't grind your mistakes on the Third Worlder. When you are around the Third Worlder, be loving, be human, be warm, be accepting -- just exactly the way human beings should be treated.

Whether they are Third World or not.

345

Right.

The whole thing of categorizing, categorizing white people, Third World people, the Jewish people is an artificial labeling. Temporarily, maybe it's necessary to regain a lot of the human identity or the cultural identity that's been lost, but actually what a Third World person is is just a person. Anybody, a white person, or Jewish, etc. are all just people. We are all very much the same.

Which doesn't mean that the groups don't need to caucus separately to gain their strength and identity and work out their programs and *then* communicate with each other. The goal of it is our separate identities and our overall unity.

Thank you very much. I didn't know I was going to get all that when I asked you up.

I'd like to tell everybody. . .

How to Free Oneself
From Unaware Racism *

We have known for a long time, and from many indications, that the white racism which afflicts the entire white
population of the United States also afflicts our Re-evaluation Counseling Communities. This shows up in the U.S.
population in the aware and unaware attitudes towards
blacks, Asians, Latinos, and American Indians, and the very
similar anti-Semitic attitudes toward Jews (with analogs in
England with attitudes toward Indians and blacks, and in
France toward Arabs). It persists in our Re-evaluation
Counseling Communities in unaware racist attitudes.

Our efforts to include ethnic minority people in our RC
Communities and to put RC skills in the hands of the black,
Chicano and Amerindian communities and movements, have
had only scattered successes in spite of good intentions and
considerable efforts. Continuing unaware racist attitudes
on the part of white RCers must be the reason. Our
treasured few black, Asian, Chicano, Amerindian and Puerto
Rican RCers have left us in no doubt that they feel this is so.

I have been urging people at workshops for a long time
to "work on and get rid of your unaware racism" but no
great successes have occurred. Many people have felt guilty
and apologetic, but that has led only to discomfort, defensiveness, and new evasions of the issue rather than to discharge and improvement.

Finally, a workshop member at La Scherpa XXX raised
the key question. "You keep saying work on it, " he said,
"but you don't say *how. How* do you discharge unaware

*A Talk at La Scherpa XXX – December, 1973

racism? All I've been able to do is feel more guilty and that doesn't help."

At last perhaps the light begins to dawn. *How* indeed!

Many painful emotions glue down racist attitudes, but the stopper-in-the-bottle that has kept us from discharging is guilt. How can we contradict guilt and begin to discharge? How can we get this material up to awareness?

First Draft of a Manifesto
On Jewish Liberation *

1) JEWS ARE HUMAN BEINGS, PRECISELY AND IN EVERY RESPECT. Their many different cultures contain some common elements that are different than other cultures, as is true of any human culture. Some of these elements are rich and human, a treasure for all humans. Some are patterns left by oppression and need to be resisted and discharged. Jews must expect and require full respect from non-Jews and from each other. Non-Jews must take the ending of all anti-Semitism (oppression and discrimination against Jews) as their own cause, pursued in their own interests.

2) World-wide oppression of Jews is a fact. It is a social institution perpetuated by oppressive societies for profit and exploitation and is used to victimize all other oppressed groups in the populations as well as the Jews themselves.

3) Cultural institutions and traditions (myths, religious hatreds, ridicule, stereotyping, etc.) for the promulgation of anti-Semitism, though founded in economic oppression, have a certain existence and momentum of their own, once started, because of the contagious character of distress patterns, and must be challenged directly at all levels, contradicted and discharged on, as well as exposed as the agents of economic and political oppression.

4) A peculiar form of oppression has been developed and directed toward the Jewish people by the oppressive ruling classes of the societies in which they have lived and has been internalized and institutionalized by the social institu-

*First printed in Ruah Hadashah No. 1 -- July, 1976

tions and official leaderships of the Jewish communities. Their oppression is basically identical in purpose and effect with all other oppressed, but its form has served to isolate the Jews from their natural allies, the other oppressed peoples, and has made them peculiarly vulnerable to genocide and extermination.

The essential elements of the special oppression of Jews are as follows:

a) For two thousand years they have been denied a national homeland, a national existence, a base from which to organize their struggle for survival in a world in which all nations have battled to conquer each other and exterminate each other's peoples or cultures.

b) Under a continuing, overhanging threat of extermination, maintained by institutions for the continuing promulgation of murderous anti-Semitic propaganda among the general populations, (institutions which are alternately official and unofficial, but which never cease to operate in oppressive societies), Jews are offered the hope of survival if they will cooperate with the oppressive forces and serve as their agents (officials, administrators, cultural leaders, merchants, bankers) in the oppression of the general population. Forced into this role, the Jewish communities and individuals serve as "visible agents" for the oppressing forces.

c) As an inducement to and in assistance of carrying out this "visible agent" role during the periods in which this role is forced upon them, Jews are allowed and encouraged to maintain and develop traditions of being a chosen people, traditions of excellence, of scholarship, of high culture, of scientific, artistic, and economic success for some members of the community. (The majority of Jews, of course, continue to be economically oppressed and culturally deprived during such periods, oppressed both by the general oppressive society and by its agents with the Jewish community.)

d) In this role, as visible agents of the oppressors, the Jewish communities become the focus of the unthinking resentments and hatreds of the oppressed peoples which the anti-Semitic propaganda directs towards them. They are portrayed as the actual oppressors, described as a "secret conspiracy", the Jews who are actually capitalists are portrayed as representatives of the Jews rather than representatives of the capitalists, and the resentment, hatred, and determination to throw off oppression of the oppressed is turned against the Jews rather than against the real oppressors.

e) As the resistance of the oppressed reaches a level that seems to threaten open revolt, the "support" and "protection" afforded Jews officially by the oppressing classes is withdrawn, the most open incitement to violence against the Jews is encouraged, anti-Semitism is stepped up or made the official policy, anti-Semitic administrations "win" elections or are installed, and the Jewish communities are forced into a "scapegoat" role and are blamed for all the ills of oppression. Traditionally, they are deprived of civil rights, deported, their property plundered, their institutions defamed, individual and mass murders are perpetuated, and extermination is threatened. The most familiar example of the turn to the "scapegoat" role are the pogroms in the "Pale" of Eastern Europe, and the concentration camps and gas ovens of Hitler Germany.

f) The surviving remnants of the "scapegoat" period are welcomed in new places of exile as martyrs or "apologized to" officially in the original country. They are assisted somewhat to rebuild communities and are once again encouraged to resume the role of "visible agents" of the oppressors of the country they are now in and the cycle begins once more.

g) Individual Jews have supported, been martyred for, and led almost every liberation movement of other people that they have had contact with, and some of these liberation movements have been successful. They have not led to the liberation of the Jewish people involved in a particular country, however, in part because of lack of a correct policy for *Jewish liberation.* This has, in the past, apparently been too difficult for Jewish leaders to formulate because of the depth of distress conditioning imposed on all Jews in this area. Non-Jewish liberationists have not faced the special nature of Jewish oppression and have not thought clearly enough in this area either. The formulation of a correct analysis of and policy for the situation is at present a key task for all liberation-minded people, Jews and non-Jews alike.

h) Isolation of the Jewish people from the other oppressed peoples is the key element in Jewish oppression. Forcing the Jews to identify themselves with the institutions of oppression in order to survive is a major factor in producing this isolation. The internalized oppression acts on the Jews themselves to turn away from daring to seek unity with others. The institutions of the Jewish "Establishment" and its leaders come to have a vested interest in preserving the isolation in terms of prestige, leadership, and jobs, and reinforce the isolation by cultural and religious injunctions.

i) The remarkable achievements of many individual Jews and of the Jewish culture are achievements of their humanness, operating through the slender opportunities afforded them, rather than of their Jewishness. The desperate pressure and compulsive success patterns transmitted to many members of each new generation of Jews by the Jewish culture and institutions and by parental distress patterns is actually a hindrance to achievement. The essence of being Jewish is being oppressed. One is not born Jewish. The rich tradition and culture is transmitted within the context of chronic patterns that distort reality. Isolation, fear of annihilation, self-denial and shame distort the use, understanding and effect of the fine culture.

5) Israel, promised to be the long-needed national homeland for the Jewish people, was sponsored and set up by American and British imperialism, strictly within the tradition of being a visible agent of the oppressors. Israel was allowed to come into existence on the basis of plans by the British and American imperialists that it would serve as an armed repressor of the liberation struggles of the Arabs. Arabs were driven from their homes in Palestine in a ruthless armed expropriation. The struggles of the oppressed Arabs, previously directed toward social change and becoming masters in their own lands, was successfully diverted to hatred of the Jews and of Israel. Armed conflicts were precipitated which kept the Israeli dependent on the British-American imperialists for arms, and allowed the most reactionary Arab regimes to arm themselves against their own people on the pretext of arming against Israel with arms alternatively supplied by the British-American governments or by the Russian government.

6) Now that heavily-armed reactionary regimes which the imperialists can deal with directly are solidly entrenched in most of the Arab states, and now that the revolutionary fervor of the Arab people has been temporarily distorted into hatred of Israel, a "scapegoat" role is being prepared for Israel.

7) The survival of Israel depends upon a change of policy, a change to becoming the champion of the poor Arabs against the oppressive Arab regimes and their imperial masters. This will be extremely difficult because of the accumulation of distress from past policies, *but it is possible*. Any other policy will simply perpetuate the insecurity of Israel, will keep it a pawn in the imperialist rivalries of the United States and Russia.

8) The continued existence of Israel as a nation, as a national homeland for all Jews and as a base for Jewish struggle for survival and against oppression, must be actively supported by all progressives and all oppressed peoples everywhere. This does not require ignoring or defending the in-

justice perpetrated upon the Palestine Arabs by their expulsion from their ancestral homelands in order to establish Israel. This remains a clear injustice and must be rectified. Israel is a no worse case in this regard, however, than any other present nation or national homeland, all of which were established by robbery and, frequently, genocide, of the original peoples by the invaders. (The United States and the American Indians, for example.)

A rational solution (perhaps a multi-national state) can be found which will rectify the injustice to the Palestinian Arabs and preserve Israel as a Jewish nation and national homeland.

9) The effective tools for eliminating distress patterns, both individual and social, through discharge of painful emotion and the following re-evaluation, will be a necessary and important part of the processes of:

a) Working out a clear policy for Jewish liberation.

b) Achieving working unity with all other oppressed peoples and liberation forces.

c) Ending of anti-Semitism and all oppression of Jews, as part of the ending of all oppression.

A Policy in the Making*

The publication of the "manifesto" and the two articles by Sheila Katz and their circulation in the RC Communities has had the desired effect in that discussion of Jewish oppression and of a correct policy for countering it has developed in many areas. The discussion has been most intense among Jewish RCers, as would be expected, but there has been a substantial amount of involvement on the part of gentile RCers as well. The material in this issue of the newsletter reflects only a small part of the questioning, discussion, and beginnings of education that have taken place.

ALL RCERS SHOULD BE INVOLVED

Should gentile RCers, and gentiles in general, be involved in the discussion and evolution of a correct policy for Jewish liberation, both inside and outside of RC? This is one issue that we can deal with firmly at this point. There has been opposition to this, resentment at times, but I think the answer must be an emphatic "yes!"

It is true that gentile RCers will often bring a good deal of ignorance and even unaware anti-Semitism into the discussion; but their involvement and participation is essential just in order to reveal these ignorances and these patterns. Participation will lead to the confusions being challenged and eliminated.

Such involvement in discussion is also crucial for this discussion to be effective, just as the involvement of gentiles in active support for Jewish liberation is essential. It is essential, first to counter and contradict one of the specific

*First printed in Ruah Hadashah No. 1 – July, 1976

characteristics of Jewish oppression itself -- the isolation of Jews from their natural allies. It is essential in the second place in order that the aware and unaware anti-Semitism among the gentile population (and among gentile RCers) be rooted out thoroughly by challenge, exposure, discharge and re-evaluation.

It is understandable that there have been voices challenging and resenting the writing of the first draft of the "manifesto" by a gentile. Some have correctly compared it with whites discussing with blacks what to do about black liberation or men advising women on women's liberation. There is a danger of unawareness and patronizing in all these and it must be watched for and challenged.

There is a third essential factor here, however. The internalizing of Jewish oppression is so intense and with such deep roots that there are likely to be areas in the evolution of a correct policy that are very difficult for Jews themselves to think about, where the "outside the pattern" viewpoint of concerned and thoughtful gentile RCers may very well be helpful. The assistance is well worth the risk.

This article itself, in which I continue to offer summary viewpoints about the development of an effective Jewish liberation policy on all fronts, is intended to be an example of this. Just as the draft of the manifesto has been criticized vigorously by almost all Jewish RCers who have participated in the discussion, what I am saying in this present article will undoubtedly be subjected to very critical analysis and dissent. Part of what I am saying presently may be revealed as incorrect as a result. I intend to continue to speak out, however, and I intend to vigorously defend any of the positions which still seem to me rational after criticism. I will refuse to yield on any of them on any basis such as "thinking about this should be left to Jews".

I think it is crucial that all gentile RCers put their best thinking to these issues. I invite them to. I hope all Jewish readers of this newsletter will invite gentile RCers to participate, *not in all discussions*, because it is essential for safety and freedom that many discussions of these issues take place only in the presence of Jews, but *in occasional discussions* where the opinions of the Jewish caucuses and gather-ins are presented to the whole RC Community. These should be thought about and questioned by the gentile members of the Community and only accepted by the whole Community when there is a general consensus on their correctness.

In summary, I think, for general reasons and because of the special isolating nature of Jewish oppression, that the evolving of a correct policy for Jewish liberation requires the participation of non-Jews.

THE POSITIVE VALUES OF BEING JEWISH

The most common and, I think, most important criticism of the "Manifesto" was that it was too negative about the nature of being Jewish. Many felt that it treated being Jewish as if it were all oppression and patterns, and neglected to affirm and appreciate the treasures of Jewish culture and Jewish life. I think this is a correct criticism. The ethical, moral, familial, and pro-human values of the Jewish cultures and traditions need to be appreciated fully and explained in detail to Jews and non-Jews alike. The commitment to righteousness and the tradition of living as an example of appreciation of, and caring for, all humans is of long standing and is a valuable model to all peoples. The positive sides of being Jewish need to be celebrated, explained, and demonstrated.

I think it is crucial, however, that the element of isolation not be accepted in this area any more than in any other. These treasures of Jewishness should be held out for all to participate in and all to emulate as a contribution of Jews and Jewish culture to the general community, both of RC and the society at large. To say this can contradict some of the internalized distress of isolation and will "feel" to some Jewish RCers as if I am challenging the "right to exist as Jews", but I think that with some discharge, my position will be seen to be the correct one. The fears installed by isolation can very easily appear as fears of *being included*, fears of *not* being separate, fears of losing one's identity, as any chronic pattern tends to appear as its opposite. In my opinion separateness and isolation must be challenged here as well as everywhere else. The richness of the Jewish cultures, the good things about Judaism and the importance of Israel as a national homeland for the Jewish people would, correctly, be viewed as contributions to the whole world's culture.

AT LEAST THREE SEPARATE, THOUGH RELATED, ISSUES

I think that many contributions to the discussion have made it clear that in formulating a correct policy we must deal with at least three broad areas. It seems plain that, in reality, being Jewish is a phenomenon distinct from, though connected to, Judaism as a religion, and from the existence of Israel as the national homeland for all Jewish people. Many leaders of the Jewish religious establishments might insist that the first two are one; the present leaders of Israel might insist all three are one phenomenon; but I think it is plain that in Jewish lives and thinking as well as in interaction with the whole society that they are three separate phenomena.

Large numbers of RC Jews identify themselves as being Jewish, and either possess to begin with, or recover after discharge, a strong sense of Jewish identity, who have little sense of participation in Judaism as a religion. Judaism as a religion does accept converts who may call themselves Jews but whose cultural background and thinking is quite distinct from that of "birthright" Jews and this is a real phenomenon even though such converts at present are few in number. By far the greatest number of Jews in the world are not Israelis but are technically full-fledged (though often oppressed and discriminated against) citizens of the United States, the Soviet Union, and other countries where they live, even though they support the existence of Israel as a homeland and feel strong ties of sympathy and culture with it.

Once we separate these phenomena for analysis it needs to be said that they are, of course, closely connected and interrelated and each must be examined in context with the other two.

BEING "JEWISH"

The "draft manifesto" said that "the essence of being Jewish is being oppressed". Both agreement and disagreement have been expressed on this point. It seems to me that most of the disagreement has been a reaction to the lack of a positive affirmation of the values of Jewish culture, which was discussed above. I think the crucial element in the statement is correct *about the present status of Jews*. In the future, when oppression has ended, being Jewish should and will be a matter of choice. Under present conditions this choice is lacking. Jews who attempted to "assimilate" in the past, to give up their identities as Jews in order to merge with the culture of the majority of the people where they were living, were pressured to do so by oppression, discrimination, and fear and were in most instances prevented from doing so by the same oppression, discrimination, and fear. It seems to me that in a future, rational society Jews must have a free choice to continue with a developing Jewish culture or adopt another culture or (much more likely) make a rich Jewish contribution to a general culture to which all no-longer-oppressed peoples will make significant contributions. It seems to me that the good things of the Jewish cultures must, on any rational basis, be open for sharing by any other people who wish to participate in them, and that resistance to this as a policy for the future can spring only from external and internal patterns of isolation rooted in oppression and the resulting distress.

JUDAISM

Judaism is, of course, one of the great world religions. It is the straight line development of the early Hebrew religion from which also stem Islam and Christianity. (These three "Religions of the Book" have much of the Old Testament in common). Many of its merits are common to Christianity and Islam and it has a number of outstanding unique values, among which I would place first the emphasis on learning and the search for rational solutions. Judaism deserves respect and appreciation in the first place (as does any religion when viewed properly) as a channel of human beings' intuitive desire to associate themselves together and commit themselves toward the upward trend in the universe, toward being "good". It deserves special appreciation for its development of a vast written literature, for its traditions of learning, and for its role as an uniter and comforter and strengthener of a great people enduring long-term, and often devastating, oppression.

Again, here, I think that a rational attitude toward Judaism both by its adherents and by other people is to appreciate it, to make its treasures available to all, and to refuse to let it act in an isolating manner. I think it is wrong to treat it as something only its present adherents can understand and appreciate, but instead urge that its precepts and tenets be widely circulated for acceptance. This may seem to imply that synagogue congregations should become proselytizing bodies seeking to recruit gentiles to the religion of Judaism. In a sense I think that this is exactly what should happen to counter the old patterns of isolation and withdrawal. It seems plain, however, that being Jewish, though related to the practice of Judaism as a religion, is in the present conditions of the world a cultural phenomenon. It must be dealt with outside of the confines of Judaism as a religion as well as inside.

ISRAEL

One basic position in the "manifesto" has gone unquestioned so far in the discussion but is, of course, at controversy in the wide world. This is that the existence of Israel as a national homeland for the Jews must be defended by all people everywhere regardless of any injustice involved in its founding or any wrongness in its present policies. This is presently rejected by all or nearly all of the Arab states' governments and political leaders. I think it can and will be accepted by the Arab *peoples* with persistent explanation and the use of the tools of RC.

Any role of Israel as an excuse for western domination of the Arab world *cannot* be accepted. Any policies of Israel supporting such a role must be changed. They must be changed by the people of Israel. *Only* thus can the presently intense Israeli-Arab hostility begin to be overcome.

We must urge the Israeli people to repudiate any such present policies of the Israeli government and leaders. We must reject the present policies of the governments of *all* the Arab states for the destruction of Israel. We must reject the conflict-perpetuating policies in the Middle East of the American government, of the Soviet government and of their French, British, etc. junior partners.

This is a sharp break with the "allying oneself with the oppressors in order to survive" policy. It may even seem to be an isolating direction, but it is not. The Israeli *people,* the Arab *people,* the Jewish population in other countries, and the progressive peoples of all countries will eventually rally to and support such a correct policy. The formulation, communication and winning of adherents to such a policy may be difficult. To begin with it may be hard for it to even be heard. It will eventually be heard and supported, however, since the basic interests of the Israeli, Arab and Jewish peoples are the same and are the same as the interests of oppressed peoples everywhere.

A great deal of painful emotion, despair, anger, and fear, both within individuals and embalmed in the Israeli, Arab and Jewish cultures will arise to resist this proposal. There is one overwhelming argument in its favor, i.e., *no other policy will work.* To continue with other policies is not only to perpetuate conflict but it is to threaten and weaken Israel's continued existence as a national homeland.

THE EMERGENCE OF ISRAEL IS A NATIONAL LIBERATION MOVEMENT

The proposal that Israel's policies become truly progressive in every way, become supportive of the liberation of the Palestinians and other Arab people as well as of the Jews, is a correct one. Support for Israel's *existence*, however, must not be conditional on her having progressive policies. The struggle to establish and maintain Israel is a *national* struggle, not a class struggle. All classes of Jews, capitalists, middle-class, and workers are united and must unite on this central issue. All ethnic groups, the Sephardim, the Ashkenazi, the Western European, and the American Jews have a common stake in the maintenance of Israel as a nation, serving as a national homeland for all Jews.

Non-Jews must not require more progressive policies from Israel as a condition of support than we require of any other of the emerging nations, many of whose policies are far more reactionary or conservative than those of Israel. The tendency to do so is an expression of the anti-Semitism which has been inculcated in all Western and Arab cultures for centuries and must be sharply exposed and resisted. This is an area of unthinkingness for many of the "left" movements of the world, which have often called the very reactionary Arab and other Third World regimes "progressive" in part because they were national movements (for which they merited support but which did not make them progressive), but mostly because they were "against Israel". This is folly. This is acceptance of anti-Semitism on an international scale. This can only perpetuate weakness and division among all peoples seeking liberation.

More progressive policies for Israel should be insisted upon by all Jews, Israelis, and supporters, but *only within the framework of unconditional support for Israel's existence.*

We non-Jews have a special responsibility and opportunity for initiating proposals for Arab cooperation with Israel among our Arab friends and for clarifying the policies of our own governments in that direction.

PROGRESSIVES EVERYWHERE MUST SUPPORT JEWISH AND ISRAEL PROGRESSIVES

The widespread failure of non-Jewish progressives to recognize and support the existence of Israel as a *national* liberation struggle has left its Jewish and Israeli progressives in an intolerable position. These have supported progressive issues and the liberation struggles of other people wholeheartedly. Many of them, natives of the "newly liberated" Arab countries, were leaders in the first stages of the liberation struggles of these countries. Now they often face isolation and attack from other Third World leaders and progressives, in what amounts to completely thoughtless rejection of the justice of Jewish national liberation, a rejection that can only be an expression of long-standing anti-Semitism, unfaced, unchallenged, and not thought through.

ANTI-SEMITISM, A THREAT TO ALL PEOPLE

The particularly poisonous form of racism and oppression that is called anti-Semitism has been developed over the centuries as a weapon of oppressive societies against *all* peoples, *all* progressive movements, *all* liberation struggles. Jews were scattered in many countries, without a national homeland and with a culture (and cultural patterns) that made it comparatively easy to set them apart from their neighbors and single them out. To turn the resentment of oppressed peoples away from their oppressors and against the Jews became a standard and effective tactic of oppressors everywhere.

Religious slanders were circulated against them. (Many Christian churches had a long history of anti-Semitism.) Myths and superstitions were widely published. The "fear of anyone different" was used to push anti-Semitic buttons.

We non-Jews in RC are unwilling heirs to this heritage of anti-Semitism. It must be counseled away at least as assiduously as we counsel ourselves out of white racism.

Gentile RCers *should not* request Jewish counselors to listen to this.

(We have a new, more effective technique, developed for white racism, that can be adopted here. This technique is, briefly: to have the client make good contact with an incident of himself or herself being oppressed [i.e. being the victim of one-way, socially enforced mis-treatment because of membership in a particular group]; then an incident of standing up against anti-Semitism, refusing to collude with it, or remain silent in the face of it; and then [and only then] reaching an incident of "going along with" anti-Semitism or remaining silent in the face of an expression of it. The safety afforded by the first two steps seems to bypass the occluding guilt and allow the human heartbreak at such monstrous ideas to discharge voluminously.)

We non-Jews in RC must certainly act *at once* against any stereotyping or other unaware anti-Semitic *behavior*, without waiting for completion of our discharge.

In a very few caucuses, Jewish RCers have apparently been pulled to the kind of "other-end-of-the-pattern" mistake which most liberation movements tend to fall into temporarily. We have seen, temporarily and in a few places, tendencies to "hate-males" feminism, or "give-Whitey-a-taste-of-his-own behavior" proposals for black liberation, even in RC.

Among Jewish RCers, the few expressions of this have taken the form of resenting Christian festivals, calling for RC to reject any expression of Christian culture, etc. These are understandable, but, I think, mistaken. Christianity is *not* anti-Semitism, though it has often been mis-used as a cloak for it. We in RC should, in my opinion, not reject celebration of Christmas, but should celebrate all religious festivals which are traditional among any co-counselors including, of course, the festivals of Judaism. This is the direction of unity, of mutual understanding.

Self-pity among any people newly aware of their oppression is understandable and can bring discharge in a
session, but it is mistaken in its estimate of reality and
mistaken as a program for liberation. We more and more are
coming to realize how oppressed *all* people have been and
this leads to much more effective unity than any games of
"We've been more oppressed than you" or continuation of
old resentments.

WHAT CAN WE DO ON POLICY?

It seems to me that important first steps to prepare for
effective change in Jewish and Israel liberation policies are
currently being taken in the discussion at workshop caucuses,
support groups and gather-ins, in the pages of this newsletter
and with the Jewish Liberation Workshops.

Later developments cannot be predicted exactly. The
future always has some surprises.

I think it is useful, however, to speculate on probable
developments and the directions that we can take in antici-
pation. One is to communicate our policy proposals widely
in the RC Communities and in any gentile groups where we
can be listened to well at this time. We can circulate the
proposals throughout all reaches of the Jewish communities
in the West (and to whatever extent opportunity presents,
within the Eastern European areas), and to all the progressive peoples' forces in all countries. Particularly we need to
find ways to make these proposals known (not necessarily
with an RC label) within Israel, within the Jewish organizations in the United States, and within the Arab countries.

We must be careful not to unthinkingly adopt the
policies of Jews on the "left". We must avoid and urge them
to avoid, any modern version of the past Jewish "left"
mistake of becoming the champion of other peoples' causes,
(this time perhaps the cause of the Arabs in general or the

Palestinians in particular) while avoiding the hard work
necessary to change the policies of the Israeli nation and its
supporters in the Jewish populations elsewhere.

A correct policy on Jewish liberation must be fought for
in the establishment circles of Israel as well as in the circles
that are more likely to be receptive to it. It must be advanced
and fought for within all the reaches of the Jewish establishment groups in the United States. It must be proposed
to middle-class Jews as well as to working-class Jews. What is
decisive is that every Jew who agrees with this policy should
insistently and thoughtfully seek to have it adopted by *all*
Jews and not give up until this is effectively achieved.

Once we have agreement on the main outlines of a
correct policy, I propose that we make strenuous efforts to
secure conferences between the Arabs who may be open to
such a policy and Jews who are promulgating it. In particular,
I propose that we organize conferences between Arab and
Jewish RCers.

NEW DEVELOPMENTS ARE CREATING OPPORTUNITIES

Events are moving so rapidly in the Middle East at
present as to outstrip our necessarily slow discussions. The
central importance of the Palestinians' struggle is becoming
clear. The Palestinians, both within and without the present
borders of Israel, can be won to a correct policy if one is
offered from the Jewish and Israeli side because they are in
touch with the reality of the oppressive nature of the ruling
forces on both sides of the present conflict. Perhaps concrete
support for an Arab Palestine nation adjacent to Israel with
full rights for the Arab and Jewish minorities in both nations
would be a realistic proposal.

The Jewish Liberation Workshop in September should
go a long way towards clarifying our policy. There will be
many more such workshops. This one is necessarily small
but it will be a most important start.

Jewish Liberation
Is Everybody's Concern*

I am here as Reference Person of the entire Community of RC. I speak, without any hesitation, for that entire Community, in offering a warm welcome to the first Jewish Liberation Workshop. The RC Community, for all its difficulties and for all the distresses it still has to discharge, is firmly committed to completely ridding itself, and the world, of anti-Semitism patterns both within RC and outside. We have much work to do in that direction, but the commitment to Jewish liberation has been made on behalf of the entire RC Community.

The Community has also committed itself to general liberation. There is a growing understanding and acceptance that human re-emergence means freedom from oppression, and that no one can be free from oppression as long as anyone else is oppressed. This reality is sinking in slowly, and the practical implications of it will be a long time in being worked out. But it is an actual situation and presently true that a very sizable movement of intelligent people, a movement that seems able to reach every section of people that it has tried to reach, has attained the point of commitment to the liberation of every human from every form of oppression. My appearance here, and one of my roles in being at this workshop, is exactly to be a symbol of the total support of the entire RC Community to Jewish liberation.

AN OUTSIDE VIEWPOINT

It is an unusual situation to be here, of course, as the only Gentile present. It's not entirely without precedent. I was the only male present at the first International All-

*Report at Jewish Liberation I – September 19 - 23, 1976

Women's Workshop. I was the only Caucasian present at the first International Asian Liberation Workshop, and I was the only white present at the first Black Workshop. The good experiences at those workshops have emboldened me to request to be present at this one. I think there is value in having someone from outside the particular kind of oppression present in a liberation workshop like this, to furnish a different viewpoint. Whether I can fill that role, of course, will be determined in the next few days.

I want to first try this morning to look at being Jewish from a non-Jewish point of view. After this, I want to present what I think is a very real and enduring safety: the safety of present reality.

WHAT IS DISTINCTIVE?

What is distinctive about the people called Jews? Are they a distinct race? They certainly are not. Their genetic background is completely varied. There are Chinese Jews who in every particular are Chinese. There are black Jews who are in every particular black and African. The great bulk of the Sephardic (or "Oriental" or "Eastern") Jews as constituted at present, are probably Berbers and Arabs in their genetic lineage, indistinguishable genetically from the Arabs and Berbers among whom they lived until recently in North Africa. They are converted Arabs, converted Berbers.

The Ashkenazi are suspected by many scholars to be largely Kazar in their ethnic or genetic background. The Kazar were a middle Asian people who converted to Judaism. Later, when they had migrated to Eastern Europe, they were joined by a wave of German Jewish refugees who brought with them a more advanced culture. Their everyday language changed to Yiddish, a medieval form of German, and a particular culture developed. Everywhere that Jews have lived, people around them have become converted to Judaism and intermarried with them, so that any long term settlement of Jews has acquired very much the same genetic background as the people among whom they lived. Not only have surrounding peoples become converted to Judaism and to the Jewish culture everywhere that Jews have lived, but also, large numbers of Jews have become assimilated into the surrounding cultures. Everywhere in Jewish history, in the early nations of Samaria, Israel and Judah, and many times and places later, over and over, people of Jewish culture, Jewish religion, have become assimilated.

Sometimes they stayed assimilated and sometimes they re-emerged again as Jews. Becoming "Maronite" Christians or "New" Christians made it possible for large numbers of Jews to persist and survive under Spanish oppression. Many of these stayed assimilated and others re-emerged again as Jews in parts of Europe and America when it became safe to do so. (These were the founders of the early Jewish settlements in the Americas.)

Are the Jews unique because of language? No. They speak Arabic dialects. They speak medieval German in large numbers. They speak Russian, they speak Chinese, they speak Japanese. As they constitute a new nation, they speak Hebrew.

SURVIVABILITY

What *is* distinctive? It seems to me from out here to be inescapable that what is distinctive about the people called Jews is a culture, a culture that is ever-changing and has many, many diverse expressions but which has common and long-lasting elements as well. As part of this culture, there is a religion. This also is ever-changing and has many diverse expressions, but has an important persistence and commonality to it.

Where the original Jewish nations and Jewish cultures were constituted, in ancient Palestine, there were many other very similar peoples. The people who assembled into the first Jewish nations and the fountainhead Jewish cultures were remarkably like the other groups of people among whom they lived in the ancient Middle East. All of these groups, all of these cultures, were continually at war with each other, conquering and becoming conquered, being captured and sold into slavery, re-emerging from slavery, becoming vassal states of the ancient empires, being independent for a time, then becoming conqueror states, in great shifts back and forth. The early Jewish peoples went into exile frequently, emigrated to all parts of the Mediterranean world, were sold into slavery as groups and as individuals. Sometimes they stayed where they were enslaved, and were assimilated by the surrounding cultures. At other times, they emerged from slavery and founded new, distinctly Jewish settlements in the places they had been dispersed to. This happened repeatedly, long before the Diaspora.

The other peoples around them suffered very much the same fates. This was the way society functioned in its early slave stage. Continual war. Rome is well-known to us simply because it was the particular slave society that came out "top dog" in a long sorting process in which every slave society city-state tried to conquer and oppress every other slave society city state. This was simply the "normal" process, the meat grinder that all slave societies went through at that time.

What was distinctive about the people called Jews was simply that their particular culture, of which the religion was an important part, had a high enough survival value that it refused to be wiped out. Nearby cultures, very similar in many respects, were wiped out, over and over and over again. Islands of the Jewish culture were also wiped out, by assimilation or by extermination, over and over again, but never the whole culture completely. The Jewish culture has had a high enough survival value at each stage of history up until now, that the Jews have perisited as a cultural group. It seems to me that this is the essence of it.

How high a value you place upon the religious aspects of the culture and how high a value you place on the other aspects will vary in judgment for every person who takes a look at the question, and will be different for every different viewpoint. But taking the culture as a whole, including the religion, it's obvious that the people who followed this culture survived better than the similar people of other cultures who lived around them. There *was* a survival value in holding on to this culture or in adopting it.

Part of what we need to do in working out a rational program for Jewish liberation is to assess correctly the positive values of that culture, the parts that are *truly* pro-survival. (All of us here have been thinking about this in more or less aware ways.) We need to do this not only for the survival and the liberation of the Jewish people, but for the benefit of all people. The Jewish culture is a treasure house for all people, has always been used as such. It has always been a treasure from which surrounding people and cultures have borrowed and borrowed and borrowed.

Looking at the religious aspect, for example, many ancient religions were spin-offs of the Hebrew religion. Some of them still exist, such as the Samaritans in Palestine. But also such huge institutions as Christianity and Islam borrowed almost all of their roots from the Jewish religion. Mohammed had read widely in Jewish literature. Most of the good elements of Islam (and there are very good elements in the Islamic religion), can trace their roots to the Jewish religion. Almost all of the good elements of the Christian religion, of course, come from such wholesale borrowing. Christianity uses the Old Testament as the foundation of everything, and it is completely a Jewish literature. But there are many other positive elements as well: the tradition of excellence, the caring within the family, the community support, the love of scholarship and the written word, the tradition of justice, the undying, though necessarily by now occasionally rigid, hope for a positive future for all. These elements, even on quick examination, have *high* survival value.

If we re-examine Jewish history, and do not let ourselves be too engulfed in the horrors and defeats, I think we will see elements in Jewish culture which have had profound survival value for the Jewish people and will have for all people. I think that because we have, at last, the tool of the discharge and re-evaluation process, we can begin to separate and distinguish the pro-survival elements in the culture from the elements that have interfered with survival--that have cooperated in non-survival, in the extermination and the assimilation and the other defeats which the Jewish people have suffered with such intensity and frequency.

No other people suffering a small fraction of the defeats which the Jewish culture and Jewish people have suffered, have survived. This kind of thing happened to many, many peoples, but never to the same people hundreds of times over, with their still persisting. This is a real source of tremendous pride. Every Jew can be enormously proud of Jews having endured.

NON-SURVIVAL CULTURAL ELEMENTS

With discharge and re-evaluation, I think we can begin to separate some of the things that are non-survival that got glued in with the positive elements of Jewish culture by the distress. This is, perhaps, one of the key contributions which RC can make to Jewish liberation. All of us have sensed, or we wouldn't be here, that with discharge and re-evaluation we can reclaim our vast pride in being Jewish without feeling obligated to go on making the same kind of mistakes that have over and over again led us to the brink of extermination.

Humanity is today on the verge of moving toward an economically unoppressive society, a classless society. This has great significance for everyone, because class oppression, economic exploitation, economic oppression, is the great grand-daddy of all other oppressions. It is the one which spins off all other forms of oppression. The oppression of women was a spin-off from the institution of class oppression. It began early, under slavery, with the enslavement of women, but it persisted under feudalism and under capitalism, with many hangovers from the slavery and feudal days. Any special oppression is deeper because of the class oppression underlying it. Racism began as a tool for maintaining class oppression, for dividing the oppressed. Mistreatment of children is a spin-off from class oppression. Now the great motive power behind all forms of oppression is on its last, shaky, rotten legs. The collapse of capitalism is well underway.

If all of us who are wage workers (and most of us *are* wage workers, even though we might have been trained to think of ourselves differently; the college professor sells his labor for a portion of what his labor produces, just like the machinist), if all of us in this key, oppressed role supported capitalism to its utmost; if we cheerfully worked for lower wages and took pay cuts and were loyal employees; and if all women agreed to continue in their oppressed role; and if all Jews agreed not to protest against anti-Semitism, but accept it as their lot; and if all blacks said thank you for the mistreatment every time they turned around, capitalism would *still* fall flat on its face in a very short period of time. Its internal contradictions are bringing capitalism to an end, and there is no possible way this can be avoided.

So we have this basic factor in the world, that the great, motive power of all oppression is on its last, shaky legs. There are great dangers, of course. There have always been dangers. Capitalism killed off the majority of the population of many countries in Northern Europe in overthrowing feudalism, and capitalism as a system cared not a whit that the battles and the plagues that followed decimated most of the population as long as the system survived. It's conceivable that the red button will get pushed and the missiles will fly and a majority of the world's population could die. It isn't likely, but it's a possibility to take into account. The possibility shouldn't add to our terror because the overwhelming probabilities and the overwhelming forces lie with the people.

The *objective* situation has been ready for a long time for a liberated humanity. Only the subjective situation, which has been so puzzling because it's so difficult to take apart, has held us back. At last we can come to understand why the subjective situation has been so difficult to change, because we've discovered at the heart of it that familiar (to us) entity, the distress pattern. It's plain now that all oppression has persisted at any time only on the backs of installed distress patterns. Only the distress pattern allows oppression to continue. Only the distress pattern allows stupidity to continue. Only the distress pattern allows an oppressive society to continue. One has to be conditioned by the installation of a distress pattern to be willing to be a victim, or one simply would not be a victim.

KEY INSIGHTS FROM RC

We're reaching some important general conclusions in RC that are quite valid, but would be difficult for people to believe because of the distress and discouragement that's been put upon them. One of them is: *Given a correct policy, any situation can be successfully handled.* Any time that things are not going well for us, any time we have frustrating difficulties (I don't mean having to do hard work--you know the difference between working very hard, but knowing things are working; and having frustrating difficulties), *any time that we're having frustrating difficulties, we can safely conclude that there is something wrong or incomplete about our policy.*

This understanding has useful implications. Any time a group of us, whatever we're doing, are feeling frustrated, it's time to stop and have a think-and-listen. Ask, what possible things could we do different than we are doing now? Even five or ten minutes of this can make a big shift. *Only persistence in patterned behavior leads to defeat.*

It's true that you can take isolated sample situations such as "there you are in the swamps of Vietnam and it's kill or be killed"; but you had to act stupid a hundred-and-fifty times first, to get into that situation. The path forked a hundred-and-fifty times, and you took the wrong path every time, in order to get to that.

Inside a distress, it doesn't seem like that, I know. It doesn't *seem* like it to me, either, but it has to be true that, given a correct policy, any situation can be handled successfully. We have the tools at our disposal now. We'll have better tools. We're continually improving them. But we have enough tools at our disposal now to say flatly that we can always determine a correct policy.

RESPONSIBILITY OF NON-JEWS

We non-Jews have a lot to do about Jewish liberation in the non-Jewish sphere. In RC, the non-Jewish RCers have a great deal of awareness yet to gain and work to do in looking at the anti-Semitism which has been systematically installed over a long period of time in all cultures, in order to get rid of it. As far as I have any influence (and I have some), we will be tackling that.

If we tackle it in the RC Community, it will get tackled outside. Because what has been lacking outside, too, is a correct policy. I think you'd be amazed if you knew how thoroughly and completely almost all non-Jewish people would welcome a good policy against anti-Semitism, one that they could understand and use. How shallow the roots of anti-Semitism are among Gentiles! I don't know, from where you are, if you can conceive of it, but I can say flatly: the roots are very shallow.

WHAT DOESN'T WORK

It's the primary responsibility of non-Jewish RCers to do something about this. But also, since I have *this* audience to talk to, I'd like to say that from out here, it seems very plain to me that with the strength of the Jewish culture and the tradition of being smart and the actuality of being smart, and the tradition of scholarship and of high education and a community feeling, that some very terrible patterns have to be operating, to have brought about the defeats that you have suffered. I don't think there is any question about it. I think we're at a point where we can look at and begin to differentiate the strength of being Jewish from the self-defeating patterns of being Jewish, and we can really live the one and discharge the other.

In the little leaders meeting we had just before this, a reference was made to the "heaviness" and the "thing" that most Jews feel. At one point, I said that another name for the "thing" is terror. How could it be otherwise? It seems to me that everyone, every Jewish person I know in RC, is operating brilliantly on top of a sheet of icy fear; that there is complete terror in there. How *could* it be otherwise? I have my own terror. The people I come from lived in terror all their lives, too; but not in the same way, not with the same intensity, not with such uniformity.

What can we say about the terror, which is, I think, the biggest thing that we have to strip off? Well, that it can be discharged, just like any other terror. What is difficult in discharging it? The lack of a safe place to stand while you look at it. We've known for a long time in RC that you can't "bail the ocean while you're drowning in it." This has become a key point of counseling--to find a place to stand while you bail the ocean; to find some ground, some bottom under your feet.

Is there safety? I think so. What are the elements of safety in RC? One, I think, is the one I just tried to say-- correct policy will always lead to successful survival, and we have the tools for determining a correct policy when we use them. This, I think is the *basic* safety.

NO REAL CONFLICTS

What's a second element of safety? That there are no, *no* contradictions between the survival of non-Jews and Jews.

ANTI-SEMITISM HURTS EVERYONE

Three, that it's demonstrable, though it has not been well enough demonstrated or often enough demonstrated or widely enough demonstrated by far, that anti-Semitism is a knife at the throat of every oppressed person, and is primarily directed at the majority of the oppressed, not primarily at the Jews, although they suffer the most from it. Anti-Semitism is primarily a tool of oppression of everybody.

Is anybody surprised by that? Let me just point it up a little bit. Anti-Semitism is the model for the divide-and-rule tactic which has been the only thing that maintained oppression for a long, long time, probably for hundreds of years by now. Only the conditioning of each group of the oppressed to oppress every other group of the oppressed has allowed oppression to continue. And anti-Semitism was where this all developed.

Why? Well, in the objective conditions that existed the persistence and strength of the Jewish culture led to its spread throughout the world. Almost everywhere in the Western and Arab world, in the Turkish Empire, in India and Indonesia, were groups of Jews whose culture set them clearly apart from the surrounding people, who were few in number, conditioned to isolation, conditioned to a victim role individually and as groups, carrying the victim patterns, and with no national homeland to intercede for them. With this condition existing in enough places, it was undoubtedly inevitable that some oppressive ruler would come up with the "brilliant" notion of turning the fury of the other oppressed on this small group as scapegoats. Who knows when it was first done? But it was very quickly learned by adjacent rulers from the one ruler, the unknown "genius" who thought it up the first time, and it spread over almost all the world, and has been used again and again and again.

It was used by the secular authorities. It was also used by religious authorities who were indistinguishable from the secular authorities in earlier times. It was used by the Eastern Christian churches and by the Roman Catholic churches, and it was used by the Protestants and by the religious leaders of Islam. But, whoever was the spokesman or tool, it was always used by and for the basic group of oppressors, the economic exploiters, for whom the anti-Semitic religious leaders were simply fronts. From the use of anti-Semitism as the early, experimental divide-and-rule tactic, which, found successful, was widely spread and inculcated as a tool for dividing the oppressed, divide-and-rule has spread to be used against every other group.

Here at Madison last spring, for the first time in RC, we made a simple step forward by asking, "How are you oppressed?" Instead of saying, "We will have the following liberation groups", we said, "How are you oppressed?" and we found about twelve new kinds of oppression. I think most of you have read the amazing reports of this which were printed in *Present Time*. At Arundel (England), a few weeks ago, we had thirty-three reports on thirty-three kinds of oppression. The oppressive structure is being revealed so clearly. Here at Madison we heard fifteen groups of the population (there were eighty people here--a substantial sampling) stand up and say, "This is how the rest of you are making our lives unbearable day after day in your unaware attitudes and actions," and each time all the rest of us listened in amazement and dismay.

The realization is becoming clear that each one of us is conditioned to put down and oppress people in all the other groups except our own. And that the oppressor society has no real strength except as the installer and manipulator of the conditioned patterns to make us all do the dirty work for the oppressor.

The real oppressor is the outmoded society. Even the members of the ruling class in this oppressive society suffer terribly from it. Both at Buck Creek and Arundel we had reports from the Upper Middle Class Caucus, and the distress and oppression by the society these RCers reported were very real. We had some old patterns grumble at first, "Why are we doing this stuff? We should be reserving our attention to think about South Africa. They have no right to grieve about their petty grievances," and so on. But that was wrong, and after a little discussion, everybody understood that it was old, divisive patterns talking.

Everybody is oppressed. *Everybody's* life is ruined by living in an oppressive society, *everybody's!* Even the members of the oppressing classes can be reached intellectually (individually, not as a class, of course) to want to end oppression.

So it can clearly be demonstrated that anti-Semitism is the cutting edge of the main mechanism for oppressing *all* people. It can clearly be demonstrated that all working class people have an *immediate* stake in overthrowing and eliminating anti-Semitism completely. It hasn't been done yet; but the job needs doing, and it can be done. Until we understood the distress pattern and the means of dealing with it, people were helpless. You can look back at all the well-meant attempts that have been made in this direction and see how they came a cropper again and again and again in the face of the un-understood mechanism of the distress pattern. Well, the ugly thing isn't un-understood anymore. We know what to do about it. And it's sticky getting at the pattern where it lurks behind our mind at the back of our head, and so, as always, we're going to be mainly working on these this week. But we can see the back of each others' heads pretty well.

So, we can demonstrate logically and clearly to everyone in every stratum of society, (and when the logic fails to get through, we can help people discharge until it does), that anti-Semitism is not only nonsense, that anti-Semitism is not only shameful, that anti-Semitism is not only destructive, but that it is a weapon aimed at the heart of that particular individual. We can show that anti-Semitism has operated, continues to operate, and until it is eliminated, will operate as a complete disservice to that particular person. We can do that. I think that's an element of our safety. It gives us lots of work to do, but that's an element of safety.

RECLAIMING POWER

Probably the element of safety I'm most excited and hopeful about is the final realization of the importance in the lives of all of us of the conditioned powerlessness. This comes home with special force on Jewish oppression.

When the breakthrough to realizing the role of powerlessness came (the story of how it occurred appeared in *Present Time*), I went back and looked at what I'd been writing for the last six months and found I had been using the word over and over again, but I hadn't *heard* it.

It was a decisive breakthrough to realize that this great, grey, fuzzy glunk that carpets all our floors and papers all our walls and tiles all our ceilings and greys all our windows and smogs all our outdoors is not natural, is not reality, but is the result of intense, severe distress, systematically installed on every single human being during childhood. It is permanently liberating to realize that the glimpses we've had of human nature in small breakthroughs on personal and small group issues, that humans are inherently full of initiative, taking charge of everything, and laughing at any opposition, is accurate in the wide world on the big issues, too.

Now the great, grey gobs of goo are still hanging everywhere. We haven't gotten them discharged yet. But if we can see powerlessness as non-reality, if we can see it as an acquired, removable thing, then we *can* get rid of it.

The longest delay that I can remember in our seeing a problem clearly, and then finding a way to effectively work at it, was last year, when the International Community at Buck Creek really committed itself to work on white racism, and it took ten months before we found a way to really do it.

That took ten months. So maybe it will take a while to find all the good techniques for eliminating powerlessness. Maybe the powerlessness patterns will turn out to have more confusing layers below the top layers that we have begun to understand. Probably, as with all patterns so far, once we think we've really mastered them, they will sneak up our back a few times and be running us again before we even notice it. But we will find ways to completely eliminate powerlessness.

What are the key elements in the patterns conditioned on Jewish people which lead them to cooperate in their own oppression? There are many of them. You have told me about invalidation, self-blame, disunity, feeling like outsiders, terror, impending doom. What's one of the key elements? What's certainly one of the biggest grey gobs of goo? It has to be powerlessness, doesn't it.

This powerlessness must be the source of another ancient destructive pattern, the one that says that cooperation in being the visible agent of the oppressors is the only way one can survive and allow one's people to survive. Of course that has to spring from powerlessness. This agreement to support reactionary policies is, long range, one of the most destructive policy patterns, always buying short range survival for a few, but long range destruction for many. This has to be rooted in powerlessness. It has to be.

Can we cut this pattern right off at the root by eliminating the powerless conditioning? If we can, we can stop piecemeal protesting or being critical of the particular manifestations of this pattern and eliminate it at its powerlessness source. We can stop being content with saying, "Kissinger, you shouldn't have done that," or "Israel shouldn't have supported South Africa." We don't have to go around picking the twigs and branches. We can get right to the root of it, and say, "Jews, take back your power." Will we have to discharge? Yes, a lot. But I think we can do it.

ENDING ISOLATION

As we discharge the powerlessness and take back our power, the isolation pattern is going to have to go. It seems to me that isolation is the cutting edge of the distress that has kept us from an effective Jewish liberation policy. I hear from Jews I co-counsel with, "But it's so deep! You cannot ever trust anybody else but other Jews to support you!" I don't doubt that it's that deep. Certainly non-Jewish RCers have to prove in practice, as well as in our intentions, that the non-Jewish RC community is going to discharge its anti-Semitism patterns, and make Jewish liberation a central point of its knowledge and concern. That's going to take some doing. It's not enough, by far, that I, as a leader, take the position I do. This is still a little inside a tradition of Jews cooperating with non-Jewish leaders or officials who "officially" take a stand against anti-Semitism, but never really reach their own memberships. We can't settle for that. Non-Jewish RCers must become *active* against anti-Semitism, in RC and in the wide world. Every bit of involvement of non-Jewish RCers in actively supporting liberation policies is going to be important ground for you to stand on in discharging the isolation distress patterns.

But we don't have to wait for that. *You* don't have to wait on it. The isolation can be contradicted right now along with the powerlessness. Sheila and I had a little discussion on the draft statement Number 2. She drafted it as a statement from "We Jews", and I said no, and she agreed to change it. After she read it to a meeting in Boston, she again said she thought it ought to be a statement from Jewish RCers. And I again said no. She is not entirely convinced, and I anticipate a lot of discussion on this issue. But I want to say that I think it's crucial that this statement be a statement of the entire RC Community because isolation is the key element in Jewish oppression. Of course, the black RCers speak for themselves, Asian RCers speak for themselves, the women speak for themselves in RC, and there will be many statements made just by Jewish RCers about Jewish liberation, and correctly so. I think it profoundly correct tactics, however, for the RC Community as a whole to speak for Jewish liberation at this point. Our basic, fundamental statement on Jewish liberation needs to be a statement that every Gentile RCer can sign, as well as every Jewish RCer; needs to be in the form of a united statement of the whole Co-counseling Community.

Isolation as an expression of internalized oppression has arisen for very definite reasons. It was imposed from the outside to begin with. Once imposed, it was hardly surprising that self-isolating conclusions were drawn and became recorded and passed on from generation to generation. *But,* liberation does not lie that way. Isolation must go. At least half the key job has to be done by non-Jewish RCers, done by refusing to accept the isolation from outside, by discharging their own anti-Semitism imposed by the culture, and insisting and assisting others to do likewise. But no Jewish RCer needs to wait on actions from outside. Excuses for not taking the initiative oneself comprise one of the stickiest of patterns, and one that slows everybody's re-emergence whenever it gloms on to an individual.

Certainly we must never accept that something outside is stopping us. That *has* to be nonsense. We have enough glimpses of reality to be able to say that very flatly. Logically, it's impossible for anything else to be true than that each one of us is indeed mistress or master of the universe. If any one of us thought clearly enough and adopted correct enough policies *and put them into action,* that alone would eventually guarantee the freedom of the world and the end of all distress patterns. We have enough glimpses of reality to say that "philosophically and logically, it has to be true that if any *one* of us, any one human being, thought clearly enough, was well enough informed (and that's not difficult these days), discharged where it was difficult to think, and put these clear thoughts and the resulting policy into action, communicated it in a way that other people could hear and join in the action; that one of us alone would be sufficient to determine the future of the world, the liberation of humankind and the end of distress forever."

It has to be true. There are by now too many glimpses of the capacity of even one individual human intelligence, let alone the power achieved by the linking of intelligences in the ways that we've begun to learn to do it, for it to be otherwise.

REALITY OFFERS SAFETY

So, what I would like to say is that reality is real and reassuring; that the terror associated with being Jewish is simply installed distress. It can be discharged completely.

I want to say that isolation is your enemy no matter in what friendly guise it appears. It appears, I know, as safety, as survival, as the only possible response to rejection. It will appear in every possible pseudo-survival form, but it's your enemy. Isolation is your enemy no matter in what guise it appears.

I want to say that anti-Semitism can be shown to be, and can be heard by everyone to be, the enemy of all people and the immediate enemy of that particular individual, and that there is no individual who could not be mobilized against it, could not become a dependable ally in the struggle to eliminate it.

I want to say that the great, underlying oppressor, the economically exploitive society, the prime mover of all other oppressions, has lost its capacity to maintain itself and is well on its way out of existence.

There is enough safety. There is enough safety in our ability to think, our ability to relate, and our ability to discharge. If we remind each other of this safety, and support each other, we can discharge the heaviest terrors. In a workshop like this all-Jewish one, there is a little bit of a tendency to pool our distresses and to resonate with each other's fears. "Where are you going to find somebody outside the terror?" a couple of people have already asked me, and already told me, "You're not enough, Harvey." But I don't need to be enough, because reality is enough. We have to scrape the frost off it, wipe the dirt off it, get our heads out of the fog of our own fears. We will have to be skillful counselors to each other to help each discharge each one's particular fears and confusion and uncover the reality, but the reality is there.

There is enough safety now to discharge all the pseudo-reality of our distress. The reality that is left is handleable.

KNOW YOUR STRENGTHS

When I think of Jewish liberation from a general perspective, I don't think, "At last, safety for Jews!" I think, rather, "Aah haah! An army of tough and able ones who have joined the general fight!" Because, of course, I'm concerned with the liberation of everyone. I've long been concerned with working class liberation, and more and more, I'm coming to understand the others. It is simply time that human beings be free.

As each group enters upon its liberation struggle, each comes with all kinds of handicaps imposed on it by its particular oppression. If you look at the blacks struggling for liberation, you see the tremendous invalidations and feelings of worthlessness and ignorance that have been installed on them as a group, and which they have to struggle out of. You see the fragmentation of Native Americans and so on. Each has to counter the effects of the particular oppression they have suffered. Well, the liberation front is growing. If you read the *Rough Notes from Liberation I & II*, this marvelous transcript of a workshop a year ago last April, the first general liberation workshop, you can see there in embryo a liberation front of a wide variety of people. The working class, largely quiescent as yet in the United States, is ready to move. The blacks, the Chicanos, the Puerto Ricans, the Native Americans, the children, the older people, the students, the intellectuals, the immigrant national groups, the middle class, are all facing unbearable problems that cannot finally be solved without a fundamental transformation of society. There is a liberation front in preparation. Its ranks are forming. Its unity is being forged. We in RC have a great contribution to make to this, because we have the means of solving the problems that have frustrated and divided every other attempt at unity before. As Jews join the liberation front, casting aside all the traditions of isolation, casting aside

385

the tradition of having to ally themselves with the oppressor in order to survive, taking their places in the ranks of the other oppressed--think of the strength they bring!

Do you have any notion how strong you are? Do you have any notion of how strong you appear from out here? I like to be up front in any struggle, but as you move, I'm going to have to run, to keep from getting trampled.

ISRAEL

Let me just say a word about the oppressive role of Israel. We heard about the dilemma of Israel over and over last night. It's a dilemma that I've shared. In the past, I bought largely the attitude of the rigid Left, that Israel's role toward the Arabs was an imperialist plot foisted upon the liberation struggles of the Arabs, and my confusion was understandable. Looking more basically at the situation, however, I think, "How could I be so unthinking?" I and most of the world's Left have been very foolish. This is true, I think, of all the Left sentiments that decry Israel's existence --we have all been the unwitting victims of long-standing anti-Semitism patterns that are very pervasive. And as with any conditioned pattern, anti-Semitism doesn't care what vehicle it rides. It will sneak into a Left policy just as happily as it will into a Right policy.

NATIONAL LIBERATION STAGE

The key issue here--and you should tell this firmly to your Left friends, who are good people, but whose confusion cannot be excused--is what stage of liberation or revolution the Israelis are engaged in. Is it nationalist or socialist? Don't be confused by the names political parties give themselves, since the word "socialist" as used in such contexts has no relation to what we are saying.

It's been clear, in revolutionary or Marxist theory for a long time, that any nation emerging from national subjection must progress through national emancipation, which is essentially a capitalist revolution, achieving national independence, before it can proceed to a socialist revolution, which involves taking power by the working class people and their allies and proceeding to the abolition of classes. Any nation still in feudal conditions or under foreign rule, which is the modern counterpart of feudalism under conditions of capitalist imperialism, must go through successive revolutions. Feudal institutions must be overthrown. National independence must be achieved before the nation can proceed to class revolution, to the abolition of classes, to the establishment of socialism. Yet, the sectarian Left around the world has over and over and over again made the mistake of demanding of Israel that it be a socialist state. As of now, it *can't* be. Jewish liberation at this point is national liberation, and it's very clear, from the standpoint of socialist theory, if you brush aside the anti-Semitism and look at the reality, that the safety, the liberation of the Jews, requires a national homeland.

ISRAEL'S EXISTENCE CRUCIAL

We heard this last night in everything everybody said. No matter how uneasy they were about Israel's reactionary policies, they were glad that Israel existed. ———said, if I remember correctly, that it was crucial to her own re-emergence that Jews had stood up and fought somewhere. I think she meant, fought with the possibility of victory, with the actuality of victory, which is an essential ingredient. There has been no shortage of fighting bravely by Jews. What is new is fighting and winning. (I hope to talk, a couple of mornings from now, about the fighting ability and about the brave battles of the Jews, historically.) The liberation of a national homeland and the existence of a national homeland are essential for Jewish liberation.

It would be almost impossible for Jewish liberation to take place without a national homeland. Does this require that every Jew immediately go to Israel and take up arms for the survival of that nation on the ground there? No, of course not. Jews have the right to be residents of any place on earth and still claim their national homeland with pride, just as the Croatian or the Serbian or the Norwegian has that right; to live anywhere on earth and yet be very proud of their national homeland, their national traditions, even if nation and tradition have only lately been re-established.

Is it important that Jews everywhere support the existence of Israel? Of course. Is it important that Gentiles everywhere support the existence of Israel? Of course. It's essential for the freedom of all people that there be a strong national homeland for the Jewish people. It is important that every Arab support the existence of Israel as a national homeland for the Jews? Of course. Arab liberation cannot succeed without Jewish liberation. It's possible to demonstrate this, and it's possible to demonstrate this to Arabs. Many attempts in this direction are going on in little ways, and with confused policies, but enough to indicate the need for Arab-Israeli and Arab-Jewish unity.

ANTI-SEMITISM IN A "LEFT" CLOAK

Is it essential that Israel have better policies than it has had, in order to survive? Yes, but that is point number two. You cannot deal with point number two until you are very clear on point number one. Point number one is that regardless of how wrong Israel's policies are or may be at any particular time, regardless of how oppressive the Israeli society is of the Eastern Jews, or of the wage workers, or of the Arabs; regardless of how wrong Israel's policies are in being an appendage of American imperialism, or in supporting the racism of the South African white minority state, regardless of any other wrong policy, Israel's existence must be supported. Point out to your rigid Left friends (it will help) that the Left has supported the most reactionary regimes in Africa because they were *national* governments, because however rotten and reactionary they were, they were *national liberation* governments, whose people had a right to their own independence even under the rottenest of governments. The Left has in general correctly supported this policy. Left Jews have in general supported this. Jews have often been in the forefront of the struggle for the liberation of the North African Arab states. Over and over, Jews took the lead in these national liberation movements. Often they were expelled very shortly after the liberation was achieved, but in general, they have not regretted their support. They knew that liberation was necessary for the Arab peoples there.

Why apply a different standard to Israel? Why say you can only support Israel if it has correct socialist policies? Nonsense! This has to be anti-Semitism. It has to be endemic, pervasive, sneaky anti-Semitism. We don't have to make any apologies for Israel at all. In the fullest sense of socialist theory, Israel's existence must be supported and guaranteed, even if it was completely reactionary, even if it was rotten in its foreign policy, in its treatment of minorities, in its class oppression. Israel's existence must be supported as a national homeland for the Jewish people.

BETTER POLICIES CAN THEN BE REQUIRED

Then, and only then, we can say that Israel must become the champion of Arab liberation. It must become the champion of a national homeland for the Palestinian people, whose territorial integrity is guaranteed by Israel, if necessary. We can say that Israel needs to help establish a bastion for real Arab liberation.

Having taken the first stand, we can say to Israel, "Get rid of these nutty old policies of being an appendage of the imperialists and a pawn in the imperialist game. Start using the strength of the alliances right next to you. Look at the realities of Palestinian existence, and of the great need for the Arabs to have a base with which to fight against the reactionary regimes installed on them by the American imperialists and the Russian imperialists." Then we can be critical of Israel's policies, and make suggestions for better ones. But we can only do this, having given our complete support to point one, that Israel's *existence* must be maintained regardless of how wrong its policies or practices are at any particular time.

Don't Let Patterns Sneak Into Our Policies Against Sexism *

Our women's and men's caucuses, classes, and workshops have made real progress in exposing and taking directions against the sexist conditioning which permeates our societies and which has done so much to degrade our relationships and our lives in the past. Even though this effort is, in a sense, just beginning, it has already richly rewarded our co-counselors and our Communities.

Many of our women co-counselors feel a new safety and initiative in RC. They act more freely and confidently to challenge the manifestations of sexism in and out of RC. They assume leadership more comfortably.

Some of our men co-counselors have stepped outside the competitiveness and fear of other men willed on them by society enough to realize the safe humanness possible in man-to-man relationships. They have been able to look at women with a new kind of respect, able to encourage women's re-emergence, to give up imposing their "needs" and expectations of support on women.

Patterns are persistent, however, they not only will hang on in their original forms in every possible way. In the absence of vigilance, they will also re-appear as counter-dramatizations, as new "roles" in the old patterns, or will attach themselves to new objects.

Women RCers must watch that they not slip back into old ways of colluding with male sexism, not treat themselves or other women with disrespect, not, out of "habit", auto-

*First printed in RC Teacher No. 7 – December, 1975

matically furnish support when a male "need" pattern leans on them. They need also watch, however, that they not (past the need to get discharge started) rehearse antagonisms toward, and grievances against men, not make a cause of "getting even" with men, or promoting isolation and division between humans.

It is undoubtedly correct to say that women co-counselors are in no way obligated to listen to or counsel men co-counselors on their distresses about women or their feelings, of any kind, about sexism. It is *not* correct to say that women and men should not co-counsel together. It is not correct to collude with "segregation" trends in the feminist movement as a whole.

Men co-counselors need to watch that they not automatically seek women as counselors, that they listen to women clients without expecting to make "rejoinders" (or seek to proclaim their "guilt") in their turns as clients (they can save this for their session with men counselors), that they go on sharing and trusting with other men. They need also watch, however, that they not transfer a "frozen need" for parenting from a "mother substitute" to a "father substitute" and assume that this is much progress.

The challenge to men co-counselors is not to find a new source of nurture while continuing to act as the frightened, timid, dependent little boys we once were forced to be, but rather to emerge to functioning like the *men* we really are by now, to gain to what the Victorians called "manhood's high estate" which is, after all, one of the really good varieties of humanhood.

It's Great to be a Man!*

It is great to be a human being, of any description.

It is great to be a woman, and every woman should be able to take pride in being a woman.

It is great to be a young person, a human being who has a long and satisfying and challenging future ahead of him or her.

It is *also* great to be a *man*.

I think that we must base our program for men's liberation in and out of RC on this *pride and joy in being a man.*

Society has forced men into an oppressive role towards women and children. Everyone has suffered from the patterns which have enforced that role. Understandably, the distress inflicted by these patterns can provoke a reaction against males and "maleness". We currently meet a fear that resurgent pride in being a man might reinforce the oppressive sexism we all are struggling to free ourselves from. I do not think this fear is justified.

Each one of us, in our liberations, must start with self-appreciation, with pride in ourselves. To undo any accumulated invalidation is an essential and central part of any human being's liberation from oppression. This must be true for men as well.

Do men have reason to be proud of themselves, proud of men? Yes. We have no reason to be proud of the oppres-

*First printed in RC Teacher No. 9 -- December, 1976

sive roles which the real oppressors in these exploitative societies have put upon us, but we have every reason to be proud of our essential nature. We are the adult, male members of the human race, and, though we are different from women and children, we are fully human. Though some of our attributes have been misused in the past, they need not be misused. We can take pride in every bit of our real male human natures.

In earlier times, people spoke with respect of "manhood's high estate", meaning that under the conditions then prevailing, an adult male had claim, at least, to independence, initiative, to being in charge of his life, to being a source of strength and intelligence and capability for the people around him. It is not men's labor and effort alone that have put our capital resources, our technology and our knowledge within reach of a secure, prosperous living for all human beings, but the labor and the thinking of men have certainly contributed their share. Men have done a major portion of the farming, the labor, the mining, the construction, the research, the writing, the composing, which have brought such rich stores of resource to our culture and civilization. It is certainly time that we undid the neglect of the culture by appreciating fully women's contribution in the past and enhancing their enormous potential for the future, that we recognize and encourage the contributions of children of all ages; but this does not mean failing to recognize the gifts which men have brought to all human activity.

If one is a *real man*, then of course one cannot be sexist. Our strength and pride would never be turned to oppressing or taking advantage of or exploiting another human being. If one is a *real man*, one must of course treat every other human being with complete respect. If one is a *real man*, one is strong, intelligent, gentle, caring, and honorable.

Of necessity attention in the struggles against oppression has been focused, to begin with, on the distressing roles of the conditioned sexist males in our society. All of us who are male have a great deal of crippling distress to discharge and free ourselves from, distress that has pushed us in the direction of oppressive attitudes toward women and children. But the culture has not all been negative in this respect. There are traditions in the United States of men standing up against sexism, of refusing to allow its oppressive sway over women.

In a rural community in which I lived as a boy, I overheard men talking about coping with and bringing an end to sexism on the part of one of the men in the community. This is the story as I overheard it:

> *One farmer was suspected and then known to beat his wife viciously. Her bruises were noticed by other people when she appeared at store and church. Apparently there was some community discussion, perhaps initiated by the other wives.*

> *Six husbands went as a group to visit the wife-beater. They presented themselves gravely, and asked him to promise them that the beatings would stop. The wife-beater told them to mind their own business. The spokesman for the group said that they were not prepared to accept that. Human decency required that they insist on his promise that the beatings would stop.*

> *The wife-beater sneered and asked if any one of them was "man enough" to try to make him stop. (It was the tradition of the culture, of course, that the men could not gang up on him, that combat must be individual. Individual physical combat was a question of honor.) The spokesman for the delegation stepped forward and said, "I will try." The powerful wife-beater quickly injured him so badly that he could not continue. The bully then sneeringly asked if any of the rest wanted what the first one had gotten.*

> *At this point the five remaining men formed a line, a queue. The first stepped forward and combat ensued.*

It did not go so swiftly this time, but the farmer was beaten and unable to continue. Now the third man stepped out, and the wife-beater's patterned confidence began to collapse. After a severe, battering struggle, the bully surrendered.

The men gathered around him and the spokesman said, "We want your promise that your wife will be treated well." The pale husband said, "I promise." At this, each man shook hands with him and congratulated him. The spokesman said, "You should know we will watch, and if necessary, we'll be back." The ex-wife-beater said, very seriously, "It won't be necessary." At this point, each of the men shook his hand again. After some hesitation, one said, "We'd be proud to have your family over for dinner Sunday. Can you make it?" Looking him in the eye, the other said, "I'm sure we'd like to come."

We men can appreciate the brave initiative of the women in challenging our sexist patterns and persisting in requiring us to think about them. It is time, however, that we take the initiative into our own hands, for the sake of our complete re-emergence.

Men's liberation cannot succeed motivated by guilt, nor by a "me-too" response to women's liberation, nor by a still-inside-the-pattern attempt to "take care" of each other in a dependent way to replace the "taking care" which came from women's patterns.

We must reclaim our pride. Pride in our humanness, pride in our maleness, pride in our strength and power.

It's great to be a *real man*.

Oppressed for Having Patterns*

We are becoming aware of the pervasive nature of oppression in our society. Much that has been "taken for granted" in our relationships with each other as enforced by society is now seen to be completely irrational and destructive.

Many groups of people are oppressed because of their inherent natures. The oppression of children, of old people, of Jews, of women, of Third World people, is organized on the excuse of who they are inherently.

Other groups of people are oppressed for having particular kinds of patterns. People who are in prison for "criminal" acts are being oppressed and destroyed for patterns which were not their responsibility for acquiring. People who are "mental patients" or are "ex-mental patients" are systematically incarcerated or, after release, discriminated against, for the existence of patterns which were placed upon them by mistreatment in the first place. People whose sexual patterns are a deviation from the inherent sexual behavior of human beings or from social "norms", are systematically mistreated and oppressed in a great variety of ways. Compulsive eating patterns are encouraged by society, but if the victim becomes "fat", that person suffers discrimination and oppression.

It is plain that this oppression is wrong and must be contradicted, that the liberation of all people must become our concern. These brothers and sisters are suffering from hurts that were done to them from outside. The punishment

*First printed in Present Time No. 24 -- July, 1976

and oppression simply reinforce patterns and do not, in any way, solve the difficulties which have led to the excuse for the oppression. However, some of these patterns have non-survival effects on the people around them and must be dealt with.

I think it is time that we put some real thinking to the clarification of these kinds of oppression so that our attitude here can be as supportive, as liberating and as intelligent as the ones we are beginning to evolve in the cases of oppression for inherent nature.

Is Homosexuality a Distress Pattern? *

I

As our Communities grow widely and large numbers of new individuals join them a certain number of homosexuals, that is, people who identify with the style of life described as "gay" or "lesbian" enter into the Re-evaluation Counseling Communities. These people are very welcome in the Re-evaluation Counseling Communities; they have in general become good co-counselors and good Community members.

In society as a whole, such individuals have been in the past and continue in the present to be invalidated, persecuted and victimized, both individually and collectively.

Only recently have homosexuals begun in an organized way to resist such ill treatment from society. They have formed organizations for their own defense, worked for recognition of their human rights, and insisted on respect from others for their dignity as human beings.

Homosexual feelings and actions have often been dubbed "evil" or "criminal" or "mental illness" by society. The attitudes of society's representatives have been in most cases obviously more irrational than those of the homosexuals they persecuted. It is quite understandable that homosexuals, organized for the defense of their dignities as human beings, would come to assert as policy that it is rational to be homosexual (often the more permissive term "bisexual" is used); that heterosexuals are the irrational ones; that heterosexuals refrain from the "more rational" bisexuality only through fear and social conditioning, or that heterosexuality and homosexuality are simply variations in the basic sexual nature of humans and that either can be rational.

* First printed in Present Time No. 14 -- January, 1974

In recent months this issue has begun to be pushed at RC workshops or in RC classes. Gay or lesbian individuals or (more often) heterosexual individuals who are feeling guilty over tolerating past mistreatment of homosexuals and are in penance championing what they feel is a correct program ("because the homosexuals agreed upon it themselves") have been pushing for "acceptance" by the RC Communities of the position that homosexuality is rational, that it is not a "distress pattern" that needs to be discharged and reevaluated.

We have not had a formal position in Re-evaluation Counseling on this question, but perhaps it is time that we did. I propose (for discussion and response in the next few months) the following position:

First, *that we completely condemn and oppose any persecution or invalidation of homosexuals by any individuals, by society, or by organs of society.* This does not, in itself, touch on the rational or irrational character of homosexuality. No individual should be mistreated for any facet of his or her human nature, nor should any individual be mistreated because of distress patterns which he or she wears. Such distress patterns were always imposed from without in the first place against the desire of the individual.

In this context we welcome and approve the recent action of the trustees of the American Psychiatric Association in removing homosexuality from their list of "mental illnesses". The term "mental illness" has carried, with psychiatrists and others, a sense of stigma and opprobrium which should not be attached to any individual.

Second, *that we recognize without argument that almost all heterosexual attitudes and activities as presently observed in our society are heavily patterned behavior.* Examination of the distressed character of the common sexual attitudes and behavior of both heterosexuals and homosexuals would not, in itself, lead to any clear conclusion as to whether homosexuality, per se, is irrational or not.

Third, *we note that our society in most of its attitudes tends to condemn, suppress and submerge the positive needs of human beings for touching each other and for physical closeness and then to identify any expression of these suppressed needs as sexual desires or actions when in fact they are not.* The very real needs of all individuals to touch other human beings regularly and to have close physical contact with other human beings (hugging, hand-holding, sitting close) are assumed by many individuals, who feel these needs, to be sexual in character when in fact they are not at all. Thus individuals who feel drawn to such closeness with members of their own sex can assume that they are on that account "homosexual" or may sometimes be even drawn or seduced into sexual activities on the basis of this assumption when in fact only very basic human needs that have nothing to do with sex are initially involved.

In any attempt to define homosexuality, these distinctions need to be taken into account. Perhaps we can use the words "erotic" or "sexual" to describe feelings different from the needs for closeness or physical touch. Then homosexuality might be tentatively defined as participation in erotic or sexual feelings or actions with members of a person's own sex.

Fourth, *that we conclude that homosexuality* (as distinct from the desire to touch or be close) *is irrational, is the result of distress patterns* (often very early in origin and chronic), *and will disappear by the free choice of the individual with sufficient discharge and re-evaluation.*

This conclusion is reached for the following reasons:

(1) A very substantial amount of experience by co-counselors and in particular by staff counselors at Personal Counselors, Inc., with homosexual clients over an extended period of time, is uniform in its indication that homosexual

behavior or feelings is in each case the result of sexual feelings becoming "glued" to a member of the same sex during experiences of distress, and that sufficient discharge of the distress inevitably leads to "ungluing" the identification and freedom from the homosexual feelings and behavior.

(a) Clients who have set a goal of becoming free of homosexual feelings and behavior have, in their counseling, been able to spontaneously bring up the experiences that underlie the feelings and behavior, and, assisted adequately to discharge sufficiently (this can often be a difficult process because of the tremendous amount of reinforcing distress imposed by the social attitudes and actions attacking and condemning the homosexual individual) find their attitudes and actions changing from compulsive homosexuality towards relaxed heterosexuality (not towards compulsive or distressed heterosexuality.)

(b) Clients who announce their satisfaction with being homosexual, who state that their goals include remaining homosexual, who are convinced that this is their true nature, and who begin their counseling on other distresses and problems exclusively, inevitably, once they have succeeded in using discharge and re-evaluation to free themselves from some of the other distresses, find a way to make the re-evaluation of their homosexuality a goal (often by the challenge to the counselor to "prove" they could make any change in this area), and, from that point on, function in the same way as clients described under (a).

(c) Observably any client or co-counselor who counsels to any extended degree on experiences connected with sex finds sexual feelings have become compulsively attached to some of a most diverse variety of different objects and topics and situations and remain compulsively attached to such objects until discharge and re-evaluation take place. We have had wide experience with a large number of clients whose sexual feelings were "aroused" by a great variety of "fetishes" in this manner. Equally compulsive and ridiculous but socially acceptable in our sick society are feelings of sexual arousal called up by briefly glimpsed underpants, or the "thigh, breast, or buttocks" of the Playboy sub-culture. With this in mind, it is not at all difficult to understand how erotic feelings can become compulsively attached to one's own sex and reinforced on the one hand by the rewarding and rationally needed "closeness" with another human being (otherwise difficult to attain outside the RC Communities) and on the other, by the shame, guilt, and fear loaded on the existing compulsion by social condemnation and abuse.

(d) Each individual's homosexuality (and this is equally true of all compulsive heterosexual behavior) turns out to be a unique, individual distress, the result of that person's unique, individual distress experiences. Any commonality between homosexualities seems to be imposed by the enforcing effect of social oppression or constructed by the determined efforts of the individual to "adjust" to a condition they have not known how to change. The widely-commented-on "transient" nature of homosexual relations, usually ascribed to social pressure, is, in part, the result of the incompatibility of diverse patterns, and, in part, due to the trapped human's unwillingness to settle for a reactive relationship. Individuals in homosexual relationships without resource or knowledge to free themselves from the compulsions involved will tend to at least seek variety with its hope of possible change in the frustrations suffered in the last relationship.

(e) Homosexual behavior, as observed, seems to be the closest approximation which the individual within the confines of the patterned distress is able to achieve to the heterosexual behavior which is an inherent possibility of his or her nature.

Since every cell in an individual's body is specifically male or female by chromosome structure it is very understandable that when the inherent heterosexual function is blocked (by, for example, fear of the opposite sex or by heavy distress compelling sexual arousal by one's own sex) that the "acting out" of the compulsions will tend toward some approximation or facsimile of the heterosexual behavior that would be present if the person were free to adopt it.

All reactive patterns of living that affect substantial numbers of people in a similar way because of the effects of social patterns *will* appear in the RC Communities, along with the individuals who wear them. Inevitably, demands will be made that RC and the RC Communities assume these attitudes as "rational". We have had experience in the past, for example, with such demands for (1) a "patriotic" supportive attitude toward the U.S. war in Vietnam; and (2) for acceptance of the use of psychedelic drugs as "enhancing" rationality.

There is also a kind of unthinking but vociferous pressure, particularly from middle class "liberals", which arises out of undischarged guilt, to accept as rational whatever programs are first put forward by any group of oppressed people who begin to resist oppression. These first attempts at programs for liberation are often rooted in painful emotion, are often the "flip side" of old distress recordings. They are stages, perhaps necessary, to help groups seeking liberation to "grow through". They are not something that would-be allies of the liberation forces should agree with or support.

Presently, in some localities, guilty, middle-class liberalism among RC members pushes clamorously for the RC Communities to accept homosexuality as rational "because the homosexuals themselves adopted this as a program".

I do not think we can concur. I think we must, with all safeguards against participating in any socially oppressive attitudes of the culture, maintain a distinct rational position that homosexual feelings or behavior in any situation where external reality permits another choice is distress behavior which will dissolve with sufficient discharge.

This is for all of the preceding reasons and, also, importantly, *because to do otherwise would be to abandon the victim of the pattern to the pattern simply because he or she defends it or "chooses" it.* Any victim of any chronic pattern appears to defend or "choose" the patterned behavior. The rest of us, outside that particular pattern, would betray its victim if we failed to hold out rational disagreement with such a pattern. We have, I think, a responsibility to do this even if "fussed at" or denounced by the pattern or group of patterns in the process.

There is a further important reason why we should not concur in any position assuming that homosexual behavior is "rational". In working with homosexual clients it is clear that in a large proportion of cases the distress incident that turned the accumulation of distress into a chronic behavior pattern is an incident of seduction, that is, enforcement or semi-enforcement by a homosexual individual on the person of an experience which puts distress (fear, other painful emotion) together with erotic feelings (also often with hope of "closeness", "touching", etc.). These precipitating experiences of seduction introduce the individual to a great deal of accumulating misery, not only because of the oppressiveness of society but also because of the certainty of further restimulating incidents to follow once the identification with homosexual behavior has been made.

This is a severe blow to the individual. It is part of the familiar destructive process in our society of the "contagion" of distress patterns, a process which we seek to interrupt at every turn. If homosexuality were to be considered "rational", then of course the homosexual individual could justify the introduction of another individual into homosexual practices as "helping the individual discover his or her own 'true nature' ". Such an attitude would be very damaging.

In practice I propose that individuals be welcome to our Communities if otherwise qualified and be made welcome as co-counselors. I propose that we require of them that they respect the position we adopt on this question, even if they disagree with it, that they not act disruptively within our Communities in an effort to force the Communities to a different position.

I think that we should probably require that teachers and Reference Persons or other leaders of the RC Communities be committed to discharge and re-evaluate on the homosexuality in the expectation of being free from it. This is the same requirement we make of would-be leaders on smoking or other addictive patterns; that they either be free from the addictions or committed to give up the addiction, that they not hold a position of defending it.

In practice, co-counseling by a homosexual on distress connected with sexuality is no different than it is for any co-counselor. For a long time we have been suggesting that it is very much to the advantage of any individual co-counselor to review all the memories of his or her life connected with sex in any way and discharge on any of them that show tension. This has been of great benefit to every co-counselor who has done it; it will certainly be of great benefit to every homosexual regardless of his or her opinion to begin with as to the rationality or irrationality of the lifestyle.

We can safely trust to the process of discharge and re-evaluation in every case for our Communities and for individuals.

I propose that this set of proposals be discussed and commented on widely in our Communities. I would like to hear the feedback. I propose that in a few months on the basis of this discussion we adopt a definite attitude on this question.

January, 1974

Discussion on the Proposed Policy on Homosexuality *

(Continued)

II

Is homosexuality always rooted in distress patterns, or is it simply another form of rational sexuality? The response to the article in the last *Present Time* has been large. The publication of the article has been successful in this sense, that numbers of co-counselors are thinking about the question, and others are upset about the question and attempting to think. Apparently a good deal of co-counseling on sexual patterns has resulted as a response to the article.

Some of the written responses react to the article *as if it proposed the oppression of homosexuals.* It was apparent that people writing had been unable to read the article as it was but had immediately identified it with the societal attitude of oppressing and victimizing homosexuals and so were unable to read or understand the article itself but were reacting to their fears. Many other people who obviously had read and understood the article were concerned that it might be interpreted that way by people within the community and especially by people outside.

A number who wrote as homosexuals felt that their counseling had led them to be more openly homosexual, more satisfied with being homosexual as a result of their discharge, and that their personal experience contradicted my conjecture that everyone who had been functioning homosexually would move toward rational heterosexual behavior if he or she discharged enough. In response to this I would say that a homosexual who has suffered oppression will tend to discharge the distress (defensiveness, shame, guilt, fear, etc.) related to that oppression first and will come to feel less defensive and more comfortable with homosexual

*First printed in Present Time No. 15 -- April, 1974

activities as a result. My conjecture is that continued counseling will in every case lead him or her to discharge on and re-evaluate on other areas of distress which I think are the sole source of the homosexual feelings and behavior.

I think it is worth restating that the previous article *proposed* a policy but *did not install a policy*. The proposal was for the deepest and most searching examination of the whole question by as many people as possible. There is no intention to bring the discussion to a conclusion quickly, but rather to think the whole question through as far and as deeply as we can before adopting even a tentative position.

It is possible that we should take no position on this question at all, in spite of the pressures which led to beginning the discussion. Many correspondents have suggested this. We should be clear, however, that taking *no* position will be taking *a* position, after so much discussion. The way is open to do whatever is rational, whatever that may turn out to be.

It is also clear (and I think this is one of the best results of the discussion so far), that to call homosexuality into question must lead inevitably to calling our attitudes toward all *sexuality* into question. This was proposed by many correspondents, that we should question whether or not there is any rationality in current *heterosexual or homosexual* attitudes and practices in our culture. Should we not, in fact, begin to think hard about what rational attitudes and practices related to sexuality would be? I think we can safely assume that having grown up in our distressed cultures, it is impossible for any one of us to "know *a priori*"what a rational attitude would be. It can only be thought out with the greatest effort and diligence through the thinking and inter-communication of large numbers of us.

Many people have been struck, as have I, by the conjecture that perhaps when we eliminate all distress from our sexuality we will never indulge in sexual feelings or activity except for purposes of reproduction, that a rational examination of the current uses of sexual activity and feelings might indicate in every case that the sexual feelings and activities have become a substitute for other needs which are not in themselves sexual, but which have been repressed by the cultural conditioning or by individual distresses.

We have been careful in restricting the organization of workshops on sex and sexuality. (Permission of the International Community and specific approval of the workshop leadership is required, by decision of the International Area Reference Persons workshop.) Even so, we have had some distressing aftermaths from the most carefully led workshops on the topic. Participants have returned to their communities misquoting the workshop leadership as authority for indulging preposterous dramatizations and thoughtless behavior. It seems plain that the entire area of sexuality is *deeply* distressed for all of us. It also seems clear that to discharge some or all of the easily available *embarrassment* about sex (which has usually had an inhibiting effect on the other patterns) and then conclude that we are now rational in the area and can safely act on our feelings is to greatly underestimate the amount of work we need to do and to invite some small or large disasters.

I hope that many more RCers will think and write in about this subject. I would like especially to invite people who don't automatically feel motivated to do so to express themselves. If one feels threatened or upset by the discussion, then one is motivated to write. If one tends to be at ease with the proposal one is not so strongly motivated. I think we will need thinking from all viewpoints in RC to resolve this question well. Please participate.

Can Homosexuality Be Rational Or Is It Always a Distress Pattern?*

III

This article closes the current written discussion on whether or not homosexual activity can be considered rational.

Many co-counselors have participated in the discussion, by mail, in the Communities, and at workshops. Many have expressed their opinions to me personally. The discussion seems to be at a pause, however. Little new is being put forward. The mail, at first voluminous, has now tapered off to nothing.

The written discussion by itself has not given us any basis for coming to a conclusion on the original question. It has been most fruitful, however, in the amount of thinking which it has generated and the amount of discharge that has taken place around the question. Most valuably, I think, it has revealed wide agreement that almost all present attitudes about sexuality in our culture are irrational, and that it will take a great deal of hard thinking and discussion on the part of all of us before we can even determine what a rational attitude about sexuality would be.

The question of whether homosexual co-counselors who defend their attitudes and activities as rational should be accredited as Re-evaluation Counseling teachers will be referred to the Reference Persons' Workshop in August. I expect that the decision will probably be to continue to consider each teacher applicant separately and make decisions individually in each case. (Two homosexuals have been accredited as teachers since this discussion began.)

---

*First printed in Present Time No. 16 – July, 1974

411

Two common weaknesses in the discussion are worth calling attention to. One is that many of the participants attempted to do their thinking and writing on a completely abstract basis, as if they were considering "homosexuality" and "heterosexuality" as only words or as abstract concepts. On paper, the two words look very much the same. If we do not think beyond that, then it may seem "intelligent" and "unbiased" to not justify any distinction between them. For productive and meaningful thinking, however, it is necessary that we *relate concepts to the reality* which they supposedly represent and to *think about the reality*; in this case--what homosexuality and heterosexuality actually consist of in practice.

Such "abstract" attitudes arise for a reason. It is a common practice of our flawed educational systems to encourage people, in the name of being "intellectual" to divorce their thinking and their concepts from reality. This is a serious mistake. Growing up in the cultures that we do, we must be always on the guard against this.

The other notion that reappeared continually in the correspondence and apparently was assumed to be true was that it would be irrational, unfair, and discriminatory to choose among prospects for teachers or for leadership in the Re-evaluation Counseling Community on the basis of what kind of distress patterns the prospects had or did not have. It seemed to be assumed that we should, in effect, treat all patterns and all patterned individuals alike in considering them for leadership and responsibility.

This is nonsense. It is not any person's fault if that person has a particular kind of pattern. Certainly no pattern is "better" than another (They are all completely irrational and terrible.) In terms of getting a job done, however, it is *always* necessary to choose people for the job with their existing patterns in mind.

An obvious example is the chronic *irresponsibility* pattern as compared to the chronic *responsibility* pattern. We will never judge a person of less intrinsic value because of chronic irresponsibility. In choosing teachers or leaders for the Community, however, we have always and must continue in the future to choose persons whose chronic distresses include being responsible.

Why must we? We must because we do not as yet have people available who have no chronic patterns about responsibility. The majority have been chronically hurt in the direction of irresponsibility. A minority have been hurt in a way that leaves them compulsively responsible. So we must rely on patterned responsibility until we have rational responsibility (trying always to remember to not "adjust" to the pattern of the person but instead help them to continue to work to free themselves from that particular pattern.)

Thanks to all of you who participated in the discussion. It has not been possible to publish more than a fraction of the correspondence, but a good sampling of it has been published, and I think that sample has been of interest and information to all of us.

Time To Halt Divisive Activity *

I have been meeting with gay support groups recently and have been dealing with the gay issue at workshops. At this point I would like to propose a clarification of our policy for Gay Liberation activities in RC.

TWO KINDS OF OPPRESSION

There are oppressions because of a person's inherent nature and there are oppressions because of particular patterns which are not the fault of the pattern's victim. The controversy which has been disrupting some RC classes and workshops is whether homosexuality should be listed where I list it, with oppression because of patterns, or whether it should be listed as an inherent nature. There is no disagreement (though there remains a lot of unclarity) on the fact that homosexuals do suffer oppression and that the RC communities as a whole should combat that oppression, both within RC and outside.

The position that I have stated and will continue to state whenever necessary -- that homosexuality is always rooted in deep distress and without fail will disappear by the free choice of the person with sufficient discharge and re-evaluation -- is supported, to my knowledge, by everyone who has actually worked with homosexuals thoroughly on their distress connected with sex. It is also supported by homosexuals and ex-homosexuals who have actually worked consistently and successfully on their distresses connected with sex.

*First printed in RC Teacher No. 9 – December, 1976

NEEDLESS CONTROVERSY

I have stated this position publicly in response to "demands" that RC take the other position and declare homosexuality to be rational. Discussions of this issue in RC have almost always been initiated by this demand, sometimes from homosexuals, but more often from their "liberal" supporters, that we take this position. I think it is time to have an end to this.

DISCHARGE NEEDED

Some gay RCers have said to me that they don't "feel safe" enough in the community unless the community adopts the policy that homosexuality is rational. I have replied that it is not a reasonable expectation to "*feel* safe" but rather to *be* safe and that the fear which they have to discharge is not likely to allow them to feel safe until they have completely discharged it. I have insisted that the position of the community as I have outlined it *does* give them enough safety *to work*. In such discussions, when I have insisted that we try working, starting with the earliest memory connected with sex in any way, the tension and attitude of controversy dissolves quickly in discharge and an eagerness develops to get to work on the sticky material.

DON'T SUSPEND SCREENING

I propose that screening standards be applied to gay persons coming into RC in exactly the same way as they are applied to other people, that we do not lower the standards because of a "liberal" attitude.

DON'T ABUSE COMMUNITY

I propose that homosexuals be welcomed in RC, subject to the usual screening for the depth of the distress, but with the understanding that they will *not* propagandize within RC or in RC meetings, workshops, support groups, caucuses, etc. for the position that homosexuality is rational. Otherwise, the contrary position must and will be enunciated, and if necessary, will become the official position of the RC Communities (which it has been possible to have it become anytime since the controversy first started).

Under this proposal, it will not be necessary for myself and others to repeatedly put forward the contrary position that homosexuality always arises out of deep distress and will always disappear with sufficient discharge and re-evaluation. We have not, in general, made an issue of this position except in response to the demand that we accept homosexuality as rational, but it is and will be necessary to respond if the other position is advanced. Hopefully, the issue need not continue to be divisive in workshops, classes and support groups.

HOMOSEXUAL LIBERATION NEEDED

I propose that homosexual RCers be encouraged to organize support groups, caucuses, etc. and to publish a newsletter, but that these shall *not* be used to organize support in RC for the position that homosexuality is rational or that homosexual oppression should be transferred from the category of "oppressed because of patterns" to the category of "oppressed because of inherent nature". I propose that homosexual caucuses and support groups shall be used to *work* on *a)* the oppression of homosexuals and means of organizing against it and to plan ways to urge that other RCers work to discharge their fears of and oppressive attitudes toward homosexuality, and *b)* to review and discharge on all their memories connected with sex in any way in the safety provided by being with other homosexuals, against the distress which the culture has put on heterosexual people about homosexuality.

DISCHARGE ENDS DEFENSIVENESS

In meeting recently with gay support groups and explaining this policy, I have gone further and insisted that we begin working on such memories as a basis for going ahead and organizing the support groups and caucuses. When work is actually begun, discharge abounds and there is a great relief on the part of everyone to find that they can work on this material with each other. The defensiveness which has so far prevented work in most of these groups while they cling to the position that "it is rational to be gay", disappears.

DON'T SPEAK WITHOUT KNOWLEDGE

Supporters of the "liberal" position who have been most vocal in creating the controversy (the homosexuals who are active in leading in RC are divided on the question, as you probably know, with about 40% supporting my position, but in general keeping quiet in the caucuses, because they wish to avoid the charges of "betrayal" by the others) will be told in the future that we will operate on the principle which they have used in China, "without investigation, no right to speak"; that is, unless people have actually discharged on their memories connected with sex thoroughly and intensively, they should realize that they have no business having or expressing opinions in this controversy and the workshops and the newsletters of RC will not be open to more of this.

To state it again, I propose that gay persons be welcomed into RC on the basis that they are expected to *not* propagandize for nor advocate within the RC Community or any of its groups the position that *homosexuality is rational.*

TO BE OPPRESSED DOES NOT CONFER RATIONALITY

To defend the pattern that you haven't gotten out of as "inherent" is understandable, particularly when you despair of finding support or means to emerge. The slogan "fat is beautiful" has been raised a number of places in RC. We see the phenomenon of do-gooding college students entering into prison reform programs and winding up as members of organizations like the Symbionese Liberation Army, claiming that it is rational to resort to individual terror because they see the oppression. It is not sensible and we will not have much of a community, if we go along with this.

WORK ON SEXUALITY NEEDED GENERALLY

It is evident that we must begin to work on sexuality in a serious manner throughout our communities. Possibly 200 co-counselors (that I know of) have so far really worked thoroughly on their memories connected with sex and, without exception, they report it to be of great benefit in all areas of their lives. This is as true for heterosexuals as it is for those with homosexual patterns. Apparently we are always likely to get a great deal of embarrassment discharge to begin with (remember the response to my attempt to talk seriously about sexuality at Buck Creek last summer) but we should recognize that however big the laughter discharge is, this is only the beginning of the distress which has been laid onto sexuality for all of us.

All individuals in RC are urged to bring up and work on their chain of memories in any way at all connected with sex, to discharge thoroughly on them. Until persons have done this, they frankly do not know what they are talking about in this area, no matter how firm their opinions are.

I hope to be doing some writing and a lot of demonstrating at workshops in the next few months on this particular topic.